An Exceptional Dialogue

AN EXCEPTIONAL DIALOGUE, 1925–1948

Nikolai Berdyaev and Jacques Maritain

BERNARD HUBERT

Edited in English and with an introduction by Ana Siljak

Translated by C. Jon Delogu

McGill-Queen's University Press
Montreal & Kingston • London • Chicago

First published in French as *Nicolas Berdiaev et Jacques Maritain: Un dialogue d'exception (1925–1948)*, présenté et annoté par Bernard Hubert © YMCA-Press 2022

ISBN 978-0-2280-2385-2 (cloth)
ISBN 978-0-2280-2386-9 (paper)
ISBN 978-0-2280-2387-6 (ePDF)
ISBN 978-0-2280-2388-3 (ePUB)

Legal deposit first quarter 2025
Bibliothèque nationale du Québec

Printed in Canada on acid-free paper that is 100% ancient forest free (100% post-consumer recycled), processed chlorine free

This book has been published with the help of a grant from the Queen's University Scholarly Publications Fund.

We acknowledge the support of the Canada Council for the Arts.
Nous remercions le Conseil des arts du Canada de son soutien.

McGill-Queen's University Press in Montreal is on land which long served as a site of meeting and exchange amongst Indigenous Peoples, including the Haudenosaunee and Anishinabeg nations. In Kingston it is situated on the territory of the Haudenosaunee and Anishinaabek. We acknowledge and thank the diverse Indigenous Peoples whose footsteps have marked these territories on which peoples of the world now gather.

Library and Archives Canada Cataloguing in Publication

Title: An exceptional dialogue, 1925–1948 : Nikolai Berdyaev and Jacques Maritain / Bernard Hubert; edited in English and with an introduction by Ana Siljak ; translated by C. Jon Delogu.
Other titles: Nicolas Berdiaev et Jacques Maritain. English. | Nikolai Berdyaev and Jacques Maritain
Names: Siljak, Ana, 1969– writer of introduction, editor | Container of (expression): Maritain, Jacques, 1882–1973. Correspondence. Selections. English. | Container of (expression): Berdiaev, Nikolaĭ, 1874–1948. Correspondence. Selections. English. | Container of (work): Hubert, Bernard. Dialogue between Jacques Maritain and Nikolai Berdyaev (1925–1948) | Delogu, Christopher Jon, translator
Description: Translation of: Nicolas Berdiaev et Jacques Maritain: Un dialogue d'exception (1925–1948). | Includes bibliographical references and index.
Identifiers: Canadiana (print) 2024046155X | Canadiana (ebook) 20240461614 | ISBN 9780228023852 (cloth) | ISBN 9780228023869 (paper) | ISBN 9780228023883 (ePUB) | ISBN 9780228023876 (ePDF)
Subjects: LCSH: Maritain, Jacques, 1882–1973—Correspondence. | LCSH: Berdiaev, Nikolaĭ, 1874–1948—Correspondence. | LCSH: Philosophers—France—Correspondence. | LCSH: Existentialism. | LCSH: Personalism. | LCSH: Christian humanism. | LCGFT: Personal correspondence.
Classification: LCC B2421 .N5313 2025 | DDC 194—dc23

This book was designed and typeset by Lara Minja in Minion Pro 10.5 pt/14.5pt.
Copyediting by Susan Glickman.

CONTENTS

Acknowledgments

It has been a pleasure to edit and introduce this English translation of the Nikolai Berdyaev-Jacques Maritain correspondence. I am grateful to Bernard Hubert for providing permission to publish this translation of his book, *Nicolas Berdiaev et Jacques Maritain: Un dialogue d'exception (1925–1948).* It has been a pleasure to work with C. Jon Delogu on this translation. Teresa Obolevitch provided initial advice and encouragement, and Melanie Rakovitch helped facilitate communication with YMCA Press. Richard Ratzlaff provided invaluable assistance in moving this edition through publication. The Social Sciences and Humanities Research Council of Canada provided the resources necessary for the completion of the project. Special thanks also to Alice Gianotti, Matthew Minerd, and Randall Poole for all their suggestions and comments. And as always, I am grateful to my family for their warm support.

Ana Siljak

Editor's Note on Spelling and Transliteration

The spelling of Russian names in the text will be transliterated in general accordance with the Library of Congress standard, with the exception of common spellings, such as Tolstoy and Dostoevsky. For the sake of clarity, a single spelling convention will be used for each Russian name throughout the text, with the exception of untranslated quotations and publications listed in the footnotes. This will avoid potential confusion caused by the variety of spellings used by Russian émigrés and their friends. Berdyaev, for example, signed his handwritten letters "Nicolas Berdiaev," but signed his calling card "Nicolas Berdiaeff."

Translator's Note

Nothing in my youth growing up in Cold War America during the 1960s and '70s would have inclined me to take an interest in the peripeteia of a Russian émigré who fled the Soviet Union in the 1920s and made a second home for himself in Paris, France. However, given my own flight in 1992 from the American Counter-Enlightenment that started under Reagan and has only accelerated in the last forty years, I was immediately drawn to the story of the scrappy older philosopher-theologian Nikolai Berdyaev and his friendship with a younger established French counterpart, Jacques Maritain. Their pre-email thread of letters and cards displays the blend of pragmatism and idealism they used to grow their readership, enlighten the public they wished to persuade, and have those individuals join forces so that good (a renewal of Christianity) would triumph over evil (the twin threats of Communism and Fascism in the 1920s and '30s).

Especially interesting are the many jumps between the straightforward transactional side of their friendship – "We could hold the meeting on Tuesday" – and the transcendental side (e.g., letters 42–4 on pages 61–2) where at times *je perdais pied*, I lost my footing. If agreeing on what "Ungrund" and "gnosis" mean was challenging for them, the experts, what chance did I have?

Of the many books I've translated, none has featured translation itself – between cultures, languages, heaven and earth – as centrally as this "exceptional dialogue" built on the faith, which I share, that translation, however imperfect and approximate, can and must succeed. I have done my best to retain the polite, respectful tone that prevailed between these two gentlemen who disagree on many particulars but share a commitment to using core Christian values to reform and preserve humanity from the destructive revolutionary tendencies of the twentieth century.

C. Jon Delogu
Professeur des Universités
11 March 2024
Université Jean Moulin, Lyon 3

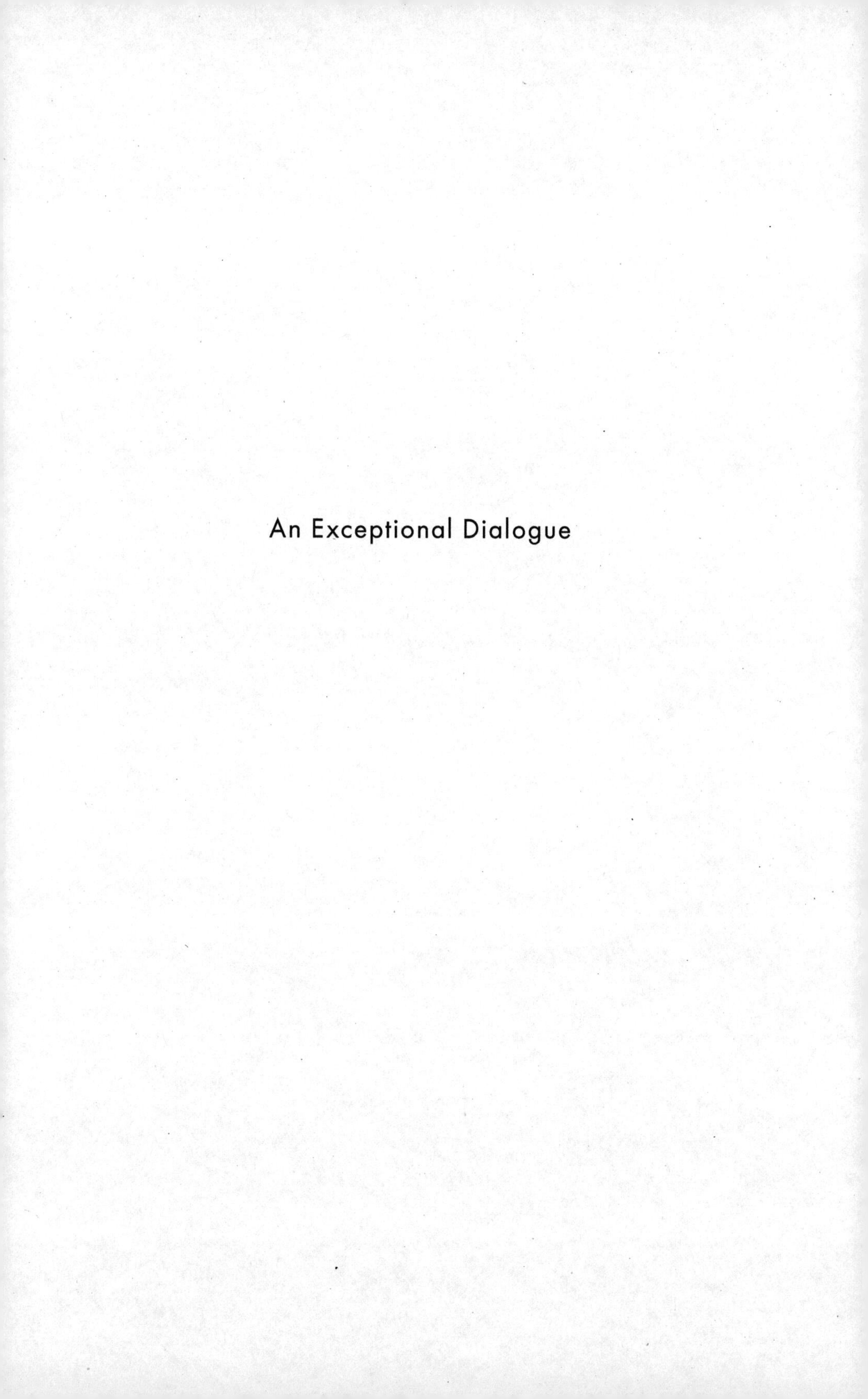

An Exceptional Dialogue

A New Christian Humanism: Nikolai Berdyaev and Jacques Maritain

Ana Siljak

IN HIS ELEGANTLY WRITTEN *Year of Our Lord 1943*, Alan Jacobs recounts a now forgotten time of intense intellectual searching in the shadow of war, during which leading Western thinkers began to seek a "renewal of Christian thought and practice" to help build a healthy postwar culture. The democratic social order they hoped would emerge out of the rubble needed a "moral underpinning" – something not easily found in the aftermath of mass death, ethnic cleansing, and genocide. A new "humanism" was needed, one that required more than mere theology, demanding the contributions of "poets, novelists, philosophers, thinkers." The characters in Jacobs's account are well known: Jacques Maritain, the neo-Thomist philosopher; C.S. Lewis, the Christian essayist and novelist; Simone Weil, the mystic; and T.S. Eliot, the modernist poet.[1]

Jacobs cites Jacques Maritain as one of the central philosophers of a twentieth-century Christian humanism: an alternative to the secular anthropocentrism that, in Maritain's view, led to the extremes of Communism and Fascism. Asserted against twin totalitarianisms, Maritain's humanism rested on his philosophy of "personalism," which refused to see the human being as a mere pawn of "the immense network of forces and influences, cosmic, ethnic, historic, whose laws we must obey." Rather, for Maritain, a person is "in the depth of his being … more a whole than a part and more independent than servile," deserving dignity and rights. The person is the key to humanism, the path to "liberation through knowledge and wisdom, good will, and love."[2]

Jacques Maritain, famous in his day, was gradually sidelined in late twentieth-century English-language scholarship, and, in at least one assessment, was "dropped from sight" and "passed by" a mere eight years after his death.[3] Lately, however, he has received renewed attention as one of the most important Catholic philosophers of the interwar and postwar eras of the twentieth century.[4] In particular, Maritain plays a central role in Samuel Moyn's controversial book *Christian Human Rights* (2013).[5] Moyn argues that the very concept of international human rights developed out of a distinctly French, Catholic philosophy of personalism in the 1930s and 1940s, a philosophy to which Maritain contributed a great deal. Moyn boldly states that it was necessary to revisit human rights "as a project of the Christian right, not the secular left."[6]

There is no doubt that Maritain's defence of the irreducible value and dignity of the person, guaranteed by the creation of humanity in the image and likeness of God, contributed significantly to a doctrine of inalienable rights transcending state borders and cultural contexts.[7] Crucially, Maritain chaired the UNESCO Committee on the Philosophic Principles of the Rights of Man, which met in 1947. Through him, the "human person" became of central value in the United Nations as an institution, which led to its adoption of the *Universal Declaration of Human Rights* (signed in Paris on 10 December 1948).[8]

In this manner, Jacques Maritain has received a much-deserved rediscovery of his philosophy. But both Moyn and Jacobs miss a crucial part of the story. Between the two world wars, starting around 1925, French Catholic humanism and personalism were also shaped by encounters with a distinctly Russian émigré philosophical tradition, notably embodied by Nikolai Berdyaev.[9]

This volume of correspondence between Maritain and Berdyaev provides us with the missing part of the narrative. The letters, which spanned decades, illuminate the nature and context of a fruitful relationship that only ended with Berdyaev's death in 1948. This was no mere casual correspondence; the two men became close collaborators on a variety of endeavours. The letters testify to their elaborate planning of ecumenical, philosophical, and theological discussions, their eagerness to read and publish each other's work, and their willingness to give and receive criticism. Bernard Hubert's essay, "The Dialogue between Jacques Maritain and Nikolai Berdyaev (1925–1948)," together with his annotations to the letters, painstakingly recovers the details of this relationship by adding information from memoirs and other correspondence. What emerges is indeed an "exceptional dialogue" of two extraordinary intellectuals.

What follows in this introduction to the English edition is a guide to the philosophies of Berdyaev and Maritain as they developed, in order to highlight what each brought to their conversation.

I will begin with the origins of Berdyaev's philosophy of personalism, revealing the central place of the Russian humanist tradition in his thought. Western suspicion of all things Russian, a continuation, after a brief hiatus, of the hostility toward all things Soviet during the Cold War, has diminished and obscured Russia's humanist discourse, though intellectual historians such as Randall Poole have written prolifically on the Russian contributions to questions of human dignity, freedom of conscience, and individual liberty.[10] It may be more controversial to claim that a Russian philosophical tradition shaped European humanist and personalist discourse in the twentieth century, and yet there is no doubt that in the aftermath of the Russian Revolution, when thinkers fled or were forced out of Soviet Russia, they brought with them distinctly Russian philosophical perspectives on a number of different subjects, including the dignity of the human person. In the 1920s and 1930s, the influence of Russian thought on European culture was widely acknowledged. Berdyaev is part of that story.

I will then turn to Maritain, who met Berdyaev after his own brand of personalism had fully developed in engagement with what Maritain saw as the essential nihilism of modernity. A devout Catholic, Maritain was determined to reassert the primacy of human flourishing based on a rereading of Thomas Aquinas. Neo-Thomism grounded the value of each human being in a God-given "intelligence" designed to encounter the divine. The similarities between the views of Berdyaev and Maritain are striking in this respect; despite the development of their personalisms out of separate Christian traditions, their insistence on the value of the human person in the face of the political and social movements of the interwar era was extraordinarily alike.

It is important to add that, despite their clear and mutually acknowledged philosophical differences, the letters confirm contemporary accounts of the two men being close friends.[11] The Maritain and Berdyaev families were frequently guests at each other's homes, and their relations were undoubtedly aided by the similarities in their households (both Maritain and Berdyaev were married, without children, and lived with their sisters-in-law). Also, Raïssa Maritain, her sister Véra, and Lydia Berdyaev were all converts to Catholicism. As is obvious from the letters, Maritain was often called, and called himself, "Jakov Pavlovitch," and Berdyaev's wife, Lydia, insisted that Berdyaev felt closest to Maritain of all of the French philosophers, because he was the most "Russian" among them. As a result, their respective philosophies emerged as a product of dialogue, and the ideas of each were formulated under the influence of the other, either sympathetically or with respectful opposition, depending on the topic.

It is precisely this kind of frank, warm "exceptional dialogue" that encourages a reassessment of interwar personalism. Not only is the personalist tradition important for its track record defending human rights against the extremisms of the Russian Revolution and of the pre–World War II era, but it also models a civil and open conversation with opponents – and even enemies – appropriate for any politically divided age. The final section of this introduction will gesture towards the value of a personalist contribution to contemporary debates about liberalism, revealing the lasting importance of both Jacques Maritain and Nikolai Berdyaev for the history of philosophy.

Nikolai Berdyaev and His Existentialist Anthropodicy

Born in 1874, near Kiev (present-day Kyiv)[12] in Ukraine, Berdyaev grew up in the tumultuous intellectual atmosphere that suffused the metropolis. It would be a stretch to consider Berdyaev a "Ukrainian" philosopher (though some have done so), since he always identified as Russian. But there is no doubt that the milieu of Ukrainian resistance and revolution in the late nineteenth century shaped Berdyaev's philosophical rebelliousness. This was a time when nationalism and Marxism were competing for the souls of Russians and Ukrainians, and therefore many important philosophers, theologians, and revolutionaries crossed paths in that city – far from the Russian centre and from the Russian capital – and liberal and radical traditions were forged there.[13]

Berdyaev began his intellectual life as a Marxist and took part in demonstrations in Kiev in 1897, for which he was briefly arrested and exiled. He never fully abandoned Marx's critique of capitalism for its degradation of human dignity, but soon moved away from Marxism because of what he considered its dangerous side: the suppression of individual freedom by materialism and collectivism. In his words, "I identified myself with Marxism only in so far as this did not involve me in the acceptance of social and economic determinism, and, whatever the truth of Marx's critique of bourgeois society and its assumptions, he could not shake my faith in the ultimate freedom of the spirit."[14] By 1904, he embarked on a quest for a new philosophy of society and politics, which led him to the movement historians have called the Russian Silver Age, though Edith Clowes has rightly argued that it ought to be called the "Russian Renaissance" – a movement that sought to reinvigorate Russian religion and use it as the basis for a revitalized Russian culture which would include poetry, art, music, and philosophy.

Berdyaev's personalism was forged in this moment, and it engaged with a particular philosophy of the person (in Russian, *lichnost'*) that could be traced to the early nineteenth century. As Sergei Horujy has shown, in the 1830s, Slavophile and Westernizer debates revolved precisely around the meaning and value of the human person, seeking philosophical and theological grounding for a defence of human dignity in a society that seemed to hold it in little esteem. The debates of the 1830s, in turn, laid the groundwork for a more developed theory of the person in the work of Russia's pre-eminent nineteenth-century philosopher, Vladimir Solov'ev. Solov'ev brought to personalism the foundational concept of "Godmanhood" (*bogochelovechestvo*), which would prove crucial for Berdyaev. All human beings, according to Solov'ev, were created as both divine and human, spiritual and material.[15] Solov'ev's Godmanhood derived from a combination of sources, including Kabbalistic readings of the first Adam, the Chalcedonian dogma of Christ's two natures, and the Eastern patristic tradition.[16] Solov'ev appropriated for his philosophy the Eastern patristic concept of *theosis*: the insistence that, because of humanity's creation in the image and likeness of God, every human being was destined to become divine.[17] The concept of Godmanhood brought Berdyaev back into the Christian fold, and theosis was central to his philosophy of the person.

Berdyaev was one of many Russian political theorists at the turn of the century who, disillusioned with the materialist premises of Marxism, embarked on a search for a political philosophy that would eschew the materialism and atheism of socialism while also avoiding nostalgia for Tsarist autocracy. They settled on a revitalization of liberalism, particularly appropriate in a context when, for a brief period before 1917, a kind of local government activism seemed promising. One of their earliest endeavours was the Moscow Psychological Society, whose 1902 publication, *Problems of Idealism*, sought to promote a liberalism that fused Kantian idealism with Solov'ev's *bogochelovechestvo*. At the centre of their argument was the conviction that the person (*lichnost'*) was a fusion of matter and spirit, of infinite and absolute value, and thus never to be sacrificed either to socialist collectivism or capitalist utility.[18]

Berdyaev's own contribution to *Problems of Idealism* reflects this project. For Berdyaev, a crucial starting point was Kant's insistence that the grounding of ethics was always the inviolability of the person, as absolute and critical to the understanding of morality, society, and political life. Unconditional respect for each person had to stand at the centre of politics, and persons were valued for their eternal and unlimited potential to strive for betterment and spiritual perfection. Berdyaev's personalism also owed an obvious debt to Solov'ev: "A human being possesses an absolute value because he is an eternal spirit, and people are equal in value because they are of one and the same spiritual substance. Spiritual individuality possesses absolute, inalienable rights, the value of which cannot be calculated."[19] In his first years after his turn away from Marxism, Berdyaev relied on idealism as a justification of the value of the human person. Over time, however, Berdyaev's personalism became more exceptional, resting on the radical claim that "personality is a higher value than the state, the nation, mankind, or nature, and indeed it does not form part of that series."[20]

To understand this, as well as Berdyaev's passion for the full freedom of the person, it is important to elucidate his particular construction of Christian anthropology in the early twentieth century, in which there is a "religious comprehension of the Anthropos as a divine person." In *The Meaning of the Creative Act*, written in 1914, he framed his project in this manner: "Many have written their justification of God, their theodicy. But the time has come to write a justification of man, an anthropodicy."[21] This "anthropodicy" is the product of years of searching for a religious vision that would fully explore and explain the radical freedom and divinity of humans. Berdyaev's philosophy came to combine a number of seemingly disparate sources: the Kabbalah, Kant, Solov'ev, the anthroposophy of Rudolf Steiner, the mysticism of Jakob Böhme, and the Eastern patristic tradition. In the end, however, Berdyaev's anthropology rests on a very particular Judeo-Christian foundation: the biblical revelation that man is made in the "image and likeness of God." But what does the image and likeness of God entail?

In *Meaning of the Creative Act*, Berdyaev begins with his interpretation of the book of Genesis, telling the story of the creation and fall of mankind as a classic tragedy: of a being created glorious by God who loses his status as priest of all creation. Through his reading of the Kabbalah in particular, Berdyaev draws on a Jewish tradition of seeing Adam, in his prelapsarian state, as a glorious being of cosmic dimensions, possessing a "body of light." Adam's "glorious" body was commensurate with his status as the mediator between the earth and the heavens, between the created world and the Creator. Adam was created after everything else as "the reason, the sum and the high point of creation … Once man had appeared, everything was finished, both the higher and the lower world, because everything is included in man; in himself he unites all forms." This reading of Genesis is also found in the Eastern patristic writings, especially those of St Gregory of Nyssa, St Maximos the Confessor, and St Symeon the New Theologian. The latter proclaimed Adam "lord and king of the whole visible creation," and stated that Eden was created for him as "a royal dwelling." It is this teaching that explains Berdyaev's insistence that before the Fall, humanity needed no sun, for each person "had the sun within him."[22]

For Berdyaev, the story of the Fall becomes the cosmic tragedy of a disgraced king. In the Rabbinic tradition, the disgrace is symbolized by the stripping of the "garments of light" from Adam and Eve – they find themselves naked, in "garments of skin" – trapped in natural bodies. And not only man but all of creation suffered from human disobedience and man's dethronement. Berdyaev quoted St Symeon at length on the expulsion from Eden: "Then also all creatures, when they saw that Adam had been banished from Paradise, no longer wished to submit to him, the criminal: the sun did not wish to shine for him, nor did the moon and the other stars wish to show themselves to him … and all the other animals of the earth when they saw that he had been stripped of his first glory, began to despise him, and all immediately were ready to fall upon him."[23]

Postlapsarian humanity finds itself in just such a state of enmity with the natural world and in slavery to necessity. Once shining like the sun, they now depended on the external sun to give them light. For Berdyaev, anthropodicy must begin with the premise that human beings, as we encounter them, are enchained: "The human spirit is in prison," he writes in *The Meaning of the Creative Act*. This prison is the material universe, which has been hostile to human beings since the Fall, and where the land itself will not yield fruit without backbreaking labour.[24]

It is through this prism of fallenness that Berdyaev makes sense of the Enlightenment and post-Enlightenment philosophy. According to him, Kant is correct that humans are partly determined by nature; Marx is correct that we live in a "kingdom of necessity;" Darwin is correct that, in the fallen world, the "survival of the fittest" prevails.[25] But for Berdyaev, all of them fail to account for the fact that human beings retain a memory of their royal origins and their former paradisical state; they know that they are meant for more. Because each person is the image and likeness of Absolute Being, each person is, even in his fallen state, a "little cosmos, who includes everything in himself."[26] As such, each person is elevated above the empirical reality of the natural world and understands personality to be "a spiritual fact outside nature, outside this world."[27]

Berdyaev's personalism rests on the premise that human beings, uniquely of all creatures, are capable of comprehending the breadth and depth of the universe, and they know that they were not meant for a prison of necessity and labour. Human beings share a deep sense of the tragic; they feel the incommensurable distance between what *is* and what *ought to be*. Especially in later writings, Berdyaev explains our worship of scientific and technological progress as rooted in the human desire to repair the fallen world and to regain the power to rule nature. But by no power of their own can people liberate themselves from their natural prisons – indeed, the more they use technology to do so, the more unfree they become. As Berdyaev puts it, Adam is now "fettered by necessity," and "powerless to free himself ... to return to his divine origins."[28]

Liberation can only come, according to Berdyaev in *The Meaning of the Creative Act*, through the Incarnation of Christ. In homage to Solov'ev, Berdyaev begins with the premise of Christ as God-Man and builds upon it the assertion of Christ as liberator: Christ takes a natural human body, descends into the prison of nature and then, through his divinity, breaks the bonds of the natural, thereby liberating humanity from the tyranny of necessity. He restores the glorious nature of the fallen Adam (a truth revealed most vividly in His Transfiguration on Mount Tabor, where his human form shines with divine light). Christ lifts human nature into the "higher divine spheres of being" and thus reveals the power of every human being to transcend nature and achieve divinity.[29]

In this worldview, the value of every human creature is evident and transcends all other earthly values. Each person has a royal lineage and in divine potential; every person contains the cosmos in himself or herself; every person has the power to become a divine child of God. This divine potential cannot be subordinated to any other principle, natural or social, and must be fully free. Human beings were created as free rulers of creation, and even though they fell captive to nature, their freedom was restored through the incarnation of the God-man.

Freedom was always of paramount importance in Berdyaev's personalism, and indeed, he has been called a "philosopher of freedom." He was drawn to the Orthodox Christian tradition only after his deeper reading and reflection convinced him that true Christianity was the source and guarantor of liberty. But Berdyaev was very careful to clarify what he meant by freedom. Long before Isaiah Berlin made the distinction more widely known, Berdyaev insisted on the crucial difference between "positive" and "negative" freedoms. Negative freedom is a modern concept, defined as "arbitrary free will" in a world where no absolute truth is recognized. "Empty, purposeless, without an object," such a freedom is a mere "freedom from," and is therefore utterly powerless to liberate anyone. Only by recognizing supernatural reality, by "transcending and going beyond the order of nature," can human beings gain the power for true liberation. Transcendent freedom is "positive freedom," or "freedom *for*": freedom as the ability to truly know, to create, and to thus ascend to the divine.[30]

Positive freedom gives a human person the capacity to imitate God and create something out of nothing. As the image of the Creator, the person is also a "creator," called to creativity as "theurgy, God-activity, activity together with God." To support his assertion regarding theurgy, Berdyaev uses pure logic: if human beings are made in the image and likeness of God, and God is a creator, then human beings are creators as well. "God is a concrete personality," he writes, "and therefore a creator; man is a concrete personality and therefore a creator, the whole make-up of being is concrete and personal and hence possesses creative power."[31]

Berdyaev's is no pseudo-gnostic account of a humanity yearning to slip the bonds of the material world. Instead, for Berdyaev, the liberation of the human being was for the purpose of the transfiguration of the material world. He reinterpreted the Eastern patristic tradition of theosis to mean more than an ascetic pursuit of divinization for the individual. Theosis was, for him, "the transfiguration of the world," uniting the divine with the earthly, restoring what was separated, and bringing about a new heaven and a new earth.[32]

Berdyaev believed that this was the essence of the New Testament parable of the talents as well as New Testament references to "fruit" that must be brought forth. These are calls to human creativity – of bringing forth, through labour, that which was not there before. Christ reveals human creative potential, the "vocation" to use what is God-given to produce something new. Creativity encompasses "science, art, inventions, discoveries, and the creation of a new and better life." It is the "realization of God's purpose for the world and for humanity, for the transfiguration of the cosmos, for the Kingdom of God." Creation is, in this sense, a Biblical duty: "Man is called to be a creator and a co-participant in the creation of the world … God gives people various gifts, and no one has the right to bury them in the ground."[33] The creation of beauty is the central task of man as part of the restoration of the fallen cosmos; it is the transformation of life into the intimation of a new kingdom of heaven.[34]

The recognition of the spiritual, creative potential of the person is also the key to the proper ordering of each community or society, pointing the way toward living in common. Each person must not only recognize the right to freedom in oneself, but the very same right in others: "We can formulate the absolute condition of the realization of the moral good: it is the recognition of the unconditional value and right to self-determination of the human person, recognition of it as an end in itself (not as a means), together with recognition of the equal value of people." This is only possible, however, if there is a belief in the transcendent, and here he turns once more toward the philosophy of Solov'ev: "In the 'individual,' in the human person, we esteem the 'universal' … a human being honors his God in another human being."[35]

In placing the person at the foreground of his liberalism, Berdyaev rejected contemporary Russian legal, positivist, and utilitarian justifications of rights. Utilitarianism (Berdyaev uses the example of John Stuart Mill) was perhaps the worst grounding for liberalism because according to that philosophy, the person was subject to "no valuation." If carried through to its logical conclusion, the implication of utility is that one could "strip a human being of his right to freedom of conscience because the majority found it useful to do so." But it should be the other way around: all legal, political, and economic progress should have a single end – the "means for the triumph of the rights of the person." Berdyaev is quite categorical in this regard: "Ethically, nothing can justify the violation of the natural rights of man, for there is no end in the world … in the name of which the principle of the human person as an end in itself could be betrayed." Indeed, even "popular sovereignty" is entirely secondary to "the principle of *inalienable* personal rights."[36]

Throughout the early twentieth century, Berdyaev grew more critical of the kind of utilitarian liberalism triumphant in the West, and of the increasing worship of the state by his Russian liberal friends. In theory, liberalism remained the sole ideology to protect that which was central to human flourishing: "freedom and human rights … which are rooted in the depths of the human soul."[37] But whenever liberalism rejected any pre-political, absolute value for the individual, it failed to acknowledge human rights as "unconditional and inalienable." Furthermore, by rejecting the transcendental and universal basis of the value of the human person, liberalism became enamoured of the state as the sole guarantor of rights and freedoms. By 1917, Berdyaev feared that the power of the state had completely overshadowed that of the individual. Liberalism began to suppress "the freedom of the person in the name of utilitarian, governmental criteria."[38]

The human person was not only endangered by a false understanding of liberalism; it was also under attack by a collectivist philosophy – Marxism. As early as 1907, Berdyaev predicted that Marxism's danger lay in the fact that it was more than just an ideology; it was a "whole faith" complete with its own morality, its own heaven, and its own hell. Moreover, it was a religion that would demand the most violent sacrifice of personhood because in socialism, "A person is never the end and is always the means; the person … is valued only according to its utility for conquering the proletarian, socialist heavens." The socialist sees no limits to individual oppression, because "everything is permitted against the person for the sake of socialism: to deprive the person of all freedom and rights, to devalue dignity, to oppress the person, if this serves just social ends."[39] In a sense, Berdyaev foresaw Soviet Communism long before it had registered any victories or defeats. More importantly, however, he condemned Marxism just as much as liberalism for forgetting that human beings have rights because there is something "eternal" within them: "the right of the divine in the human being, his divine likeness and filial relation with God. A human being therefore only has eternal rights because he is an eternal spirit."[40]

Berdyaev had a radical view of human dignity and value. His interpretation of the meaning of "image and likeness of God" was not limited to an assertion of the value of the uniqueness of the individual; it demanded far more than a merely utilitarian "space" in which individuals would have the freedom to do what they pleased. Berdyaev's vision of human rights is more consonant with a premodern European understanding of rights as the "privileges" of a certain class or society, for example, the benefits bestowed on an aristocracy to empower them to rule. He quotes St Macarius of Egypt: "Know thy nobility, that thou art called to royal dignity: that thou art a chosen race, a holy tongue – a holiness."[41] This chosen race, for Berdyaev, was the whole of humanity.

Berdyaev's path from Marxism to Christianity led him, for a time, into a conservative, nationalist stance shared by many former Marxists. During this period, Berdyaev saw himself as a prophet of messianism, hoping for and expecting a wave of religious renewal led by Russian Christians: "Russian messianism has always been connected with Russia accepting into herself the truth of Christ and through this serving the world. Only as a Christian country, in which everyone, from small to great, suffers for God and the meaning of life, is Russia distinctive (*svoeobrazna*) and great. As a bourgeois-imperialist, skeptical atheist country Russia can be only a second- or third-rate country."[42] This nationalism was only heightened by the passionate anti-German sentiment that Berdyaev adopted during World War I, as Russia fought an increasingly losing battle on the Eastern Front. In article after article, Berdyaev demanded that Russia take her place among the European defenders against German "imperialism."

But with the advent of the Russian Revolution in 1917, Berdyaev was forced to re-evaluate the Russian nationalist project. (It is ironic that Germany was, in fact, the country that took in Berdyaev and his fellow ex-Marxist philosophers, when they were exiled from Soviet Russia by Lenin in 1922.) From that point on, Berdyaev began to write about 1917 as the necessary consequence of Russia's internal corruption and despotism, even when he deplored the Communism that followed. By 1927, he castigated "white" Russian calls for a Russian civil war against Bolshevism as a kind of "utopianism of the right." The right, he wrote, creates "a god for itself out of monarchy, out of the state, out of nationality, out of property, and out of traditional life (more pagan than Christian)." In the end, he wrote, right-wing nationalists were more danger to the Church than the left: "they are in fact preparing another enslavement of the church and another corruption of Christianity."[43] In general, he castigated all those who placed politics before their faith and their neighbours, dividing the world into binaries of "left" and "right," and "good" and "evil." Such moral judgements were "a spiritual perversion" because these were "unimportant and minor things," "third rate" when compared to God or an authentic spiritual life.

For Berdyaev, true faith required a full separation between the "Kingdom of God" and the "Kingdom of Caesar."[44]

While in Berlin, Berdyaev met Oswald Spengler and Max Scheler, and he published *Un Nouveau Moyen Âge* (literally translated as "a new Middle Ages," but rendered as *The End of Our Time* in English), which became his passport into the intellectual life of Europe.[45] This compilation of essays written between 1918 and 1922 was published in Russian in 1923 and immediately translated into German in 1924, quickly becoming popular among German and French intellectuals.[46] The very premise of the book was startling: humanity was reaching the "End of the Renaissance," an end to the humanism that had led to cultural flourishing and progress. The legacy of the Enlightenment, including materialism and positivism, had unleashed antihuman forces into the world, and culture was being destroyed by biological scientism, market politics, and technological mechanization. For these reasons, the twentieth century could be seen as akin to the collapse of the Roman Empire – and humanity was entering a "New Middle Ages." All was not bleak, however. Here Berdyaev insisted on a re-evaluation of the Medieval period, moving away from viewing it as purely a time of darkness and ignorance. Instead, it was a time of great spiritual and cultural growth, without which the Renaissance would never have happened. Perhaps, he speculated, a new Renaissance was on the horizon.[47]

Berdyaev's philosophy of the "person" is central to *The End of Our Time*. In the book's early pages, he makes an important contrast between the person and the liberal-capitalist concept of the "individual." The "individual" is a modern construct, shaped by the philosophical materialism and utilitarianism of the age, whose freedom is defined as the pursuit of material interests. But such a "negative" freedom is pure illusion, leading individuals into the bondage of capitalism.[48] Berdyaev paints a dismal picture of the liberal-capitalist universe, in which ostensibly free individuals are unwittingly enslaved to the machinery of the market.

Moreover, in a world devoid of transcendent values, individual liberty is, for Berdyaev, "simply a formula without any content." In this soulless world, individuals follow their whims aimlessly, losing all connection with one another and becoming socially atomized.[49] Paradoxically, then, "Modern history … developed individualism, and individualism has been in fact the ruin of human individuality, of personality, and we are witnesses today of what comes of an individualism that has no spiritual basis."[50]

The primacy of the individual over the spiritual led to another inevitable, if unintended, consequence of modernity: the pursuit of false collectivism, including communism and fascism. Atomism was unsustainable, so people flocked to community wherever they might find it. "Man is tired to death and is ready to rest upon any collectivism that may come." The rejection of traditional religion had led to the embrace of false religion. This was Berdyaev's first discussion in the European context, as an emigrant, of Marxism as a secular religion in which the "collectivity takes the place of the lost God." Fascism similarly bonded individuals together in an aimless and destructive but nonetheless all-encompassing supra-individual collective.[51] A true individuality – that is, personality – rests on Solov'ev's notion of Godmanhood, in which the individual "recognizes super-individual and superhuman realities and values and submits oneself to them." The recovery of human personality would be the task during the New Middle Ages that was to come.[52]

In 1925, the French writer and editor Stanislas Fumet was so taken by the book that he arranged for a French translation to be published in 1927 by Roseau d'or, Maritain's imprint at the Parisian publishing house Plon. It instantly became a philosophical bestseller, by the standards of the day: it was translated into multiple languages and was still in print in France ten years later. In his essay in this volume, Hubert marshals a plethora of evidence for the importance of this book to French thought. Berdyaev's insights into the failures of secular liberalism, the perils of capitalism, his distinction between individualism and personalism, and his view of Communism as a secular religion, all struck a persuasive chord with French philosophers, particularly Catholics.[53] One of these was Jacques Maritain.

Jacques Maritain, Intelligence, and Human Value

Jacques Maritain was slightly younger than Berdyaev, born in Paris in 1882 into a prosperous and prominent family, one ultimately conflict-torn, especially in religious matters. His grandfather was Jules Favre, a well-known politician and a founder of the Third Republic, and his mother, Geneviève, was determined to make her son a famous political figure. Maritain's parents divorced in 1885 and his father died by suicide in 1904. Baptized as a Lutheran, Maritain abandoned his faith and was a committed atheist and socialist by the time he entered the Sorbonne.[54]

His commitment to socialism was, like Berdyaev's, short-lived. Soon it seemed to Maritain that the materialist premises of his socialist faith were not sufficient for a meaningful life. This was confirmed through his acquaintance in 1901 with Raïssa Oumansoff, who had been born into a Russian Jewish family and had lost her faith after attending university. According to Raïssa, the young couple gave themselves an ultimatum to discover a higher meaning for life or to end it. The philosopher Charles Peguy saved them by suggesting that they attend the lectures of the philosopher Henri Bergson, who revealed a world far more complicated than that of the positivists and materialists. They married in 1904 and their journey to faith, and ultimately to Catholicism, began, assisted along the way by the counsel of the religious writer Léon Bloy. Due to the inspiration of Bloy, Maritain and Raïssa converted in 1906, and convinced Raïssa's sister, Véra, to join them in their new faith.[55]

Like Berdyaev's, Maritain's path from atheism to religious faith shaped his philosophical opposition to modern secularism. Where Berdyaev was steeped in a tradition that extended through the Russian nineteenth century, Maritain's philosophy was grounded in a personal reading of St Thomas Aquinas and the "tradition of Thomists," encouraged by a general revival of Thomism as a result of the efforts of Pope Leo XIII to revitalize scholasticism in the modern era.[56] In time, Raïssa and Jacques read the works of St Thomas Aquinas, and by 1925, Maritain was part of a regular circle designed to update Thomism for the modern age. His project, from that point forward, could be described, in Jason West's words, as "the creative retrieval of Aquinas for the world of today," enriched by a study of the commentators that followed, all the way to the late nineteenth century.[57]

If Berdyaev rested his philosophy of the person on his interpretation of Adam's original glory, so Maritain rested his, in accordance with Aquinas, on the unique human quality of "intelligence," the noblest aspect of the human being. In one of his earliest Christian writings, *Prayer and Intelligence*, composed together with Raïssa in 1922, Maritain describes the intellect as humanity's "most perfect possession," distinguishing human beings from the rest of the natural world, and from the "lower forces" common to both "human and to animal life."[58] The intellect is the source of the highest aspiration of humanity: "divine contemplation, or union with God through … knowledge of him."[59] It is through intelligence that people seek what is good, true, and beautiful, and it is via the intelligence that they achieve that Catholic ideal most akin to the Eastern Christian idea of "theosis" – beatitude. For Maritain, "beatitude" is, most simply, "seeing, possessing God in a deifying vision, in which the very being of God will be one with our intelligence." Moreover, right living depends, in part, on right reason: "reason is the proximate rule of our action, and every interior act of the soul which involves order and government belongs to reason."[60]

But reason could never realize itself in action if it were not for the freedom of the will. For Maritain, as for Berdyaev, freedom (which Maritain defined as free will) is both incontrovertible and of exceptional importance for the full realization of the person. In his *Bergsonian Philosophy and Thomism*, Maritain is unequivocal: "the existence of free will is the most certain fact there is," because human beings can "immediately apprehend" how they determine a course of action by a free will that "triumphs over indetermination." True free will is not, however, completely undetermined and ungoverned. The will does not choose between ready-made objects or actions in the world, but rather depends upon the intellect to reveal the possibilities amongst which the will can choose to "make one actual." Will is thus subordinate to the intelligence as "practice is to theory, action to truth," and intelligence and the will are thus "integral parts of one another." The human person is composed of both intelligence and will, so that each person can discern truth and then freely choose to enact it and make it real. It is for this reason that Maritain calls freedom a "marvelous" and "terrifying" thing: through freedom, persons "cause that to be which was not," and "intervene in the order of the world by acts of endless scope." In so doing, they participate in "divine freedom" and become "like gods."[61]

Centring the essence of humanity on "intelligence" and "will" led Maritain to a full understanding of the departure from personhood in the modern age. Where Berdyaev sought the foundations of modernity in the self-contradictions of the Enlightenment, Maritain, in his early writings, placed the blame squarely and insistently on Martin Luther and his Reformation. In one of his earliest and most passionate works, *Three Reformers*, Maritain castigates Luther for his inability to accept the unknowable nature of divine "grace." Tormented by his persistent sins, worried about the state of his soul, Luther demanded proof of his personal salvation, his "state of grace," and in the process, according to Maritain, he invented modern selfhood – the self as the seat of the will and thus the locus of salvation.

Denigrating "Reason" as a "whore" wholly captive to the wiles of the devil, Luther erased the importance of intelligence and insisted on the "individual will," unmoored from Reason, as the only force within the human being able to receive salvation through Christ. The consequences of this theology were tragic, according to Maritain. Human beings were "cut off from the universal body of the Church" and stand "solitary and naked before God and Christ," in order to achieve "justification and salvation." Faith had no intellectual component; it was pure will that lifted humanity out of otherwise hopeless depravity. The human being had to will his own redemption by "driving himself into a desperate trust in Christ." Maritain declared, in no uncertain terms, that this was "the Pelagianism of despair."[62]

But Luther was by no means the sole contributor to modernity in this regard; his German contribution was complemented by the French rationalism of René Descartes. For Maritain, Descartes is superficially Luther's opposite as the champion and defender of reason, even to the point of dismissing all other human capabilities. In his theory of "clear ideas" as the only criteria for understanding the world and the Divine, Descartes, according to Maritain, committed the opposite sin to Luther: rather than dismissing the human mind as irredeemably fallen, Descartes declared reason to be pure – in Maritain's term, "angelic" – needing no encounter with the material world to understand truth. The consequence, as Maritain saw it, was insanity: "The essence of rationalism consists in making the human reason and its ideological content the measure of what is: truly the extreme of madness."[63]

With one attacking reason and the other deifying it, these two men introduced different, but complementary, paths to the subjectivism of modernity. For Luther, self-will is the path to salvation; for Descartes it is reason. But in the end, both make humanity the measure of the divine and of salvation: "So, for modern Protestant individualism the Church and

Sacraments separate us from God; so for modern philosophic subjectivism, sensation and idea separate us from reality … Consequently, truth and life must be sought only within the human subject."[64]

These two thinkers, alongside Jean-Jacques Rousseau – who deified human emotions – combined to elevate the "individual" above matter, above church, above community in its pursuit of the good and the true. The crisis of modernity, Maritain writes (in a manner similar to Berdyaev and yet before the two met), stems from individualism. In no uncertain terms he declares "modern individualism" a "blunder" – "the exaltation of individuality camouflaged as personality, and the corresponding degradation of true personality." Much like Berdyaev's concept of "negative freedom," Maritain's understanding of "individualism" is that it is illusory, a phantom. Stripped of traditional social protections, unmoored from any anchoring faith, the modern human being is told, "You are a free individual; defend yourself, save yourself, all by yourself." Individualism pretends to offer freedom to follow one's own inclination and will, it promises "universal suffrage, equal rights, liberty of opinion," but what it gives with one hand it takes away with the other; it "delivers the person, isolated, naked, with no social framework to protect it, to all the devouring powers which threaten the soul's life." As a result, Maritain argues, individuals have gained the world but lost their personalities in the thicket of modern secularism: "Look at the Kantian shriveled up in his autonomy, the Protestant tormented by concern for his inward liberty, the Nietzschean giving himself curvature of the spine in his effort to jump beyond good and evil, the Freudian cultivating his complexes and sublimating his libido … all those unhappy people are looking for their personalities; and, contrary to the Gospel promise, they knock and no man opens to them, they seek and they do not find."[65] Maritain, like Berdyaev, insists that rampant individualism is unsustainable, and predicts that individuals will eventually succumb to tyranny of some sort: "the monarchic tyranny of a Hobbes, the democratic tyranny of a Rousseau, or the tyranny of the Providence-State of Hegel and his disciples."[66]

The true alternative was, for Maritain as for Berdyaev, the "person." Maritain wanted to recover the Thomistic definition of the person as "a complete individual substance, intellectual in nature and master of its action," whose essential value lay in the intelligence that could lead to beatitude.

Maritain explains that this is why Aquinas believed that "the word person signifies the noblest and highest thing in all nature." A person transcends the created universe by virtue of possession of "that divine thing, the spirit" and ascends to "a world above the whole bodily order, a spiritual and moral world which, strictly speaking, is not part of this universe." For this reason, for Maritain, as for Berdyaev, persons are free; they, unique among the animals, have the liberty of "choosing their end," a "supreme independence" from all the "machinery of sensible phenomena." The dignity of human beings thus lies not with their individuality, the mere fact of their separation from others and their possession of reason and will. Instead, dignity resides in their personality, that combination of divine spirit and liberty that presses onward toward the divine. In sum, according to Maritain: "As individuals, we are subject to the stars. As persons we rule them."[67]

It can be argued that "creativity" was not as central to Maritain's philosophy as it was to Berdyaev's. However, one of Maritain's earliest publications was a justification of art from a Thomistic perspective. Consistent with his elevation of the "intelligence" as the highest human faculty, he believed art to be a "habit of the practical intellect." A human being interacts with matter, shaping it toward an end – transforming chaotic nature into beauty. Like Berdyaev, Maritain argues that art makes the human being "an associate of God in the making of works of beauty." The artist develops "the faculties with which the Creator has endowed him," and thus creates something like the Creator himself, but "in the second degree." The artist is also blessed in that art is no mere imitation or rearrangement of what God has already created: "artistic creation does not copy God's creation, but continues it."[68]

At first, Maritain's Catholic revolt against secular modernity led him into the arms of Action Française, the far-right monarchist association formed by the controversial Charles Maurras. Maurras was a traditionalist, a champion of "Latinity" – a vision of Western culture as hearkening back to the pre-Enlightenment era, before individualism and democracy undermined the strength of Europe. His antisemitism was well known (and this was always a sticking point for Maritain, especially because of Raïssa and Véra's Jewish heritage). Moreover, he was not a Catholic. Nevertheless, Maritain was associated with the group until 1926. Later, Raïssa wrote an insightful assessment of Father Clérissac, Maritain's spiritual guide and the man who brought Maritain to Action Française: "In his disgust of the modern world … he trusted a movement … the spiritual dangers of which he did not discern."[69] These words could easily have described Maritain.

Pope Pius XI condemned the Action Française group in 1926, mostly because of their use of religion for political ends. Maurras and his fellow members hoped that the church would become an ally in the pursuit of Latinity, and Maurras (like Carl Schmitt) admired the church for its hierarchical and unitary cultural authority. But for Maurras, politics was primary.[70] When he condemned the pope's decree against Action Française, this was the last straw for Maritain. In a blistering letter he wrote to Maurras in January 1927, Maritain insisted that his refusal to accept the papal decree contradicted his supposed traditionalism. "You have always fought against the heresy of private judgment," he wrote, "you have always worked to give men's minds a proper feeling for authority, for hierarchy, for the *conservative order of being.* That you should be led to an attitude that is in practice strictly protestant and anarchic will be for many a horribly painful scandal."[71]

This moment demonstrated to Maritain the perils of political ideology, and it was with this experience in mind that he published *Primauté du spirituel* (The primacy of the spiritual) in 1927. In this text he boldly argued that, in all matters, things political had to be subordinated to things spiritual, "for the good of the State is not God Himself, and remains far, far inferior to the supreme beatitude of man." For this reason, he believed that Maurras's insistence on the primacy of politics was anti-Christian. Maritain also insisted that in modern secular societies, the church should remain separate from the state. The only form of legitimate temporal power for the church had to be "indirect," intervening when the spiritual needs of its flock were concerned. The likeness to Berdyaev's exhortations on the separation of church and state are striking. (When first translated, the English title of the work was *The Things That Are Not Caesar's*, very similar to the title of Berdyaev's article of the same year.)[72]

The similarity of the ideas of the two men, especially the striking confluence of thought on the person, modernity, and the state, raises the question whether these thinkers influenced each other before they met in 1925. This is difficult to determine, though it may be noted that Maritain was familiar with the Russian intellectual heritage through his wife and sister-in-law, and Berdyaev wrote on Catholic philosophy as early as 1908. It would be possible to trace common readings that influenced their ideas, but it should also be noted that Maritain himself wrote in his first letter to Berdyaev, with apparent surprise, "It is a great comfort and lively pleasure for me to see how on so many essential points, and especially the criticism of the 'modern' world, our ways of thinking converge."[73]

Collaboration and Conversation: The Interwar Years

When the men met in 1925, both of them found it to be providential – a meeting of minds that had followed similar but separate paths. From that year on, their intellectual endeavours were products of collaboration and conversation. Beginning in 1926, Berdyaev and Maritain discussed their shared passion, the place of Christianity in the modern world, and these conversations are at the heart of the correspondence included in this volume. They also participated in a series of ecumenical conversations with Orthodox, Catholic, and Protestant thinkers at the Russian Academy in Paris, until Pope Pius XI's condemnation of such conversations in 1928. After that, Berdyaev and Maritain organized more informal discussions in Paris, both at Maritain's home in Meudon and at Berdyaev's house in Clamart. At these meetings, Berdyaev met other important French intellectuals including Emmanuel Mounier, Etienne Gilson, and Gabriel Marcel. Both Maritain and Berdyaev expressed their ideas in the personalist journal *Esprit*, founded in 1932, and both were influential in the drafting of the *Personalist Manifesto*, written in 1936 by Emmanuel Mounier.[74]

The story of the interactions and collaborations of these two men in the interwar period, as narrated in Hubert's essay, is exceptionally well researched and invaluable. Using the correspondence, as well as diaries, memoirs, and published work, the introduction and annotations provide much needed information for a proper appreciation of their relationship. Hubert pays particular attention to the ecumenical endeavours Maritain and Berdyaev jointly organized, demonstrating how important the reconciliation between Christian denominations was for both. Moreover, the essay provides an excellent resource for understanding the intellectual interactions of a wide variety of Russian émigré thinkers and writers within the French intellectual milieu.

There is no doubt that Maritain and Berdyaev were very different philosophers, and not simply because they belonged to different Christian denominations. Hubert lays out in clear detail the philosophical differences that undergirded many of their debates. The Frenchman remained a Thomist and insisted on the grounding of his insights in the intelligible reason given to humanity by God. The Russian, on the other hand, grew impatient with the Thomistic system, and insisted that humanity could never be defined by reason alone – that the path of the individual to the divine was often undefinable and mystical. Even the question of the nature of God and of Being were points of disagreement between the two men. Hubert describes a humorous moment: a meeting of Catholic and Orthodox philosophers and theologians in Clamart in 1930 where Berdyaev presented a paper on the primacy of Divine Nothingness in the mystical understanding of God. As one participant noted, "Berdyaev's ideas provoke high agitation within our little circle. *French and Russians rose up speaking all at once.*" Maritain, in his letter to Berdyaev, deplored the conflict, but ended up feeling that Berdyaev's thought was essentially "an anti-intellectual existential philosophy." In the end, Maritain always adhered to a Thomistic personalism, while Berdyaev described his own personalist philosophy as "existentialist."[75]

Nevertheless, the relationship between the two men served as an important vehicle by which both of their contributions entered European intellectual history. Friends of both philosophers recognized their overlapping views. The émigré Helen Iswolsky, who knew both, declared that the similarities in the "Christian humanism" of the two philosophers was Berdyaev's lasting contribution to Western thought, not just in France but throughout the world.[76] Catholics were sometimes critical of the closeness between Maritain and Berdyaev, complaining that this relationship was moving Maritain away from his Catholic roots.[77] Subsequent French philosophies of Christian humanism and personalism were, in large part, the result of conversations between Maritain and Berdyaev. Indeed, it is possible to argue that personalism was, in some ways, a "Russo-French" philosophy.

Given that Berdyaev has yet to see a revival of the sort that Maritain has received, it is important to emphasize just how clearly these letters reveal

Berdyaev's contribution to European thought of the period. The insights found in Berdyaev's *End of Our Time* and elsewhere influenced the entire personalist movement. Berdyaev had convinced personalists of the 1930s and early 1940s that a new Middle Ages was approaching: a time of conflict in which any new Christian humanism would have to contend with the twin barbarisms of Communism and Fascism. Maritain remembered one such conversation quite well: "We were wondering how two apparently contradictory facts could be reconciled: the fact that modern history seemed to be entering, according to the expression of Berdyaev, into a New Middle Age, in which the unity and the universality of Christian culture would be found once again, and this other fact, that the general movement of civilization appears to be dragging the world toward the universalism of the anti-Christ and his rod of iron."[78] The task of Christian philosophers, then, was to defend humanism in an age of crisis – encapsulated in one of Mounier's slogans: "Refaire la Renaissance" ("Remake the Renaissance"), echoing Berdyaev's notion that the Middle Ages were the precursor to the Renaissance that followed.[79] Mounier gave credit to Berdyaev in 1939, as the war was just beginning: "Now that we are perhaps at the debut of a new Middle Ages, if you have something to say, let me know."[80]

The most openly acknowledged of Berdyaev's contributions to French personalism was his conviction that Communism was a particular threat to the person in the modern era. First expressed in *Un Nouveau Moyen Âge*, Berdyaev's views were more fully elaborated in 1932 in the first issue of the personalist journal *Esprit*. Berdyaev's article, entitled "The Truth and Lies of Communism," presented Communism as a natural result of the failure of liberal capitalism, which exploited human labour, and of the failure of Christianity, which had done little to ameliorate the suffering of the world. But he argued that Communism is ultimately evil because it "refuses the personality all value and all significance."

After publication, the article became a major topic of conversation, prompting heated debate throughout the work of all the personalists, especially Maritain. In a number of his writings, Maritain described Communism as the result of liberal capitalist atomism and the failure of Christianity: "at its origin we find a desperate protest against the dehumanization of the person … In reality, then, it must be counted as a Christian heresy."[81] John Hellman states unequivocally that Berdyaev's "spiritualist critique of communism became solidly implanted in the *Esprit* movement." The idea of Communism as a religion, and perhaps even a form of heretical Christianity, would later appear in the work of Eric Voegelin, who acknowledged the influence of Berdyaev's philosophy on interwar political thought.[82] Indeed in 1934, when *Esprit* founded a philosophy discussion group in Paris, Berdyaev was perceived as one of the most important thinkers of the time.[83]

In sum, it is important to fill the gaps in accounts of the Catholic revival of the interwar twentieth century by restoring Berdyaev to his central place. Of all the Russian émigrés in Paris and in the rest of Europe, Berdyaev most clearly shaped the conversation on humanism and personalism. Through his close connections with Jacques Maritain, Etienne Gilson, and Emmanuel Mounier, Berdyaev contributed a distinct and original Christian philosophy to the French personalist movement, which, in turn, led to the form of "person centred" Christian discourse that triumphed in the post-1945 era. In 1931, Maritain openly praised the Russians for bringing to France this "theandric" view of human beings, so central to the full understanding of the person and so opposed to the secular idea of the individual.[84] In *The Person and the Common Good*, he wrote that the distinction between the individual and the person was a long-standing one, and developed particularly by Berdyaev.[85] By the time Jacques Maritain wrote his highly influential *The Rights of Man and Natural Law* in 1942, his view of the person had evolved through encounters with Berdyaev's. One can even hear echoes of Berdyaev in Maritain's categorical statement that "A single human soul is of more worth than the whole universe of bodies and material goods … In light of the eternal value and absolute dignity of the soul, society exists for each person and is subordinate thereto."[86]

Reassessing Personalism

Maritain's prominence as a philosopher grew dramatically, especially after World War II. Even before the war, Maritain was highly sought out for lectures and talks in Europe and the Americas. When war broke out, Maritain decided to stay at the Pontifical Institute of Medieval Studies in Toronto, in large part because he feared for the safety of his Jewish wife and sister-in-law. Later he taught at Princeton and Columbia. By 1942, he published his *The Rights of Man and Natural Law*, which positioned him to become "the premier postwar philosopher of human rights."[87] He was then invited, as one of 150 prominent thinkers, to participate in a UNESCO Committee on the Philosophical Principles of the Rights of Man. Maritain chaired a meeting of the committee in 1947 and contributed a chapter on a UNESCO symposium, entitled "On the Philosophy of Human Rights."[88] As Moyn reminds us, ideas about international human rights were clearly shaped by Catholic personalist thought, via Maritain.[89]

World War II separated Berdyaev and Maritain in person, but Berdyaev followed Maritain's efforts, especially those regarding the institutionalization of international human rights. In 1945 he wrote that "the declaration of the rights of man is of Christian origin." Yet again he reiterated his call to restore the centrality of the freedom of the person in the postwar era: "A person is called to freedom, and in that freedom he achieves his full humanity. But he should not seek freedom for himself … he should seek it for others, for his brothers in their common humanity."[90]

Berdyaev died in 1948, at his desk in Clamart, France. Jacques Maritain ended his days in France as well – returning to live with the Little Brothers of Jesus in Toulouse. He died in 1970. Interest in the philosophies of Berdyaev and Maritain declined toward the end of the twentieth century, perhaps because their ideas did not seem useful for, and even contradicted, projects such as the Second Vatican Council, with which Maritain became partly disillusioned; the post-Communist reuniting of church and state in Russia, which Berdyaev would have deplored; and, of course, the resurgence in the 1980s of globalized neo-liberalism that both thinkers would have also opposed.

Now that so many of these developments have themselves been called into question, it is time for a reassessment of the personalist tradition and the rights tradition that is based upon it. Samuel Moyn and James Chappel have argued that French personalism arose in the late 1920s and 1930s, as Communism and Fascism stood out as particular ideologies hostile to the absolute value of the person. As James Chappel points out, Bolshevism, like Fascism, was seen as "a new entity that, through its totalitarian claims to dominance, abolishes the possibility of Christian spirituality as understood from a personalist perspective."[91] Both scholars place personalism in the history of reactionary, Catholic politics. Moyn even extends this to condemn the postwar human rights tradition as a whole, casting suspicion on a phenomenon that originated in a "conservative" Catholic philosophy. Moyn insists that secular progressives should be wary of supporting human rights as "part and parcel of a reformulation of conservatism in the name of a vision of moral constraint, not human emancipation or individual liberation … so that men and (perhaps especially) women could conform to God's will and moral order."[92]

But it is very important to note that though the personalists were prescient regarding the depredations of Communism and Fascism, they did not ignore the excesses of industrial capitalism and the liberal marketplace that rested upon it, and here, the designation of personalism as "conservative" bears some scrutiny. Both thinkers agreed that even democracy itself, if it ignored the dignity of the human person, ended up as "dehumanizing."[93] Explicitly borrowing from Marxist critiques of bourgeois industrial society, and following Berdyaev's argument in *Un Nouveau Moyen Âge*, both Maritain and Mounier lamented the mechanization of daily life and the commodification of values in capitalist economies. In this manner, personalists positioned themselves against all the major interwar political ideologies. At times, Berdyaev's thought rested on a Christian liberalism, and at times it tended toward anarchism. Maritain, on the other hand, advocated for a rights-based communitarian politics which placed limits both on state power and on economic exploitation.[94] But both men refused to be hemmed in by any political movement. For both, this was an intentional stance – having succumbed, in their early years, to versions of reactionary nationalism, they wished to remain independent from any political loyalties that sought to claim them. Rather than deploring the human rights movement's connections with personalism, scholars should therefore reconsider personalism's defence of a universal system of human rights.

Unlike in the West, where rights may seem to be taken for granted, a robust defence of rights is extraordinarily valuable in places where such a tradition is not well established. This was true, for example, in the Russia of Berdyaev's day. The Russian intellectual elite of the nineteenth and twentieth centuries was positioned to develop personalism as a bulwark for rights precisely because of their experience of oppression during the Tsarist and Soviet eras. As Eric Lohr has argued, those political philosophers who wished to fight for rights and dignity in Russia were compelled to look beyond their own traditions to articulate a universal theory of human rights. In Lohr's words: "If left alone, the British legal system might evolve to give the citizen expanded rights that were deeply grounded in domestic custom, law, and institutions. Left to itself, the Russian legal system had a demonstrated penchant to do just the opposite, succumbing to the arbitrary force of the tsar and state over the individual … The concept of natural rights not only gave the individual a claim against the state but also, by limiting the state, thereby protected intermediate civic and institutional realms."[95]

Finally, it should be emphasized that personalists ended up, because of their philosophy, rejecting not only Communism and Fascism, but also the temptations of Vichy, Franco, and the antisemitism that was common in their day.[96] This track record should surely count in their favour, and in favour of their philosophies.

In an era of neo-liberal crisis, the freedom and rights advocated by these two philosophers should be reassessed to see if they can provide the foundation for a new kind of liberalism: one that can transcend modern categories of "left" and "right" and provide a limit to any social or political project, whether libertarian or collectivist. Instead of modern individualism, replete with utilitarian and materialist notions, this new liberalism would recognize the fullness, dignity, and potential of every human being and make it the centre of ethical, social, and political concern.

Notes

1 Alan Jacobs, *The Year of Our Lord 1943* (Oxford: Oxford University Press, 2018), 42–3.

2 Ibid., 125–6.

3 Gerald A. McCool, "Jacques Maritain: A Neo-Thomist Classic," *The Journal of Religion* 58, no. 4 (1978): 380, 383.

4 See Sarah Shortall, *Soldiers of God in a Secular World: Catholic Theology and Twentieth-Century French Politics* (Cambridge, MA: Harvard University Press, 2021); Eduard Baring, *Converts to the Real: Catholicism and the Making of Continental Philosophy* (Cambridge, MA: Harvard University Press, 2019);

James Chappel, *Catholic Modern: The Challenge of Totalitarianism and the Remaking of the Church* (Cambridge, MA: Harvard University Press, 2018). An English-language exposition of the philosophy of Jacques Maritain by Jason West will soon be published by the Catholic University of America Press. I am indebted to him for providing a draft of portions of his manuscript.

5 Samuel Moyn, *The Last Utopia: Human Rights in History* (Cambridge, MA: Harvard University Press, 2010); Samuel Moyn, *Christian Human Rights* (Philadelphia: University of Pennsylvania Press, 2015).

6 They did so, Moyn argues, in a very particular interwar context in which political liberalism was challenged from the left and the right with the pernicious rise of early twentieth-century "totalitarianism" (here he builds on James Chappel's important scholarship on the Catholic origins of the theory of "totalitarianism"); Moyn, *Christian*, 67–71. See also James Chappel, "The Catholic Origins of Totalitarianism Theory in Interwar Europe," *Modern Intellectual History* 8, no. 3 (2011): 561–90.

7 Moyn does acknowledge Berdyaev's contribution in a footnote, claiming that Berdyaev brought with him to France "an old Russian tradition of religious personalism." See Moyn, *Christian*, 66–7, 91.

8 Ibid., 90–1.

9 The influence of Berdyaev on Maritain is often acknowledged in passing, but rarely explored. The one exception is the excellent work of Catherine Baird, most of which, sadly, remains unpublished, especially her 1997 PhD dissertation, which lays the groundwork for understanding Berdyaev's influence on French thought by showing the important points of contact between Berdyaev and the French personalists. See Catherine Baird, "Russian Personalism: The Influence of Russian Populism on French Personalism, 1930–1938" (master's thesis, McGill University, 1992) and "'The Third Way': Russia's Religious Philosophers in the West, 1917–1996" (PhD Diss., McGill University, 1997). See also Bernard Doering, *Jacques Maritain and the French Catholic Intellectuals* (Notre Dame, IN: University of Notre Dame Press, 1983), 24.

10 Randall Poole, "Integral Humanisms: Jacques Maritain, Vladimir Soloviev, and the History of Human Rights," *Vestnik Sankt-Peterburgskogo Universiteta: Filosofiia i konfliktologiia* 35, no. 1 (2019): 92–106; see also Paul Werth, "The Emergence of 'Freedom of Conscience' in Imperial Russia," *Kritika: Explorations in Russian and Eurasian History* n.s., 13, no. 3 (Summer 2012): 585–610, and Eric Lohr, "The Ideal Citizen and the Real Subject in Imperial Russia," *Kritika: Explorations in Russian and Eurasian History* n.s., 7, no. 2 (Spring 2006): 173–94.

11 Lidiia Berdiaeva, *Professiia: Zhena filosofa* (Moscow: Molodaia gvardiia, 2002), 92, 167; Jean-Luc Barre, *Jacques and Raïssa Maritain: Beggars for Heaven*, trans. Bernard E. Doering (Notre Dame, IN: University of Notre Dame press, 2005), 197.

12 This book will refer to the city as "Kiev" for the sake of preserving the historical context.
13 Oleksandr Obedkov, "Retrospektivnii analiz filosofskoi kategorii 'svoboda,'" *Humanities Studies* 88, no. 11 (2022): 59–65; Richard Gorban, "Deiaki aspekti spetsifiki doslidnitskikh pidkhodiv do religiino-filosofskogo dobroku Mikoli Berdiaeva," *Ukrainski Religieznavstvo* 71–2 (2014): 187–95. One of the key arguments for including Berdyaev in the Ukrainian philosophical tradition is that his older brother Sergei was a Ukrainophile. See Vladimir Volkovskii, "Filosofiia svobody Nikolaia Berdiaeva i liberal'naia traditsiia ukrainskoi politico-filosofskoi mysli," *Solov'evskie issledovaniia* 2, no. 42 (2014): 138–54.
14 Nicolas Berdyaev, *Dream and Reality: An Essay in Autobiography*, trans. Katharine Lampert (London: G. Bles, 1950), 92.
15 Sergey Horujy and Patrick Lally Michelson, "Slavophiles, Westernizers, and the Birth of Russian Philosophical Humanism," in *A History of Russian Philosophy 1830–1930: Faith, Reason, and the Defense of Human Dignity*, ed. G.M. Hamburg and Randall A. Poole (Cambridge: Cambridge University Press, 2010), 27–51. See also Randall Poole, "Editor's Introduction," in *Problems of Idealism: Essays in Russian Social Philosophy* (New Haven, CT: Yale University Press, 2003), 1–78, esp. 4–5.
16 Vladimir Solovyov, *A Solovyov Anthology*, ed. S.L. Frank, trans. Natalie Duddington (London: SCM Press, 1950), 15–16. Konstantin Mochul'skii, *Vladimir Solov'ëv: Zhizn' i uchenie* (Paris: YMCA Press, 1951), 10, also notes that Godmanhood is a modern philosophical development of Chalcedon.
17 See Ruth Coates, "Theosis in Early Twentieth-Century Russian Religious Thought," in *The Oxford Handbook of Russian Religious Thought*, ed. Caryl Emerson, George Pattison, and Randall A. Poole (Oxford: Oxford University Press, 2020); Randall Poole, "Vladimir Solov'ev's Philosophical Anthropology," in *A History of Russian Philosophy 1830–1930*, 136–7.
18 Poole, "Editor's Introduction."
19 N.A. Berdiaev, "The Ethical Problem in the Light of Philosophical Idealism," in *Problems of Idealism*, 161–96, esp. 171.
20 Nicolas Berdyaev, *The Destiny of Man*, trans. Natalie Duddington (San Rafael, CA: Semantron Press, 2009), 55.
21 Nicolas Berdyaev, *The Meaning of the Creative Act*, trans. Donald A. Lowrie (San Rafael, CA: Semantron Press, 2008), 79, 19.
22 According to St Symeon, Adam's Fall was partly due to his fearlessness, because he felt all-powerful due to "great glory which he was vouchsafed in abundance." St Symeon the New Theologian, *The First Created Man* (Platina, CA: St Herman of Alaska Brotherhood, 2013), 87–9, 68. See also Bogdan G. Bucur and Vladimir Ivanovic, "The Image of Adam's Glory: Observations on the Early Christian Tradition of Luminosity as Iconic Garment," RIHA *Journal* 0224 (30 September 2019), DOI: https://doi.org/10.11588/riha.2019.2.70048;

Alon Goshen Gottstein, "The Body as Image of God in Rabbinic Literature," *The Harvard Theological Review* 87, no. 2 (April 1994): 171–95; Berdyaev, *Meaning*, 65.

23 Berdyaev, *Meaning*, 72–3.

24 Ibid., 11.

25 Ibid., 75–6.

26 This belief, that man is a microcosm of the universe, is common to the Kabbalah, Böhme, anthroposophy, and the Eastern patristics.

27 Berdyaev, *Meaning*, 49–52, 61.

28 Ibid., 47, 79.

29 Ibid., 79.

30 Ibid., 153, 147.

31 Ibid., 135.

32 Nikolai Berdiaev, "Spasenie i tvorchestvo," *Put'*, 1926, http://www.hrono.ru/libris/lib_b/berdo4.html

33 Ibid.

34 Berdyaev, *Destiny*, 126.

35 Berdiaev, "Ethical," 175–7.

36 Ibid., 179.

37 Nikolai Berdiaev, "Filosofiia neravenstva: pis'ma k nedrugam po sotsial'noi filosofii," in *Sobranie sochinenii*, ed. N. Berdiaev, vol. 4 (Paris: YMCA Press, 1990), 253–596, esp. 418.

38 Nikolai Berdiaev, *Novoe religioznoe soznanie i obshchestvennost'* (Moscow: Kanon, 1999), 195–6.

39 Ibid., 128–9.

40 Berdiaev, "Filosofiia," 423, 431–2.

41 Berdyaev, *Meaning*, 82–3.

42 Christopher Stroop, "Nationalist War Commentary as Russian Religious Thought: The Religious Intelligentsia's Politics of Providentialism," *The Russian Review* 72, no. 1 (2013): 94–115. Berdyaev is quoted on page 103.

43 N. Berdiaev, "Dnevnik filosofa: o dukhe vremeni i monarkhii," *Put'*, no. 6 (January 1927): 110–14.

44 Nikolai Berdiaev, "Tsarstvo bozhie i tsarstvo kesaria," *Put'*, no. 1 (September 1925): 31–52, 51.

45 Berdyaev, *Dream*, 127. *Un Nouveau Moyen Âge: Réflexions sur les destinées de la Russie et de l'Europe* was translated by Aniouta Fumet and published in the Roseau d'or series of the Plon publishing house under the editorship of Jacques Maritain in 1927.

46 Baird, "Third Way," 284–5.

47 Nicolas Berdyaev, *The End of Our Time*, trans. Rev. Fr Donald Attwater (San Rafael, CA: Semantron Press, 2009), 16.

48 Ibid., 35.

49 Ibid., 35, 84–5.
50 Ibid., 35.
51 Ibid., 16, 39, 89. This idea, fully developed later in the *Origins of Russian Communism* and elsewhere, was greatly influential in Europe, and was adopted, in part, by Eric Voegelin. See Gerhard Wagner and Gilbert Weiss, eds., *A Friendship That Lasted a Lifetime: The Correspondence Between Alfred Schutz and Eric Voegelin* (Columbia: University of Missouri Press, 2011), 77; Eric Voegelin, *Selected Correspondence, 1950–1984* (Columbia: University of Missouri Press, 2007), 203; and Eric Voegelin, *Selected Correspondence, 1924–1949* (Columbia: University of Missouri Press, 2009), 574, 611.
52 Berdyaev, *End*, 35.
53 See Lidiia Berdiaeva, *Professiia: Zhena filosofa* (Moscow: Molodaia gvardiia, 2002), 154; Baird, "Third Way," 284–5. Berdyaev was well aware of the success of *Un Nouveau Moyen Âge* in France. See his "Young France and Social Justice," *Dublin Review* 96 (January 1935): 37–46, esp. 37.
54 Ralph McInerny, *The Very Rich Hours of Jacques Maritain: A Spiritual Life* (Notre Dame, IN: University of Notre Dame Press, 2003), 7–8, and also Jason West's unpublished manuscript.
55 Ibid., 26–7.
56 Baring, *Converts*, 24; Shortall, *Soldiers*, 31; McCool, "Maritain," 387. An excellent discussion of Maritain's continuing interest in Thomistic commentators, including John of St Thomas, is found in Matthew K. Minerd, "The Influence of John of St. Thomas upon the Thought of Jacques Maritain" (unpublished manuscript).
57 West's unpublished manuscript; Minerd, "Influence."
58 Jacques Maritain, *Prayer and Intelligence: Being La Vie D'Oraison of Jacques and Raïssa Maritain* (London: Sheed & Ward, 1928), 17, 29, 30.
59 Ibid., 33.
60 Jacques Maritain, *Three Reformers: Luther – Descartes – Rousseau* (New York: Charles Scribner's Sons, 1929), 38–40.
61 Jacques Maritain, *Bergsonian Philosophy and Thomism*, trans. Mabelle L. Andison (New York: Philosophical Library, 1955), 252, 256, 266, 271, 274. This book was originally published in French in 1913.
62 Maritain, *Three Reformers*, 35, 18. "Pelagianism" refers to the fifth-century heresy of the monk Pelagius, who asserted that the human will was sufficient to obtain salvation. Though Maritain came to regret his more violent critique of Luther, his attitude toward Cartesianism remained negative.
63 Ibid., 85.
64 Ibid., 46.
65 Ibid., 19.
66 Ibid., 20–1.

67 Ibid., 19–21. See also Shortall, *Soldiers*, 68–9; V. Bradley Lewis, "Thomism, Personalism, and Politics: The Case of Jacques Maritain," *Quaestiones Disputatae* 9, no. 2 (2019): 151–73, muse.jhu.edu/article/720330. Matthew Minerd attributes this view of human beings as above "the universe" to John of St Thomas. See Minerd, "Influence," 25.

68 Jacques Maritain, *Art and Scholasticism: With Other Essays* (New York: Charles Scribner's Sons, 1942), 9, 11, 63.

69 Quoted by Doering in *Jacques Maritain*, 12.

70 Shortall, *Soldiers*, 53–4.

71 Doering, *Jacques Maritain*, 25, 30. See also Shortall, *Soldiers*, 69–70

72 Jacques Maritain, *The Things That Are Not Caesar's*, trans. J.F. Scanlan (London: Sheed & Ward, 1932), 2

73 N. Berdiaev, "Katolicheskii modernizm i krizis sovremennogo soznaniia," *Russkaya mysl'* no. 9 (September 1908): 80–94. The English translation of Maritain's *The Things That Are Not Caesar's* includes a section on Russian Orthodoxy, which demonstrates a familiarity with Russian thought. See Bernard Hubert's essay below, 50; Lewis, "Thomism."

74 Antoine Arjakovsky, *The Way: Russian Religious Thinkers of the Russian Emigration in Paris and Their Journal, 1925–1940* (Notre Dame, IN: University of Notre Dame Press, 2013), 150–1, 164.

75 See Hubert, 60. This controversy is also described in Baring, *Converts*, 167.

76 Hélène Iswolsky, *No Time to Grieve … An Autobiographical Journey* (Philadelphia, PA: The Winchell Company, 1985), 184, and Hélène Iswolsky, *Light Before Dusk: A Russian Catholic in France, 1923–1941* (New York: Longmans, Green, 1942), 97.

77 Hubert, 90. Fr Garrigou Lagrange complained in a letter that Maritain was falling under the influence of Berdyaev and, it was implied, moving away from Thomism. See also Charles Journet, *Journet-Maritain: Correspondance, Vol. III: 1940–1949* (Paris: Editions Saint-Paul, 1998), 54. At this time, Berdyaev himself felt that he and Maritain were growing closer philosophically; see Berdiaeva, *Professiia*, 116.

78 Barre, *Beggars*, 294.

79 R. William Rauch, Jr, *Politics and Belief in Contemporary France: Emmanuel Mounier and Christian Democracy, 1932–1950* (The Hague, NL: Martinus Nijhoff, 1972), 89.

80 Association des amis d'Emmanuel Mounier, "Correspondance Mounier-Berdiaeff," *Bulletin des Amis d'Emmanuel Mounier* 33 (February 1969): 5–20, 15.

81 Maritain, *True Humanism*, 31; Jacques Maritain, *The Person and the Common Good*, trans. John J. Fitzgerald (New York: Charles Scribner's Sons, 1947), 83, 86.

82 John Hellman, *Emmanuel Mounier and the New Catholic Left, 1930–1950* (Toronto: University of Toronto Press, 1981), 101.

83 Ibid., 80, 286n44.

84 Jacques Maritain, *The Dream of Descartes*, trans. Mabelle L. Andison (New York: Philosophical Library, 1944), 186.

85 Maritain, *Person*, 24.

86 Berdyaev, *Destiny*, 13. When *The Destiny of Man* came out in 1934, Berdyaev received letters from various French philosophers about the importance of this work; see Berdiaeva, *Professiia*, 110. In 1940, after the Maritains had moved to the United States, Raïssa Maritain explicitly asked for this book to be shipped to their new residence; see Journet, *Correspondance III*, 117.

87 Samuel Moyn, "Personalism, Community, and the Origin of Human Rights," *Human Rights in the Twentieth Century*, ed. Stefan-Ludwig Hoffman (Cambridge: Cambridge University Press, 2011), 87, 90.

88 It was also published: UNESCO, with an introduction by Jacques Maritain, *Human Rights: Comments and Interpretations* (New York: Columbia University Press, 1949). On Maritain and the UNESCO project, see Paul Gorden Lauren, *The Evolution of International Human Rights: Visions Seen*, 3rd ed. (Philadelphia: University of Pennsylvania Press, 2011), 210–11; McInerny, *The Very Rich Hours of Jacques Maritain*, 140, 160, 165.

89 "Catholic influence on the Universal Declaration of Human Rights (particularly through the Catholic thinker Jacques Maritain) ... was crucial." Michael Rosen, *Dignity: Its History and Meaning* (Cambridge, MA: Harvard University Press, 2012), 53.

90 Nikolai Berdiaev, "O zatrudneniakh svobody," in *Istina i otkrovenie*, ed. Nikolai Berdiaev (Sankt Peterburg: Izd-vo Russkogo Khristianskogo gumanitarnogo instituta, 1996), 274.

91 Chappel, "Origins," 581. Ironically, Chappel argues that Maritain's argument here "prefigures" Eric Voegelin's thesis that communism is a "religion." In fact, Maritain was following Berdyaev here, as Voegelin did later.

92 Moyn, *Christian*, 10.

93 Bernard A. Gendreau, "The Role of Jacques Maritain and Emmanuel Mounier in the Creation of French Personalism," *The Personalist Forum* 8, no. 1 (1992): 97–108, 99.

94 B. Jayne Miller, "Anarchism and French Catholicism in *Esprit*," *Journal of the History of Ideas* 37, no. 1 (1976): 163–74.

95 Eric Lohr, "The Ideal Citizen and Real Subject in Late Imperial Russia," *Kritika: Explorations in Russian and Eurasian History* 7, no. 2 (Spring 2006): 173–94, esp. 192.

96 Hubert, 100.

The Dialogue between Jacques Maritain and Nikolai Berdyaev (1925–1948)

Bernard Hubert

WELL BEFORE THE RUSSIAN REVOLUTION OF 1917, within the context of the Franco-Russian alliance, knowledge of Russia had grown in France. This is clear from the well-known book by Eugène-Melchior Vogüé, *Le Roman russe* (The Russian novel), published in 1886.[1] After 1917, the exile of those Russians who had found refuge in France brought Russian and French people closer in many ways. Publishing initiatives gave Russian writers the chance to reach a wider public.[2] Solidarity associations were established in support of Russian Orthodox émigrés in France, including the Amitiés franco-russes (French-Russian Friendships), which provided material aid to Russian citizens starting in 1920; L'Union française d'aide aux Russes (The French Union for Aid to Russians), presided over by Monsignor Chaptal, the auxiliary bishop of Paris, which helped 250,00 Russians between 1922 and 1930; and the Amis des étudiants russes (Friends of Russian Students), a Lille association. There was also the work of Abbé Couturier in Lyon and the Association française d'aide aux émigrés (The French Association for Aid to Émigrés) in Nice and the Alpes-Maritimes.

In 1923 in Lille, the Saint Basil seminary was established with financing by the Œuvre des écoles d'Orient and staffed by Dominicans with the aim of helping Orthodox émigrés, but within a Catholic context. More generally, the "Roman project" of Pope Pius XI, who became head of the Catholic church in 1922 and favoured the reunion of all Christians within the Roman Catholic church, cast suspicion on the solidarity between French Catholics and Russian Orthodox émigrés. In 1926, Russian Orthodox reservations about Monsignor Chaptal and their fear of Catholic proselytizing were expressed officially by Metropolitan Evlogii (Vassilii Georgievskii), the administrative leader of Orthodox parishes in Europe.[3]

In the other direction, the Union pour la verité (Union for Truth) and the Décades de Pontigny (ten-day assemblies at the Abbaye de Pontigny) contributed to the stimulation of intellectual contact not only between Catholics and Orthodox, but also included Protestants. In this context, the meeting between the Thomist philosopher Jacques Maritain and the Russian philosopher Nikolai Berdyaev demonstrates a mutual effort at understanding through friendly dialogue in a faith-based setting. Despite philosophical differences that remained unchanged, the dialogue between these two thinkers, whose paths intersected over several years, allowed over that time a convergence of intellectual forces in the service of a spiritual renaissance of Western culture and clarified the political and social stakes to be defended in 1920s and 30s Europe, which was so unsettled by totalitarian ideologies.

The "singular"[4] relation between Jacques Maritain (1882–1973) and Nikolai Berdyaev (1874–1948) may be surprising or puzzling[5] since they were two very dissimilar personalities. Their religion, philosophy, and culture separated them, and yet a mutual goodwill would bind them together to the point of creating between them an "emotional dialogue"[6] at the heart of the spiritual renewal and the unsettling of Europe that took place between the two World Wars.

Geographic proximity (they lived in the Paris suburbs of Meudon and Clamart, respectively), an identical home life (married without children, and thus entirely dedicated to intellectual and spiritual life), a shared attachment to Léon Bloy, familiarity with Proudhon and Marx[7] but also with important spiritual figures, vast knowledge of canonical philosophy, a taste for mysticism and thirst for social justice nourished by a shared faithfulness to Christian teachings were all nutrients in the soil that allowed this "fruitful"[8] dialogue to germinate over the "long years of their friendship."[9]

After the publication of Maritain's *Primauté du spirituel* (The primacy of the spiritual), this friendship led to the accusation made by certain followers of Charles Maurras that Maritain had "fallen under the spell of Berdyaev" and was "insidiously introducing into Catholicism the reveries of a Slav."[10] On this subject, Berdyaev remarked that Maritain's "conservative Catholic adversaries criticize him for capitulating to my alleged negative influence. This is incorrect when it comes to philosophy, but there may be some truth to it concerning social and political problems."[11] Besides Maritain's sympathies for Russians, and Berdyaev's for Jews,[12] one should note that "both had spouses who had converted to Catholicism and that in both households daily operations were managed by a sister-in-law (Véra Oumansoff, a Roman Catholic, was the sister of Raïssa Maritain; Evgeniia Rapp, an Orthodox Christian, lived in the home of Berdyaev)."[13]

Other authors have noted certain "points of convergence"[14] between the two thinkers, notably in the philosophy of history[15] and on social questions,[16] by referencing a shared association with Emmanuel Mounier,[17] because Maritain and Berdyaev, each in their own way, influenced the philosophy of personalism.[18] Hélène Iswolsky notes that "the area in which Maritain and Berdyaev truly met and understood each other intimately was on social problems. They shared the same Christian humanist conception, and on this terrain there were no divergences."[19] Iswolsky also observes that "the deepest influence exerted by Berdyaev on Western philosophy was felt in the sphere of social doctrine. Along with Maritain he inspired the spiritual revolution that took place between 1930 and 1940 and contributed to the arrival in France of Christian humanism."

Above all else, Berdyaev advocated new forms of social justice. On all these questions, Berdyaev agreed with Maritain's thinking. Like Maritain, Berdyaev defended personalism (which is based on a Christian anthropology). His conception of a completely Christian society, expressed in his book *Un Nouveau Moyen Âge: Réflexions sur les destinées de la Russie et de l'Europe* (published in English as *The End of Our Time*), developed in parallel with Maritain's doctrine as expressed in his *Humanisme intégral* (*Integral Humanism*).[20] The arguments of the two philosophers in favour of economic justice are identical, as well as their desire to see Christian morality applied to the working classes.

The points of convergence and divergence between the two thinkers – the one originally attracted to socialism, the other to communism, with

Maritain later becoming a fervent Catholic and Berdyaev returning to the Orthodox faith[21] – become clear as one follows step by step the exchanges between these two philosophical writers, examining their correspondence, noting their mutual exchange of books, often with elaborate dedications, and observing the quotations that each would use of the other's work in their own writings.[22] By taking account of these various documents and the allusions to Berdyaev in Maritain's own notebooks, the *Carnets de notes* (Notebooks), and in the published *Cahiers Jacques Maritain* (Jacques Maritain notebooks) for the years 1929 to 1936, as well as the pages devoted to Maritain in Berdyaev's *Essai d'autobiographie spirituelle* (published in English as *Self-Knowledge: An Essay in Autobiography*), it is possible to follow, despite irremediable philosophical differences and different itineraries, the path of their friendship and their shared struggle when confronting the bourgeois and communist worlds.

Several stages can be identified within the course of their dialogue, composed of personal conversations, epistolary exchanges, collaborative publications in their respective journals, participation in meetings organized by one or the other, and interventions in public debates. These all took place with a friendly tone of respectful sharing that stretches over the twenty-year period of a companionship that can be divided into several distinct moments: 1) the first contact between the writers; 2) interfaith Franco-Russian meetings in Paris and then in Clamart; 3) the debate over Descartes and Cartesianism at the Studio franco-russe, with the emergence of discordant epistemological positions; 4) their interpretations of the work of Dostoevsky; 5) their support of the review *Esprit* and the problem of communism and their disagreement on the question of liberty; 6) the place of Raïssa Maritain in the exchanges between "Jakov Pavlovitch" (Maritain) and "Nicolas Alexandrovitch" (Berdyaev); 7) *Humanisme intégral* (*Integral Humanism*) versus *Cinq Méditations sur l'existence* (*Solitude and Society*); 8) the combat against antisemitism and their final exchanges.

1925–1927: The First Contact Between the Writers

A Meeting under the Auspices of Jeanne and Léon Bloy

While he was in Russia, where "the dominant tendency of Russian thinking from 1900 to 1922 [was] an energetic though brief spiritualist reaction against the materialist scientism that had reigned over the second half of the preceding century"[23] and where, traditionally, cultured minds of the Russian intelligentsia were split into two large intellectual schools, "the liberal and Western school" versus the "Slavophile school,"[24] Nikolai Berdyaev, who "was repulsed by all conformism,"[25] rejuvenated the thinking of the time by engaging with "all aspects of modernism: idealism, spiritualist research, neo-Christianity, and new literary tendencies."[26] This was how Berdyaev had become familiar with the authors of a "secret France" that he used to call the "revolutionary reactionaries."[27]

As Olivier Clément remarks, "among the leading examples of this secret France [Barbey d'Aurevilly, Baudelaire, Verlaine, Mallarmé, Villiers de l'Isle Adam, Léon Bloy, Hello, Huysmans], Berdyaev had a decided preference for Bloy."[28] In 1914 in the review *Sophia*, Berdyaev had written a long article devoted to Bloy, "the knight of poverty."[29] Attentive to Bloy's critique of the bourgeois world, Berdyaev saw in him "a Jew, not a Hellenist, an idol-breaking prophet, a 'fool for Christ' who bears witness as much through his tragic life as through his writings."[30] "[A]mong the points of convergence between Maritain and Berdyaev," Bernard Marchadier underscores two: "an anti-bourgeois stance and an aspiration toward a political-spiritual revolution. The anti-bourgeois stance that they both professed took its inspiration from their common teacher, Léon Bloy."[31] And as Clément underlines, "among the sparks that the pamphleteer ignited, three themes seem fundamental, three themes that converge in Berdyaev's thinking, either deepening it or perhaps awakening it. They are the suffering of God, bourgeois life as a metaphysical category,[32] and the prophetic expectation of Man and the Holy Spirit as Paraclete."[33] Clément also notes a complicity between Berdyaev, a philosopher of the person, and Léon Bloy for whom "the sense of God is inseparable from that of the irreducible unity of each person."[34]

Berdyaev, a former Marxist[35] and "inspirer of Orthodox religious renewal,"[36] was expelled from Russia in September 1922 along with other intellectuals "aboard one of the famous 'philosophy steamers.'" In his homeland he was "one of the typical figures of the early twentieth century,"[37] and as such made a brief stay of two years in Berlin which turned into the first stage of his exile.[38] Then "starting in 1924, new migration took place, displacing Berlin from its role as the intellectual capital of the diaspora" of Russian emigration, with a shift to Prague, Belgrade, Sophia, and especially Paris, which had already welcomed a first wave of Russian émigrés and now became the "pole of the Russian diaspora in Europe."[39] Nikolai and Lydia Berdyaev arrived in Paris in 1924 as part of "the second wave of émigrés, often composed of socialists who had supported the revolution at its inception,"[40] as opposed to the reactionary monarchist Russians who had been the first to leave with the aim of pursuing a pre-1917 Tsarist restoration. 1924 was a critical year[41] for the Russian immigrant community in France that numbered approximately 50,000 people.[42] "They moved into a modest Parisian hotel in the summer of 1924. With the help of Prince Trubetskoi, Berdyaev and his wife were able to quickly change addresses and occupy the ground floor of a charming furnished house in Clamart where they lived for four years."[43] Once in France, Nikolai and Lydia were soon introduced to Jeanne Bloy[44] by Stanislas and Aniouta Fumet,[45] who in turn introduced them to Jacques and Raïssa Maritain, both godchildren of Léon Bloy.

Berdyaev was originally from Kiev and belonged to a land-owning noble family. He had a French grandmother, Mathilde de Choiseul-Gouffier (1805–1867), a daughter of the Count of Choiseul-Gouffier. Like other Russian intellectuals,[46] Berdyaev "spoke fluent French, a talent that helped him considerably in his relations with Paris intellectuals."[47] Starting in 1924 with his arrival in Paris, where a large contingent of Russian intellectuals had landed[48] as well as the administrator of Russian Orthodox parishes in Western Europe, Metropolitan Evlogii,[49] Berdyaev was introduced to Charles Du Bos[50] at the home of Lev Shestov; and he transferred his Academy of Religious Philosophy, created in Berlin and supported by the Young Men's Christian Association (YMCA),[51] to the Russian Center of Paris (at 10 Boulevard Montparnasse). It is in this centre that Berdyaev gave his "weekly courses on historic and philosophical subjects," but it was also the location of public meetings, as well as the headquarters of the YMCA Press that Berdyaev edited and that published roughly four hundred volumes in Russian, many of which were forbidden and censored in Soviet Russia.[52]

In his *Essai d'autobiographie spirituelle*, Berdyaev recounts the origin of his meeting with Maritain when he was fifty and Maritain just over forty years old: "I met J. Maritain at the beginning of my stay in Paris in 1925.[53] The widow of Léon Bloy introduced us. I had always been very interested in L. Bloy, and an article of mine brought him some attention in Russia. Soon after our arrival in Paris, Lydia wrote to Madame Bloy, who had been a Protestant of Danish origin and then became a fanatical Catholic, and who was entirely devoted to preserving the memory of her husband. She was a remarkable woman in her own way and a friend of Maritain, a Protestant convert to Catholicism and godchild of L. Bloy. I was familiar with some of Maritain's writings that seemed representative of Thomism in France. It was said that he had a large influence on Catholic youth. Madame Bloy offered to go with me to see Maritain."[54]

In an entry for Sunday, 29 March 1925, Maritain noted that Berdyaev was in Meudon and spoke of "the tragic death of [the Russian poet Alexander] Blok."[55] In September 1925, in the first issue of the review *Put'* (*The Way*),[56] which he was editing, Berdyaev included a book review of Maritain's *Réflexions sur l'intelligence et sur sa vie propre* (Reflections on intelligence).[57] The book was published in 1924 and, according to Berdyaev, marked a "renewal of classic Catholicism." The volume is present in Berdyaev's Clamart library with several passages underlined but no dedication. However, starting in 1925 and continuing to 1948, roughly fifteen of Maritain's publications and a book by Raïssa Maritain were sent to Nikolai and Lydia Berdyaev with a dedicatory inscription or homage by the author.[58]

If, as he wrote, Berdyaev was "thrilled to meet Maritain,"[59] it was nonetheless, at first glance, "paradoxical," as Gérard Lurol would say, "that Jacques Maritain and Nikolai Berdyaev could get along. For Berdyaev, Maritain represented Thomist rationality, a scholastic and deductive way of philosophizing, whereas he considered himself to be of an emotional and intuitive nature that he called existential. And yet they were happy to make each other's acquaintance and professed a mutual affection."[60] Stanislas Fumet, a close friend of Maritain and the first to have met Berdyaev in 1924, never imagined that these two philosophers would get along.[61]

First Letters and Interfaith Meetings at the Russian Students House

The correspondence between Nikolai Berdyaev and Jacques and Raïssa Maritain began in 1925 and ended in 1946. The letters of Jacques and Raïssa Maritain are not in the Berdyaev archives in Clamart because they were repatriated to the Russian State Archive of Literature and Art in Moscow.[62] As for the letters of Berdyaev to Jacques and Raïssa Maritain, they are kept in the Maritain collection of the National Library of the University of Strasbourg (BNU). From 1925 to 1938, Berdyaev's letters to the Maritains testify to their geographic proximity when they lived in Clamart and Meudon, respectively. After 1939, once the Maritains had left Meudon for the United States, the correspondence continued with several letters and a final one from Berdyaev dated 25 August 1946 confirming that a food package had arrived in Clamart.

The first meeting between Berdyaev and Maritain in 1925 took place the same year that the Pontifical Commission for Russia was created in Rome under the direct supervision of the Pope. Also in the same year, Metropolitan Evlogii helped to found the Saint-Serge Institute for Orthodox Theology in Paris, bringing together distinguished professors including Sergei Bulgakov, George Florovsky, Boris Vysheslavtsev, and Georgii Fedotov.[63] It was in this context, which invited Catholics to discover and understand Orthodox spirituality, that Maritain and Berdyaev met, as is confirmed by their epistolary exchanges of 5, 7, 9 and 19 October 1925. It is precisely in 1925 that one finds the dedication "To Monsieur and Madame Nikolai Berdyaev, in tribute with respectful sympathy in Christo JESU, Raïssa and Jacques Maritain" inscribed on the first page of the Maritains' 1925 publication *De la vie d'oraison* (*Prayer and Intelligence*), a book that Berdyaev annotated with lines in the margins on several pages.

Starting in 1926, a collaboration between the two thinkers began. Having already organized meetings of the Free Academy of Spiritual Culture of

Moscow that he founded and presided over from 1919 to 1922,[64] Berdyaev again played an important role in Paris in association with the liberal Orthodox intelligentsia and the YMCA[65] that supported the review *Put'*. In this context, Maritain accepted "the invitation of Nikolai Alexandrovitch [Berdyaev] to a first series of monthly meetings, to be held starting in January 1926 with Lev Zander at the Russian Students House"[66] located in rue Dupuytren in Paris. A letter from Maritain to Berdyaev dated 4 January 1926 informs him that Maritain has "taken care of recruiting some friends for monthly meetings on Thursdays." In his letter Maritain lists the names of Raïssa, Stanislas Fumet, Reverend Gillet, Abbé Beaussart, Madame Noële Denis-Boulet, and Roland Dalbiez.

Maritain was unable to participate regularly in these monthly interfaith Thursday meetings of Catholics, Orthodox, and Protestants that continued until January 1928.[67]

Reciprocal Publication in Their Respective Reviews: Put' *and* Chroniques

In January 1926, in the second issue of the review *Put'*, Berdyaev published "Metafizika i mistika,"[68] a Russian translation of Maritain's article "Grandeur et misère de la métaphysique" (The majesty and poverty of metaphysics) that had been published in the first volume of the Roseau d'or in December 1925.[69]

In 1926, Berdyaev had received from Jean Cocteau his *Lettre à Jacques Maritain* (Letter to Jacques Maritain) that was published in January of that year with the dedication "à Nicolas Berdiaev, hommage de Jean Cocteau." This *Lettre à Jacques Maritain* is annotated by Berdyaev, whereas the copy of *Réponse à Jean Cocteau* (Response to Jean Cocteau) dedicated by Maritain "à Nicolas Berdiaev, son ami Jac. Maritain," sits in the Clamart library with no annotations and its pages not even completely cut open.

For his part, Maritain published a text of Berdyaev's under the Roseau d'or imprint. On 6 March 1926, Maritain wrote to Berdyaev as follows: "I am returning your manuscript so that you can look over the corrections (in red ink) that I propose. Generally, they only concern matters of form and style. On three or four points, however, I thought it necessary to explain and specify further the ideas presented. I tried to do so while remaining faithful to your line of thought. I hope I've succeeded, but I prefer that you judge for yourself if all is well here … Finally, there's the question of the title 'La culture, la civilisation et la transfiguration religieuse' strikes me as rather heavy. I offer you two simpler alternatives: 'La sagesse de l'histoire' or 'Philosophie de la culture.'"

Berdyaev's text entitled "Le destin de la culture" (The fate of culture) was published in August 1926 in the second volume of the Roseau d'or[70] alongside other essays by Humbert Clérissac, Max Jacob, Henri Massis, Jean Cocteau, Julien Green, Paul Sabon, Léopold Levaux, and Georges Bernanos.[71]

In "Le destin de la culture," Berdyaev diagnoses a decline in European culture as being at the origin of "bourgeois and irreligious civilization" that he denounces, with the help of Khomiakov, Dostoevsky, and Konstantin Leont'ev, as the triumph of Mammon,[72] noting, for example, that "the ardent hatred of a Léon Bloy against the bourgeois mentality is nothing other than the defiance of an artistic and religious soul against modern civilization."[73]

Besides the reciprocal dissemination of their respective writings, the exchanges between the two thinkers also discussed mysticism[74] – an important subject for Maritain, who, at the end of 1926, would publish his article "Expérience mystique et philosophie" (Mystical experience and philosophy)[75] in the *Revue de philosophie* edited by the philosophy department of the Institut Catholique de Paris.

Un Nouveau Moyen Âge *and* Primauté du Spirituel *Published in the "Roseau d'or"*

It is thanks to Raïssa Maritain that her husband first encountered the Russian edition of Berdyaev's book, published in Berlin in 1924. On 4 March 1925, Maritain wrote to Berdyaev: "My wife has begun to read and translate out loud for me your book about the new Middle Ages. It is a great comfort and lively pleasure for me to see how on so many essential points, and especially the criticism of the 'modern' world, our ways of thinking converge. I would have liked to offer you a copy of my book *Théonas*, in which I develop ideas about Progress and Revolution that are similar to your own, but unfortunately it is out of print ... Rest assured, dear Sir, of my cordial and sincere sympathy in Xto JESU. Jacq Maritain."

The task of translating Berdyaev's book, *Un Nouveau Moyen Âge*, was far along in the summer of 1926, as is clear from what Maritain wrote to Berdyaev on 9 August 1926: "I am as sorry as you about what you have expressed to me about the translation of your book. I think the best thing would be to write to Fumet to say that you find the translation faithful but too literal, and that you believe a total reworking is necessary to make the French, in style and substance, an equivalent of the Russian text." Aniouta Fumet, who was of Russian origin, carefully made the precise and literal translation.[76] Aniouta and Stanislas Fumet probably worked on improving the text but Maritain did as well, since he wrote to Berdyaev on two occasions (2 and 6 November 1926) to inform him that he has been "immersed in the translation of your book";[77] that he was rereading carefully; and to tell him that he would like "to see [him] briefly before handing over the translation of [the] book, which I just finished reading, to the printer." Maritain further noted, "Your study is of great importance, and I would like it to appear in a French version that is as readable and as striking as possible."[78] Fifteen days later, on 24 November 1926, "the Russian thinker Nikolai Berdyaev,"[79] as Maritain refers to him, made a written request to meet with Maritain.

Early in 1927, Berdyaev's *Un Nouveau Moyen Âge* was published by Plon in the collection "Le Roseau d'or"[80] edited by Maritain (along with Stanislas Fumet, Frédéric Lefèvre, and Henri Massis). It included a brief introduction by Aniouta Fumet presenting Berdyaev to French readers.[81]

By publishing *Un Nouveau Moyen Âge*, which quotes the work of Léon Bloy,[82] Maritain was making a selection from among Berdyaev's books published in Russian before 1927 and later translated into French such as *L'Esprit de Dostoïevski* (*Dostoievsky: An Interpretation*, 1929),[83] *Le Sens de L'histoire* (*The Meaning of History*, 1948),[84] and *Le Sens de la Création* (*The Meaning of the Creative Act*, 1955).[85] Berdyaev's historical-philosophical reflections about Russia and Soviet communism constituted only one part of his published works,[86] and they were on the margins of his most personal philosophical thinking, which only became fully accessible to French readers much later.[87]

Un Nouveau Moyen Âge, the book that "established the reputation of Berdyaev in the West,"[88] and whose success was "striking,"[89] overflows with themes that were developed in all his writings: the idea of doubling and an "interior breaking" of man that emerges in the Renaissance and worsens in the Modern era; the difference between a Catholicism that secured for the Middle Ages the transition between Antiquity and the Renaissance and a set of Orthodox teachings that did not experience the Renaissance and must hope for a new Middle Ages; the affirmation that in modern times "man without God ceases to be man"; the choice for the Russian people between Christ and the Antichrist because "by their spiritual development, it is an apolitical people that only aspires to the culminating point of history"; the nature of socialism, which "has a messianic character," and the significance of Russian communism, which "demands a society of a sacred nature, a submission of all facets of life to the religion of the devil, to the religion of the Antichrist"; the nature of revolution and how none has "ever succeeded"; the primacy of morals and the present urgency "to affirm the primacy of spiritual activity over political activity"; the prophetic vision of Dostoevsky who "understood that socialism in Russia was a religious question"; the calling of Russia "whose people bend toward the Kingdom of God … which explains not only its virtues but also many of its vices"; the purification of the Orthodox church, whose "internal light and its mystical foundations remain unshakeable"; democracy, which is "extreme relativism, the negation of all that is absolute"; the proletariat or "class messiah, a new messiah, organizer of the terrestrial realm."

Stanislas Fumet wrote a long review of "this powerful and somewhat prophetic book" of Berdyaev,[90] who, "in the name of a Christian idea of man," claims to observe not "a simple crisis of humanism" but diagnoses "the end of humanism," "which consisted in separating man from his eternal roots, by removing him from all deep subordination" thus leading man to a detachment from his inner life. This decline of humanism, which carried with it "the seed of its own destruction," took place in stages, such that "the time that flows from the Renaissance to the end of the nineteenth century was only the test of humanism that resulted in its somber defeat," the death of humanism, and "this 'end of the Renaissance' that Berdyaev announced to be immediately followed by a 'new Middle Ages.'" For Fumet, the originality of Berdyaev lies in the insight that "by losing God to find himself, man fatally must also lose man, because man only exists as an image and resemblance of God." In sum, as an exegete of history, Berdyaev reveals the exhaustion and defeat of humanism: "Here we are in the new Middle Ages. The moment when the abyss is unmasked. Today no confusion is any longer possible. The grand experiences that we have just undergone, the World War, the Russian Revolution, have ripped off the last veils that Berdyaev calls the veils of the day, the veils of clarity *that hid the mystery* … At present, the veils of clarity are dissolved. Night has come, the night that reveals the abyss and allows one to distinguish the stars, the night that leads Berdyaev to say that we have entered a new Middle Ages."

Given this diagnosis by the Russian thinker, one can understand that the Swiss theologian Charles Journet, a great friend of Maritain, thanked Berdyaev for writing *Un Nouveau Moyen Âge*, and marked his appreciation by sending him his own book, *L'Union des Églises et le christianisme pratique* (The union of churches and practical Christianity; 1927) with a very explicit dedication: "To Monsieur Nikolai Berdyaev, in homage and with very respectful sympathy for his beautiful book, *Un Nouveau Moyen Âge*, Ch. Journet."[91]

Maritain and his wife Raïssa went to Clamart to meet Berdyaev on Tuesday, 22 March.[92] On 24 April 1927, Maritain alerted him to "the two long articles on *Un Nouveau Moyen Âge* by M.F. Deschamps in the Brussels publication *Revue catholique des idées et des faits*," adding, "Your book is being enthusiastically received in Belgium."

Evidently, by publishing *Un Nouveau Moyen Âge* in the Roseau d'or collection, Maritain and his friend Fumet had facilitated the establishment of an audience in France for Berdyaev, who, according to Pierre Pascal, was "the only Russian thinker at the present time accepted in the Western world and exerting real action on it."[93]

By the end of July 1927, some months after the publication of *Un Nouveau Moyen Âge* and its claim that "the most urgent task at the present time is to affirm the primacy of spiritual activity over political activity,"[94] Maritain also published his *Primauté du spirituel* in the Roseau d'or.[95] In this work Maritain quotes "the Russian philosopher Nikolai Berdyaev" about what the latter "called a new Middle Ages,"[96] and notes his surprise that "the

Western public is unfamiliar with Russian speculative thinking. The names of Khomiakov, Solov'ev,[97] and Berdyaev have barely reached it."[98] The subject of a new Middle Ages – in other words a spiritual renewal after the crisis of modern times and the disillusion that ensued – was a theme taken up elsewhere by Maritain.[99]

Primauté du spirituel, whose purpose was to present a theory of spiritual power and temporal power and their correlation, included an annex entitled "On Russian Orthodoxy."[100] In that postscript Maritain, echoing the writings of Berdyaev, observes that "few events in the history of the world have had such a mysterious and tragic importance as the spiritual test now weighing on Russia and the Russian church. If the Bolshevik revolution, essentially directed against God, is a clear sign of Man in a state of sin, may not the vast movement of faith fostered by the Russian church – with such great sufferings, and so much blood, so many martyrs and heroic stories – be the announcement and preparation of some great work of Christ and the Holy Spirit?"[101] Maritain then adds, "Nor is it without reason that Providence has dispersed across Europe such a large number of Russians exiled from their country and so many young people eager for religious renewal. It is in the name of Christ and with the love of Christ that we should go with them, to recognize ourselves through them, and help each other to gather together, within each of us first of all, all that has been disjoined."[102]

When Maritain wrote these words in 1927, he was already in contact with Russian Orthodox émigrés in France, some of whom, notably Evgraf Kovalevskii[103] and Vladimir Lossky,[104] often came to Meudon on Sunday afternoons. As Maritain states, it was with the love of Christ that he reached out to them, having already experienced the obstacles that could arise around such meetings. Indeed, "besides the internal difficulties that could affect Orthodoxy itself inside the host country," Maritain wrote that he was aware of

> all the obstacles that rise up against unity, the prejudices and missteps that may be alleged on both sides, the strong and unjust animosity that a great number of Orthodox theologians feel toward Catholicism, and especially the peril of spiritual subordination under the national and the political as happens in certain theories such as

> Eurasianism.[105] There is but one Church, with Christ himself as its head and the Pope holding his place here below: all the divine grace that circulates in separate forms of Christianity joins them invisibly (*voto*) to this unique Church. However, this virtual belonging must still be realized in the external unity of dogma and of supreme spiritual governance, and that will not happen without many difficulties. But God does not place in the heart of his children certain profound desires to then leave them always frustratingly unfulfilled. As long and as slow as is the work he desires, the obscure efforts pursued here and there, in the simplicity of the spirit of the Holy word, for a better and more fraternal mutual understanding, will not be fruitless.[106]

Was it from this perspective that Maritain envisioned a particular program for the interfaith meetings with Russian Orthodox émigrés in France? A paragraph in *Primauté du spirituel* offers a clue: "It seems that among intellectual Russians today, who are very sensitive to the criteriological problem, there is an awakening of a desire for philosophy properly speaking. This is an important phenomenon in which we would hope Catholics, and in particular the disciples of Saint Thomas, will manifest an appropriate interest. Their special role would be to show the Orthodox how the Catholic conception of nature and grace, and the Thomist idea of human nature (unlike the closed Stoic conception), is open and able to be completed – and in fact completed and elevated by grace – and is in accordance with the authentic demands of the Christian spirit and those of philosophy."[107]

In truth, the intention was at best to state a goal, because the difficulties to overcome to reach that horizon were numerous, as Maritain also states:

> The more one deepens these questions, the more one realizes that the principal obstacle to a union consists in a misunderstanding, namely the confusion of the spiritual temperament of a culture, either here or there, with the Church, which is universal. The spirit of Orthodoxy is not the same thing as the Russian spirit; the spirit of Catholicism is not the same thing as the Latin spirit. When things are truly well understood on both sides, unity is within reach … When someone such as Seraphim of Sarov teaches that the goal of a Christian life

> is the *acquisition* of the Holy Spirit, he is saying the same thing as a Saint John of the Cross, and both are saying the same thing as Saint Paul. The best, and the most urgent way to get to know each other, for the Orthodox and Catholics, is to identify and love each other through the most holy representatives of their spirituality.[108]

In this text from 1927, one sees a sketch of the future program of the interfaith meetings between Orthodox and Catholics that Berdyaev and Maritain will organize in Clamart, "on themes no longer theological or ecclesiastical, but mystical and spiritual."[109]

1928–1931: The Interfaith Meetings in Paris and Clamart

The First Interfaith Meetings in Paris

Chapter 10 ("Russia and the Western World") of Berdyaev's *Essai d'autobiographie spirituelle* devotes several pages to Maritain and the interfaith meetings they organized: "In Paris, for several years, there were interfaith meetings that I initiated. Orthodox believers would meet with French Catholics and Protestants in the 'Russia House' in Boulevard Montparnasse. For the first time, Christians of different faiths could discuss religion with each other. It was also in this Russian atmosphere that Modernist and Thomist Catholics could discuss matters together. There were no painful historical memories of struggles attached to Russian Orthodoxy. In the early phase, the elan and interest around these meetings was considerable. In fact, there were too many people and the meetings ran the risk of becoming too 'fashionable.'"[110]

Berdyaev also notes: "Everyone understood that we were a Christian oasis in a non-Christian world. These meetings manifested the essential union in Christ and at the same time the variety of types of religion, philosophy, and spirituality. Collaborating actively were many noteworthy participants such as Reverend Gillet, later the leader of the Dominicans, Father Laberthonnière, who championed Catholic Modernism, and especially Jacques Maritain about whom I will have more to say. There were even important Protestants such as Pastor Boegner, the head of the Reformed Church of France, Professor Lecerf, the only Orthodox Calvinist … and Wilfred Monod representing a radical current."[111]

There exist two letters from Maritain to Berdyaev from this period of interfaith meetings in Paris. In one dated 11 January 1927, Maritain wrote in a postscript: "Could I ask you to please invite to the meeting on Thursday the 20th the following two friends: 1) Louis Massignon, 21 rue Monsieur; 2) Nikolai Nabokov, 3 rue de l'Estrapade." The second letter, dated 24 April 1927, concerns the meeting of 4 May, for which the plan was to have Florovsky give an introduction on "the idea of creation and the Orthodox conception," and then Maritain, doubting his own memory, added: "Maybe M. Kartashev remembers better than I?" which confirms that professors at the St Sergius Orthodox Theological Institute were also involved in these meetings.

1928: New Interfaith Meetings in Boulevard Montparnasse

First launched in January 1926, the interfaith public gatherings of Catholics, Orthodox, and Protestants proved over time to be rather disappointing. Moreover, the Magisterium in Rome intervened through the encyclical *Mortalium Animos* (6 January 1928)[112] expressing reservations about these public interfaith meetings. The consequence was "the withdrawal of all the invited Catholic theologians"[113] from these meetings. In addition, Maritain was reluctant to have modernists and Protestants participate in the interfaith meetings. In a letter to Berdyaev dated 5 March 1928, he states his preference to restrict participation in the interfaith meetings to Orthodox and Catholics:

> I am writing to you about our interfaith meetings. I must tell you frankly that I am personally incapable of continuing to put up with the contributions of Father Laberthonnière. They create an abnormal, completely intolerable atmosphere. The respect that I owe the person and priest prevent me from describing the theories that he defends in the terms they deserve. There is a higher question regarding what we owe to holy truths, which a priest is not permitted to consider

> simply as he wishes. Life is too short for me to add to ordinary pains the burden of hearing the dogmatic statements of modernism (and of liberal Protestantism).
>
> I am prepared to collaborate actively and with all my heart on anything you might organize between the Orthodox and Catholics, because, however opposed they might be on many points, they at least have a common veneration for the revealed deposit and holy truths of Faith. Then we can collaborate and do useful work. With the modernists and the Protestants (with the exception of Father Lecerf) it is completely impossible, as experience has made abundantly clear, it seems to me.[114]

Thus, another type of interfaith meeting, private and by invitation only, was started at an address in Boulevard Montparnasse and continued during 1928 and 1929.[115] Maritain made his contribution to this new series of gatherings with the permission of Monsignor Chaptal,[116] the auxiliary bishop of Paris in charge of foreigners. The bishop supported these meetings in so far as they permitted "a reduction of prejudices" and "a means of defending … the Catholic Church" among "the Orthodox who directed the movement of minds in Paris."[117] At the end of 1928, in a letter to Berdyaev dated 19 December, Maritain writes, "For the other meetings in the Boulevard Montparnasse, I think your idea of three lectures on the nature of the church is very good." Maritain includes the names of four possible speakers: Father Lebreton, Father David Lathoud, Abbé Journet, whom he calls "one of the best theologians of the day," and Olivier Lacombe, a layperson. He then adds, because mindful of the situation that followed the publication of the *Mortalium Animos* encyclical: "When you have made a decision, let me know. I probably ought to write to Monsignor Chaptal if we want a priest as lecturer and a sufficiently large Catholic audience. About the audience, I will furnish you with a list of twenty-five people to invite."

1929: Launching the "Intimate" Tuesday Meetings in Clamart

Starting in November 1928, alongside the interfaith meetings in the Boulevard Montparnasse, another type of informal, smaller, "*intime*" meetings on the topic of mysticism and spirituality was established in Clamart.[118] The first of this series took place on 29 January 1929 and the last on 19 January 1932. Between these two dates, for "three years,"[119] fourteen sessions were led by Berdyaev and Maritain. According to Pierre Van der Meer, "At the study meetings held at the home of Berdyaev, the discussions ... sought to achieve a rapprochement and mutual understanding between Occidental Catholic thinkers and non-dogmatic Russian Orthodox Christian prophetism."[120]

"Having the impression that the interfaith meetings [in Boulevard Montparnasse] were losing their point," Berdyaev writes, "I organized meetings in my home. It is thanks to Jacques Maritain that this was able to happen."[121] Indeed, their friendship, their habit of holding these meetings in their homes, the proximity of Meudon and Clamart, their respective lifestyles, and the Russophile character of the Maritains,[122] all allowed the two men to naturally envision this fruitful collaboration.[123] In his *Essai d'autobiographie spirituelle*, Berdyaev comments on the initiative of these meetings: "I had the idea of organizing more intimate gatherings on themes not so much theological or ecclesiastical, but instead mystical and spiritual. I suggested to Maritain that we organize them at my house. He willingly accepted and took charge of the French side of the meetings, on condition that there would be no Protestants. These intimate meetings devoted to the study of mysticism were very enthusiastic occasions and generated much interest. We had new participants, notably Charles Du Bos[124] and Gabriel Marcel,[125] Massignon, a specialist of Muslim mysticism, and Gilson,[126] a great specialist of Medieval philosophy. The atmosphere was friendly despite some divergences."[127] Hélène Iswolsky reports that also participating in these meetings was "a group of Orthodox who mostly belonged to the Russian Institute of Theology of Paris."[128]

Sometime before the first of these intimate meetings devoted to the study of mysticism, Maritain reached out to several of his friends about participating in this new format and announced to Berdyaev on 28

November 1928 that he "already had the agreement of Charles Du Bos, Abbé Altermann, and Jean de Menasce," adding that "the best day for all those [he had seen] would be Tuesday afternoon." Twenty days later, on Monday, 17 December 1928, Berdyaev "organized with Maritain but also Bulgakov, Fedotov, and Florovsky a first informal meeting between Catholic and Orthodox thinkers at his home in Clamart."[129] The same day in Meudon there was an "evening meeting with the Russians."[130] Again on 19 December, Maritain wrote to Berdyaev to suggest the names of suitable people to be invited to the intimate meetings: "I think it would be advantageous to invite Gilson. Fumet and Dermenghen are obvious. I inform you that not far from your place (93bis route de Clamart in Issy) lives my colleague Abbé Simeterre, a professor of the history of ancient philosophy at the Institut Catholique." Quite quickly, a letter from Berdyaev to Maritain dated 27 December 1928 addressed the organization of the first intimate meeting scheduled for January 1929 in Clamart. Now that they agreed on the general theme of "Occidental and Oriental Mysticism," they needed to choose the specific subjects to be discussed. In his letter, Berdyaev asked Maritain if he would take charge of "inviting all the French Catholics" or if he should also "write to some, such as Gilson and Du Bos."

It should be noted that for Maritain, these monthly interfaith meetings on Tuesdays, also called intimate meetings, were not only in addition to the Sunday meetings "with the Russians" in Meudon[131] mentioned in Maritain's notebooks, but also to the Boulevard Montparnasse meetings that often took place on Monday. Moreover, from November 1929 to April 1931, there were also some sessions at the Studio franco-russe. Thus, in the same letter, such as the one for 27 December 1928, Berdyaev planned an intimate meeting for 29 January 1929 and mentioned the "Montparnasse meetings" that were still going on, proposing to "begin with the lecture by Pastor Boegner" – a meeting that took place on 18 February 1929[132] – while also suggesting "it would be very good to have Abbé Journet speak." The project of a lecture on the Church by Abbé Journet at "The Montparnasse Russian Students House" came up in several letters by Maritain and Charles Journet between 9 January and 19 April 1929, and it was eventually scheduled for 6 May 1929.

In a 7 January 1929 letter to Berdyaev, Maritain confirmed the date of 29 January, 4 p.m., for the first intimate meeting at the home of Berdyaev.

He wrote, "The title 'Mysticism and Its Relations with Religion' strikes me as very suitable for the first meeting. I think the best thing would be for you to do the first introduction yourself." On 11 January, Maritain insisted again that Berdyaev do the introduction: "I think it would be much better for you to speak. Not a lecture, just an introduction laying out the goal of these meetings and opening things up for discussion. In any case, I think it would be preferable to have the first presentation be done by a Russian (Florovsky perhaps if it really bothers you to speak yourself. But I am sure the French would prefer to hear you)." Maritain also specified what he thought best regarding the invitations to Massignon and Gilson and allowed himself to invite Olivier Lacombe. This first "Russian meeting at Berdyaev's" took place on Tuesday, 29 January 1929, with an "excellent presentation by Berdyaev," noted Maritain.[133] An allusion to this meeting is contained in the note from Maritain to Berdyaev on 5 February where he states, "I was delighted with the meeting at your home and especially by your presentation."

In a note sent on 5 February, Maritain told Berdyaev, "I spoke with Massignon by telephone, and he would be happy to make some introductory remarks next time," while also stating that for a future interfaith meeting in Montparnasse "it would perhaps be best to wait for me to first see Monsignor Chaptal." The second intimate Tuesday meeting at Berdyaev's, on Western and Eastern mysticism, was discussed in a 10 February 1929 letter in which Berdyaev states that "someone simply must act as moderator in order to prevent the anarchic tendency of our discussions." He then asked Maritain, "Should I go ahead and inform some of the French participants or will you do it yourself? It would be wonderful to have Monsieur Du Bos at our meetings." For the next Montparnasse interfaith meeting, Maritain sends a "note in haste" to tell Berdyaev, "I saw Monsignor Chaptal and he had no objections; he merely requested that I share with him the list I had made for you of the Catholics being invited. I just sent off the list to him." And for the intimate meeting, Maritain specifies that "Massignon is ready to do an introduction at your home on *Christine l'Admirable* … The date he proposes is Tuesday 26 February." In a postscript he adds, "I think that you could invite Henry Gouhier (the best disciple of Gilson) to the Clamart meetings." In fact, the second meeting at Berdyaev's is eventually scheduled for 5 March 1929.[134] Maritain writes on 23 February to communicate the names of the French participants: "Massignon, Du Bos, de Menasce, Abbé Altermann, Gouhier, Olivier [Lacombe] … I could also add Jean Daniélou (a university *agrégé*),[135] Dom Vincent Padovani of the Compagnie de Saint-Paul," while letting Berdyaev be in charge of inviting "Fumet, Abbé Simeterre (if you think it proper to invite him), Dermenghen."

During 1929, a succession of meetings took place. After the 5 March meeting, a third Tuesday meeting at Berdyaev's happened on 16 April 1929: "Florovsky spoke about Byzantine mysticism and Gregory Palamas."[136] And at the fourth such meeting on 4 June 1929 Maritain led a discussion on Saint John of the Cross.[137] The meetings were interrupted for the summer, and in July 1929 Maritain published his long article "Bergsonisme et métaphysique" with the Roseau d'or[138] and sent a copy to Berdyaev that remains in the Clamart library with annotations on every page. Then at the end of summer, Maritain noted that he went on Saturday, 5 October, "at 5 p.m. to Berdyaev's with Raïa."[139]

The "intimate" meetings only resumed in December 1929. Maritain agreed to them in a letter to Berdyaev on 18 November: "Yes, Tuesdays around 4 o'clock once a month at your place strikes me as entirely suitable for these intimate gatherings. Personally, 3 December as our first day works well for me. I am delighted at the prospect of hearing the presentation of M. Ilyin on the question of Sophia." As was now their custom, they divided the work of sending out the invitations. Maritain invited "Massignon, the Abbés, the young people," while Berdyaev took on inviting "Gabriel Marcel, Fumet, de Pange." In a note dated 29 November 1929, the "well-known Orthodox philosopher"[140] attempted to schedule, in consultation with Maritain, the date of the fifth meeting for Tuesday, 10 December 1929, in Meudon – "at your place," Berdyaev wrote, but it took place in Clamart.[141]

At the end of 1929, there was a last effort to prepare an interfaith meeting at the Boulevard Montparnasse location. Maritain wrote to Berdyaev about it on 18 November: "On Monday 9 December I am unfortunately not available, as I have an appointment that cannot be moved. But on the 16th I'm free. It would please me if it were possible for that day to schedule the lecture by Father Bulgakov at the Montparnasse location. As for the continuation of the interfaith meetings, I confess that I no longer see much purpose in them. It seems to me we have already gotten what we could from that approach.

We can speak again later about that." In fact, the card from Berdyaev of 29 November 1929 alluded to another date, "the 23rd or 30th of December," for the "lecture by Father Bulgakov"; but no interfaith meeting in Montparnasse seems to have taken place at the end of December, nor afterwards.

1930: Passionate Exchanges

In a notebook for Sunday, 12 January 1930, Maritain wrote, "Evening Russian meeting. Nika [the musician Nikolai Nabokov] speaking on Russian Soviet literature."[142] On Tuesday, 21 January 1930, Maritain jotted down in his notebook, "Meeting at Berdyaev's with Raïa."[143] It was the sixth intimate meeting about mysticism. On Sunday, 26 January, Berdyaev was present in Meudon.[144]

In an exchange of letters between Maritain and Berdyaev from late January to early February 1930, the two men discussed the program for upcoming meetings. It appears that only M. Puech "has agreed to do a lecture for us on Pseudo-Dionysius and Neoplatonism," but "not before the second half of March." Berdyaev then added, "And it is impossible to hold the meeting without your presence. When are you returning from Ireland?" In reply, Maritain advised Berdyaev to ask M. Puech to what extent Pseudo-Dionysus is Neoplatonic and to what extent he is Christian.[145] Three weeks later he added, "Let's hope that M. Puech's presentation will not be too HISTORIC as that term is understood at the Sorbonne."[146] The seventh intimate meeting was scheduled for Tuesday, 27 March at Berdyaev's.[147] One wonders whether it was entirely successful, because on 27 March Maritain wrote to Berdyaev, "I plan on writing to Father Théry for a new presentation on Pseudo-Dionysius."[148] On the eve of that seventh meeting, Berdyaev, Bulgakov,[149] and Maritain were present at a session of the Court of Cassation about the union of the churches, but they were so disappointed they left during the middle of it.[150]

A new intimate meeting on mysticism was scheduled and on 21 April Maritain encouraged Berdyaev to do the introduction. "Certainly, an introduction by you on the problem of negative theology will be of great use to us. It is an absolutely central problem." This eighth meeting was held on Tuesday, 13 May 1930, but the tone or atmosphere of this meeting bothered Maritain, who raised the matter in a letter to Berdyaev the next day stating, "I still have a painful impression of yesterday's meeting. I was troubled to see that you were led to express thoughts that are deeply important to you within a less than peaceful setting that did not allow for a thorough discussion. That is why I prefer to say nothing about the serious question of evil that touches on God's reserved mysteries. I hope that my other remarks did not upset you. Even if I do not think the same way you do, know that I understand the problems you raise and have a great deal of respect for your thinking."[151]

In a notebook entry for 13 May 1930 Maritain records, "At Berdyaev's at 4:30, his presentation on negative theology. Participants agitated. Poor Berdyaev lays out the essence of his thinking (which is not orthodox) in a disputatious atmosphere. Very interesting for me however. It pushes me to write on these topics (Personality, Evil). From the point of view of faith, the first reproach against this *Ungrund* of Böhme is its desire for a deeper, hidden divinity, which is a human and philosophical notion! Not the three figures of the Trinity. In the end Weigel will say that the Trinity is God in his relation to creatures!!"[152] From his perspective Berdyaev noted, "My presentation on the mysticism of Böhme and Angelus Silesius provoked some disquiet. A priest and professor at the Institut Catholique said to a woman next to him, 'This is how heresies are born.' At times I felt I was irritating Maritain; some of my statements were a challenge for our friendship."[153]

Jean de Pange reported in his *Journal* for 13 May that Berdyaev gave "a presentation on negative theology and German mysticism: Eckhart, Tauler, Weigel, Böhme, and Angelus Silesius." At the end of his short review of it, de Pange notes, "Berdyaev's ideas provoke high agitation within our little circle. *French and Russians rose up speaking all at once*."[154] The French were probably more surprised than the Russians, who seemed to be more accustomed to agitation in gatherings, in the manner of the three brothers Karamazov with their father in the presence of the *starets*: "All those present were moved, except the *starets*; all rose with emotion."[155]

In a letter to Berdyaev on 14 May, Maritain raises two important points: one regarding the control theology exerts over mysticism, the other about the notion of *Ungrund*: "On theology's oversight over mysticism: it is to the extent that the mystic utters, in his way, theological propositions or, if you like, enters into the cataphatic domain, that theology checks him, as it were. And if it is to be done correctly, this oversight must take into account the distinctive characteristics of mystical language, in other words by first of all translating into properly theological propositions the *speculative affirmations* with which the experimental language of the mystic is filled."[156]

Maritain next explains his position on the notion of *Ungrund*:

> The fundamental criticism that I would make about this doctrine is the way it seeks in God something *deeper* than what *God himself revealed about himself and his intimate life*. What pride! About the intimate life of God we can know nothing more than revelation allows. And revelation tells us that God is one in three persons; it tells us nothing about an *Ungrund* that would be deeper. In truth, Böhme gives a *human* idea – myth, symbol or concept, call it what you want – but in any case a *human* idea of *Ungrund* primacy over the dogmatically revealed truths and over the *divine* idea (the idea of the Holy Trinity); he is the one falling into cataphatic excess. *Gottheit*, *deitas*, that is the *Trinity*, there is nothing deeper in God. It is what reason cannot reach, what the Son must reveal to us (whereas unity is something reason can recognize).

On 23 May, some days after a meeting in Meudon "with the Russians,"[157] Berdyaev responded to Maritain's letter stating, "I did not have the impression that the atmosphere at our last meeting was insufficiently calm. Russians always discuss matters passionately. I confess it is difficult for me to speak calmly when the topic is the problem of evil and suffering. I am deeply torn apart by this problem."[158]

Relations were always extremely courteous between the Thomist philosopher and the one Maritain referred to in 1930 as the representative of "an anti-intellectual existential philosophy."[159] On Sunday, 19 October, Maritain wrote to Berdyaev, and they met on 21 October in Meudon.[160] In November 1930, Berdyaev invited Jacques and Raïssa: "My dear friend! We would so like to see you both at our place … We can speak then about the topics of our meetings."[161] On Thursday, 4 December, some days before a meeting in Meudon with Hélène Iswolsky,[162] Jacques and Raïssa Maritain went to Clamart and they "decided to resume the Tuesday meetings at Berdyaev's."[163]

The meetings started again with the ninth session taking place on Tuesday, 16 December 1930: "At 4 p.m. at Berdyaev's, Olivier [Lacombe speaks] on the principle of identity, intelligence, and logic."[164] A short time later, on Sunday, 21 December, Berdyaev went to Meudon after dinner.[165]

1931: The Resumption of the Tuesday Meetings

Maritain and Berdyaev, each on his own, invited Étienne Gilson to the tenth meeting.[166] Starting Tuesday, 20 January 1931, the meetings resumed. Maritain did a presentation titled "On Philosophy, Theology, Mysticism."[167] In his *Carnet de notes* Maritain records the following: "20 January. Meeting at Berdyaev's. After my presentation on Saint Thomas and philosophy 'in faith,' Berdyaev turns to Gilson, counting on him to contradict me, reminding him what he had written about Thomism and about Saint Thomas as a precursor of the philosophy of pure reason. To everyone's great surprise, Gilson declared that if he had spoken thus, he was mistaken and that he was entirely in agreement with me. (He had in fact considerably changed his position in the later editions of *Thomisme*.) Raïssa and myself felt very touched by the attitude of Gilson and his uprightness in correcting his position himself. Our bonds of friendship began that day."[168]

The eleventh "meeting at Berdyaev's"[169] took place on Tuesday, 24 February 1931, noted Maritain. The twelfth meeting was scheduled for Tuesday, 24 March 1931: "meeting at the home of Berdyaev who presents his thinking about religious anthropology and to whom I respond at length."[170] Six weeks later, on Tuesday, 5 May 1931, was the thirteenth meeting "at Berdyaev's (Father Augustin Jakubisiak speaks about predestination)."[171]

During the summer of 1931 the meetings were interrupted, and before resuming again in the fall, the two philosophers exchanged several letters. The correspondence stored in the Maritain archive includes a brief postcard note dated 29 October 1931 in which Berdyaev proposes coming to the Maritains' on Sunday, 8 November. Maritain had written to him on 27 October and invited him to come discuss the meetings: "I must speak to you about our meetings. I am so overwhelmed with overdue work and so completely exhausted that I doubt it will be possible for me to regularly attend our meetings this year, neither at your place nor the ones like we used to have at the home of Du Bos with Gabriel Marcel. I am very upset about it all, but it seems materially impossible for me to maintain my former consistency. However, I certainly do not want this to disrupt these meetings which are so beneficial. The trouble is that Massignon is in the same situation I am in. We have to find French philosophers who can attend regularly, and that is what I'd like to speak with you about."

After 1931, what became of these intimate meetings that "were so especially interesting when Maritain and Berdyaev led the conversation"?[172] A fourteenth meeting is mentioned for Tuesday, 19 January 1932: "Tuesday 19. Afternoon meeting at Berdyaev's. My little Raïa comes."[173] It would be the last meeting, but other occasions would come up that allowed Maritain and Berdyaev to pursue their exchanges on other topics.[174]

Even if some expressed their regret,[175] the intimate Tuesday meetings on mysticism reached an end at the turn of the year between 1931 and 1932. The interfaith meetings in Boulevard Montparnasse did not last long either. In 1931, the Russian Orthodox community in France experienced a significant institutional crisis, with the breakdown of the canonical ties between the Metropolitan Evlogii and the Patriarchate of Moscow that was subordinate to Soviet power, and Evlogii's request to the Patriarchate of Constantinople for canonical hospitality.[176] This rupture contributed to "the disintegration of the first Orthodox French community and the deterioration of the bonds between the different protagonists of the religious revival."[177]

The overall assessment of these meetings was positive because the mutual discoveries of Catholics and Orthodox allowed early prejudices to be overcome while at the same time acknowledging the challenges of interfaith dialogue. In fact, the Tuesday meetings on mysticism had to be relaunched at the end of 1930. In any case, several of the meetings would leave their mark, such as the one of 13 May 1930 on the mysticism of Böhme that gave rise to the passionate discussions and exchanges that clearly revealed some notable doctrinal differences. Also memorable was the meeting of 20 January 1931, during which Maritain and Gilson adopted a common position on the philosophy of Saint Thomas Aquinas that would become a strong link in their friendship. Above all, it is worth noting that the meetings were a true laboratory of thought among Christian philosophers and therefore a community in which Maritain, Berdyaev, and others could concretely experiment with the exercise of Christian philosophy, at a time when the debate about the notion of Christian thought was at the forefront, notably at a meeting of the Société Française de Philosophie in Paris on 21 March 1931.[178]

27 January 1931: The Debate at the Studio franco-russe on Descartes and Cartesianism

Philippe Chenaux offers an important reminder of the challenges of the day: "The encyclical *Mortalium Animos* (6 January 1928), by condemning all forms of Catholic ecumenism that might be connected to a 'pan-Christianism,' had a cooling effect on the ardour of [ecumenical meetings], though it did not reject the necessity of contact with separatist Russian Orthodox believers. Two circles attempted to foster this dialogue in the Paris of the 1920s: one rather informal circle was centered around Maritain and Berdyaev; a second more institutional one was known as the Studio franco-russe."[179]

THE STUDIO FRANCO-RUSSE

In answer to the question "What is the Studio franco-russe?" Léonid Livak responds, "It was a set of public debates by writers and intellectuals – both French and Russian émigrés – that took place in Paris between 1929 and 1931 with the aim of allowing a succession of views to be expressed that would identify essential points of moral rapprochement and possible intellectual collaboration between the elites of the two countries."[180]

Following the example of the Décades de Pontigny of Paul Desjardins,[181] the Studio franco-russe meetings took inspiration from "the great humanist tradition that would place diverse opinions in opposition while respecting freedom of thought."[182] The Studio franco-russe[183] was created following a literary gathering on 30 April 1929 with the support of the organization called Humanités contemporaines, founded by the politician J. Probus Corréard, co-director of the review *L'Intransigeant*, which also supported the Studio de la poésie, the Studio de l'histoire, the Studio du théâtre, the Studio de la philosophie, and the Studio social.

The main organizer of the Studio franco-russe was a close associate of Berdyaev, "the Russian poet and journalist Vsevolod Borisovich Foht (1895–1941) who signed his French writings 'Wsevolod de Vogt.'"[184] A second leader was "the French poet and novelist Robert Sébastien [born in 1903] from the Jacques Maritain circle."[185] The Studio franco-russe organized monthly debates animated by the generation of "young writers and intellectuals in exile."[186] "These monthly debates ['on the last Tuesday of each month'[187]] took place regularly over two periods: from November 1929 to May 1930,[188] and from November 1930 to April 1931. The public was sizeable, sometimes surpassing the three-hundred-seat capacity of the Musée social located at 5, rue Las Cases in Paris's seventh arrondissement."[189]

"The Studio franco-russe meetings took place entirely in French. The subject of each meeting was announced in advance. Two speakers – one Russian, one French – would prepare and present their points of view on the problem in question. Then de Vogt and Sébastien would initiate a debate that was open to anyone present in the room. Many French and Russian writers and intellectuals were expressly invited and occupied the first rows that were reserved for them. The hosts would invite them to intervene first, which underscored the 'elitist' nature of the Studio sessions."[190] Furthermore, as Léonid Livak noted, all the parties who gathered at the Studio at that time, "Russians as well as the French, had a particular interest in the spiritual and notably Christian revival in Western culture more than in the totalitarian ideologies that dominated the political and intellectual landscape of the time."[191]

According to Pierre Van der Meer, at the Studio franco-russe "the debates … were very lively: Russians and French, elderly gentlemen and very young men would converse about the given subject – Dostoevsky, André Gide, Tolstoy, Solov'ev, Lenin, the Church, Marxism, fascism, literature, sociology, or religion with a chaos of opinions and systems of thought for or against. The customary atmosphere in the crowded room was one of passionate agitation. At the same time, one might hear outbursts of applause and whistling, protests and acclamations."[192]

THE DEBATE OF 27 JANUARY 1931

During a Studio franco-russe meeting on 31 May 1930 with René Lalou, Vogt, and Sébastien, Jacques Maritain promised "an anti-Descartes [presentation] for January 1931."[193] In an entry for Thursday, 22 January 1931, he recorded in his notebook, "Worked on Descartes for Studio franco-russe (next Tuesday)."[194] On Tuesday, 27 January 1931, Maritain attended the Studio franco-russe and together with Boris Vysheslavtsev gave a "memorable" lecture on Descartes.[195] That evening, Maritain noted in a entry dated 27 January, "Lecture on Descartes, evening at Studio franco-russe. My little Raïa is there, with Véra, Hill, Madame Millot, Nine, many friends. Raïa is pleased with my presentation. Vysheslavtsev defends Descartes. He makes him into a mystic. Intervention by Berdyaev … by the Russian philosopher Gabrielovich, Lacombe speaks out perfectly, with firmness, tact, courage. I answer back to everyone as best I can."[196]

Maritain's lecture, entitled "Descartes and the Cartesian Spirit," eventually became chapter 5, "The Cartesian Heritage," of *Songe de Descartes* (*Dream of Descartes*, 1944), first published in 1932 and reviewed in the journal *Put'* in 1934.[197] This lecture and that of Boris Vysheslavtsev, along with the intervention of Berdyaev and Maritain's reply to Berdyaev, as well as other interventions, and finally the concluding remarks by Maritain, were all published in a February 1931 issue of the *Cahiers de la quinzaine* that sold more than one thousand copies. This is the only written trace of a properly philosophical public debate between the philosophers from Meudon and Clamart. It was a debate in which all the speakers clearly contested the value of Cartesianism, but with fundamentally divergent views about the critique and the value of Descartes's intuitions.

Maritain's presentation on "Descartes and the Cartesian Spirit" concludes on "The Cultural Significance of Cartesian Dualism" with an evocation of Dostoevsky's thought as analyzed by Berdyaev, including a direct mention of the Russian philosopher. Maritain noted that after the Cartesian dualism "which brings with it both a naïve optimism and an anthropocentric materialism regarding civilization … thinking had made considerable progress. Never has man better scrutinized his positions. Never has man experienced such a tormenting nostalgia for liberty. Yet how would he truly know liberty? His own personality escapes him. He is subject to the doubling up that Berdyaev so well described in the most profound pages of his book on Dostoevsky."[198]

Next, calling to the Russians in the audience, after first reminding all that Descartes had accomplished three important ruptures: "rupture of thinking with being, rupture of the movement of the soul with wisdom, rupture of the human composition," Maritain declared, "I believe that Russian philosophy deliberately distinguishes the theandric conception, which recognizes that the Word became flesh and places all things under the sign of the Incarnation, from the anthropotheist conception, which holds that man becomes god and which orders all things toward this conquest of divinity. It is true that human affairs go, in fact, necessarily in the direction of one or the other of these two conceptions. Well then, Descartes gave to anthropo-theism its philosophical legitimacy. And that's why we are at war with him."[199]

It remains the case, as Maritain underlined, "that Marxism, in [his] view, represents the latest and most active form of anthropo-theism."[200] Maritain then invited "each to do his own soul searching": "Perhaps modern Russian philosophy would do well to approach the subject of Hegel in the manner we have tried to approach Descartes. In any case, I ask our Russian friends to accept the argument that if Cartesianism was in modern history the French sin, there is something more besides this sin in French thought. I ask them also to distinguish as is required, in other words absolutely and radically, the rationalist conception of the world, which had its great sage in Descartes, from the Catholic conception of the world, whose preeminent sage was Saint Thomas Aquinas, and which is not compartmentalized to the Latin or European worlds but holds for the Orient and for the Occident."[201]

After these words by Maritain, it was the Russian Boris Vysheslavtsev's turn.[202] This longtime friend of Berdyaev presented Cartesian intuition as part of the universal principle of doubt and the *cogito*, later taken up and transformed by Husserl in his phenomenological reduction. Vysheslavtsev also placed this Cartesian intuition in relation to the ancient wisdom of India.[203] In his presentation entitled "Descartes and Modern Philosophy," after first discussing the Cartesian ego as part of a "phenomenological reduction,"[204] Vysheslavtsev turned to the Absolute that constitutes the keystone of Descartes's thinking. For Descartes, "God, the Absolute, does not need to be proved, it is instead the world and nature whose reality must be proven. Because one may doubt that things exist, but one may not doubt that the Absolute Being exists. The Absolute is irreducible, it completely resists reduction to phenomena, as much as the self and even more so. The reality of the Absolute is for Descartes an immediate intuition, something self-evident that presents itself at the same time as that of the self."[205]

Vysheslavtsev next examined the relations of the self or ego to the Absolute or God, and he presented what he called "the Russian interpretation of Descartes," an interpretation "more ontological, more absolutist, more mystical and much closer to Descartes."[206] Thus, according to Vysheslavtsev:

> After "phenomenological reduction," after universal doubt, there remains only two beings: the self which is not the Absolute, and the Absolute which is not the self; the self, as dependent, and the Absolute as independent ... This *dependence on the Absolute* is something unique in the world: it is absolutely different from all other natural dependence, such as the dependence on things, on men, on nature. One must liberate oneself from all dependence on sense to contemplate the dependence on the Absolute. The *via purgativa* of mystics is the method to attain "the independence from things," the independence from the world. The *via purgativa*, the obscure night of the great philosopher is the *epoché*, the *doubt*. It frees us from all things temporal, material, and natural, reducing them to appearances, to phenomena; we must rise into another dimension, the third, where the spirit senses itself in the spiritual atmosphere of thought and freedom, very high, above the world of phenomena. Such is the surprising dialectic of Descartes and of all great mystics – Hindoo and Christian – having attained the summit of independence, they find themselves absolutely dependent, because they have encountered the Absolute.[207]

This Russian interpretation of Descartes may seem astonishing, but it may be found consonant with the perspective of Vysheslavtsev for whom "this *axiom of dependence* is evident, but not rational. It is the mystical intuition of the Absolute which is irrational; it is the meeting with the *Deus absconditus* [the hidden, unknowable God]. One experiences before it the singular sentiment of profound astonishment, or of a fright before the Abyss. This has been called the *Mysterium tremendum* (Rudolf Otto) and the 'feeling of absolute dependence' (Schleiermacher)."[208] In the end, this ultimate intuition of the Absolute is itself of a religious nature because, for Vysheslavtsev, "in theological language, this feeling of dependence is the immediate intuition of the *created* being who feels itself bonded with the *uncreated* being, with the *Creator*; and this liaison is the *religio*."[209]

One may note here that the Russian interpretation of Descartes proposed by Vysheslavtsev has a religious dimension. Moreover it is his theological vision of man that authorizes Vysheslavtsev to make criticisms of Descartes, by distinguishing, on the one hand, the profound intuitions of the first part of his writings, and on the other, the "Cartesianism": in other words, the second part of his writings, in which organic life is dissociated in the sense that "this second part of his philosophy, which constitutes his sin and misery, is his system of two substances, his geometrical and mechanical manner of understanding organic life, of considering plants and animals as automatons without souls or life ... Cartesianism only accepts and develops this second part of the works of Descartes that no longer has any value. If Thomism is fighting against it, we are absolutely in agreement. Eliminating Cartesianism is necessary to see the true value of Descartes."[210]

Following the initial presentations, the themes developed by Vysheslavtsev were partly taken up by Leonid Gabrilovich, and later Maritain responded to questions raised by this Russian interpretation of Descartes. It is important to note the intervention Berdyaev made at this meeting. Directly after Vysheslavtsev's presentation, the moderator Wsevolod de Vogt initiated the first phase of the debate by giving the floor to Berdyaev. Among the diverse questions raised by Berdyaev, his main point was as follows: "Descartes created European rationalism, without a doubt. It is the negative side.[211] But Descartes also established within European philosophy the problem of the subject. If we compare the philosophy of Descartes to scholastic philosophy, and not only to the philosophy of Saint Thomas but to scholastic philosophy in general, we will see that in the latter, and in Thomism also, the most remarkable dimension, the problem of the subject, was never thoroughly set forward. For example, if we take the question of clear and distinct knowledge, for Thomists clarity and distinctiveness are always in the object itself. It is being, the object itself that is clear and distinct, but if there is no clarity and distinction in the subject, that leads to nothing."[212]

Berdyaev declared himself to be "completely anti-Cartesian," while also stating, "I defend Descartes from a completely special point of view, I could say from a historiosophical point of view"[213] in the sense that "the advent of Descartes is an act in the drama of philosophical knowledge," because "when the problem of the subject is posited, then the realist, objective point of view is surpassed. It is a moment in the history of the philosophy of knowledge."[214] Berdyaev considered that the "the philosophy of Descartes is not at all a philosophy of mind, but that the philosophy of mind became possible after the problem posited by Descartes. It is precisely a historical point of view. There is a new experience, a new problem that gets posed, and it is the dynamism of philosophical thinking that manifests itself in this way."[215]

Berdyaev specified his thinking further by saying:

> The spirit was revealed in religious life, and the scholastic is certainly penetrated by the spirit that was revealed in religious life. It is what constitutes his grandeur. But in philosophical thinking, purely philosophical, the philosophy of spirit did not yet exist at the time of the scholastics. The life of spirit needed to be discovered also in philosophical thinking and by philosophical thinking. This means that the revelation of the spirit, which is absolute from a religious point of view, begins to enter into the domain of life and must enter into the domain of philosophy. This happens through a dramatic occurrence, in stages, by a succession of actions. Cartesianism is ultra-rationalism. It has nothing in common with the philosophy of spirit, and I found that what Monsieur Maritain said about the outcome of European culture that derives from Descartes – almost all that he said – is correct, at least from my point of view. But it is all the same unjust toward Descartes, who must also be judged from another point of view.[216]

Maritain's reply to Berdyaev came next, and it points to the underlying philosophical difficulty of their respective interpretations of Descartes. Because if Maritain "thinks, indeed, as [his] friend Berdyaev does, that there is a drama around knowledge,"[217] he nevertheless recalls that

> Philosophy of spirit (if one means by that knowledge of the life proper to spirit, entrance into the depths of thinking), existed, in his view, really and truly among the scholastics. What the scholastics did not do is to distinguish with complete explicitness the problems of this philosophy. They were treated, but they had not been named as such with their own separate noetic universe. Thanks to Descartes, thanks even to the errors of Descartes, these problems were introduced in a striking, manifest manner in the preoccupations of modern times. The importance of the world of reflexivity was not recognized until the time that philosophies emerged erecting reflexivity in everything and as absolute, and enclosing speculation inside insolvable enigmas. If you like, put more simply and succinctly, there is a movement of the history of thinking, that reason by itself could suffice; but on account of the weakness of philosophers and the weakness of human reason, it is sometimes necessary for the devil to push the wheel.
>
> Well, in the case of Descartes the devil pushed the wheel. In other words, thanks to Cartesian idealism and rationalism, a new problem was put forward (alas, poorly put forward), a problem that we ought to respect, that remains, that is crucial to address, but that is intimately linked in Descartes to fundamental errors, and that one cannot resolve correctly other than by articulating it in a different way than idealism has done. I believe that what is called philosophy of spirit, insofar as we imagine that this philosophy did not exist in antiquity, is the distinctive problematic of idealism, formulated in relation to idealist preconceptions and the idealist system. In other words, a problematic that was poorly formulated, it is the spirit enclosed on itself that cannot manage to get beyond the postulates of idealism and which, as a result, necessarily goes from drama to drama.
>
> When it is said that the ancients only had a philosophy of the first dimension, a philosophy of the object, of things, I also think a

> mistake is being made about the profundity of ancient philosophy. We imagine that their realism was a simple realism of common sense, a naïve realism. That was not at all the case! The philosophy of Saint Thomas is neither a purely objectivist philosophy, in the sense that I have just indicated, nor a philosophy of spirit in the idealist sense. It is important to note here that clarity is not only in the object for Saint Thomas; that is completely incorrect. Evidence has its root in the thing, but only expresses itself in spirit which gives itself the thing present as object. It is the radical and potential intelligibility of things that becomes actual in spirit. Material things are potentially intelligible. They must pass into spirit by the vital act of intellection to attain all the light that constitutes evidence. For Saint Thomas, things are not clear and distinct, there is no evidence in action except in spirit, which supposes the entire theory of intelligence and an array of considerations that are properly psychological or noetic that take us very far from naïve realism [applause].[218]

Note that this public debate with Berdyaev underlines well the point of divergence between the author of *Réflexions sur l'intelligence* and the "existentialist" Russian thinker – while each in his own way declared himself anti-Cartesian, both focused on the question of the nature of knowledge.

During the discussion that followed, other speakers intervened[219]: Désiré Roustan, Leonid Gabrilovich, René Lalou, and Olivier Lacombe, who responded to Boris Vysheslavtsev on a point related to Hindu thinking. As for Leonid Gabrilovich, he stated his wish to "in a way complete and detail further the defensive enterprise undertaken by [his] friend Monsieur Vysheslavtsev."[220] To this end, he remarked:

> Monsieur Berdyaev said it was strange to see a Russian defending Descartes, because Descartes is the philosopher who has had the least success in Russia within Russian philosophy. This is true. But allow me to ask you, what is Russian philosophy? … I would like to claim that so-called 'Russian philosophy' has been built completely in Weimar and Jena. What is generally called Russian philosophy – and I know whereof I speak – is to a great extent an outgrowth of German

> idealism, especially of the sort shaped by Schelling and Baader. Yes, this problem of Russian philosophy is still a big question. For my part, I openly confess that I consider there to be no Russian philosophy at all [laughter]. There is the Russian spirit which has posed problems of considerable importance. Here we can observe a noticeable degree of congeniality between Russian thinkers and some great French philosophers. True Russian philosophy is that of our greatest writers, notably Tolstoy and especially Dostoevsky. This true Russian philosophy has asked the same questions that have been asked in France by the great French philosophers, by Pascal for example – and in this regard we find ourselves on common ground. But Russian philosophy as a system, fortunately or unfortunately, has never existed, does not yet exist, and perhaps, we can hope, will never exist in this form as system.[221]

In the end, two points emerged from this debate over Descartes. First, even if there was a partial convergence of Maritain and Berdyaev's positions in that both declared themselves anti-Cartesian, a significant divergence persisted around the central question of the philosophy of knowledge.[222] In truth, Maritain's "critical realism" of the natural light of intelligence stood in opposition to Berdyaev's "mystical realism" according to which truth is perceived and possessed in and through spiritual experience.[223] Secondly, this sharply contrasted confrontation of Jacques Maritain's thinking with Russian thinking allows one to better see how the mystical interpretation of Cartesian thinking favours a religious philosophy consistent with the thinking of Dostoevsky that exalts the autonomy of the human subject and his freedom.

1932: Interpretations of Dostoevsky: Berdyaev, Maritain, Journet

Fyodor Dostoevsky

In a letter addressed to Maritain on 22 February 1928, Berdyaev broaches "the possibility of publishing [his] book in the 'Roseau d'or,'"[224] but Maritain does not follow up on Berdyaev's request. For his part, Maritain published some pages on Dostoevsky entitled "Dialogues" with the Roseau d'or. He noted, quoting André Gide, that "Dostoevsky is not strictly speaking a thinker; he's a novelist." For Maritain, "André Gide explains well how, though awkward at expressing his thoughts in his own name and in abstract terms, Dostoevsky mixes them into the skin and bones of his characters and has them live through them. They are not the ideas of a philosopher, contemplative ideas, they are the ideas of an artist, ideas in action. This is exactly right, so long as one also adds that this novelist is a novelist-theologian, a novelist-prophet." Indeed, above all a novelist who "writes to heal."[225] Or, as Eugène-Melchior Vogüé puts it, "Dostoevsky is a psychologist of the spirit who plumbs the horrors of human life that "the human soul retains completely in sight" and whose "preferred landscapes are the outskirts of large cities and miserable streets."[226]

Maritain then hurried to his conclusion: "So then, let us be mindful, while trying to get clear on his thoughts, not to misconstrue the admirable complexity of the creative synthesis or ascribe too indelicately to the artist as coming directly from him that which is from him only through and in the material he enlivens and that which manifests his thought only through the rays refracted a thousand times and by the total distribution of the light and by the parts left in shadow as much as by the light."[227]

The Spirit of Dostoevsky According to Berdyaev

In 1929 the publication by Éditions Saint-Michel[228] of Berdyaev's *L'Esprit de Dostoïevski* contributed to the dissemination in France of the thought of the author of "The Legend of the Grand Inquisitor."[229] Recognized as "the one who assimilated Russian thinking by presenting to the French public authors such as Khomiakov, Leont'ev, and especially Dostoevsky,"[230] Berdyaev sent his *Esprit de Dostoïevski* to Jacques Maritain on 25 May 1930.[231] We know Maritain had read it by 17 October, some days before a meeting with Berdyaev.[232]

In 1920, while a professor at the University of Moscow, Berdyaev "gave a year-long seminar on Dostoevsky at the Free Academy of Spiritual Culture."[233] It is easy to understand, as Olivier Clément remarked, that "the fundamental intuitions of the great religious philosopher [Berdyaev] are Russian in the grand literary tradition of the nineteenth century, above all from Dostoevsky and the Christ figure in the Legend."[234] Indeed, starting with the foreword to the *Esprit de Dostoïevski*, written in Moscow in 1921 before being translated and published in France in 1929, Berdyaev announced his debt to his master Dostoevsky because, as he writes, "at the base of my conception and my perception of the world, there has always been the idea of freedom. And within this original intuition of freedom, I would always rediscover Dostoevsky as though in his chosen homeland."[235]

In his *Esprit de Dostoïevski*, Berdyaev organizes his chapters around several major themes: Dostoevsky's spiritual dimension, Man, Freedom, Evil, Love, Revolution, Socialism, Russia, The Grand Inquisitor, Christ and the Antichrist, and finally Dostoevsky and us. Across these themes, Berdyaev analyses in succession the question of Dostoevsky's new art and his philosophy of religion. He then underscores Dostoevsky's discovery, which Berdyaev characterizes as in part an irrational freedom whose roots resemble the *Ungrund* of Böhme, and in part the freedom of choice for the good. Then Berdyaev investigates the way in which Dostoevsky conceived of human freedom, which, to be true to itself, invites man to resist all social organization, notably socialism and the Marxist revolution. Berdyaev also examines attentively the necessity, for Dostoevsky, to resist all forms of spiritual constraint such as those he attributed to the Catholic church, which the great Russian novelist judged was safeguarding freedom less well than the Orthodox church.

Most of the themes developed by Berdyaev in the volume on Dostoevsky had already been nourishing his reflections on future possibilities for Russia in his *Nouveau Moyen Âge*, with a particular emphasis on freedom, since "the theme of man and his destiny, for Dostoevsky, is freedom."[236] It is thus once again on the crucial question of man's freedom, artfully dramatized by Dostoevsky in "The Legend of the Grand Inquisitor," that Berdyaev concentrates.[237] He states in the introduction that "The 'Legend of the Grand Inquisitor' in particular had made a big impact on me as a youth; and to such an extent that for the first time, I turned to Christ, and it was as he was represented in the 'Legend' that he appeared to me."[238]

The chapter entitled "The Grand Inquisitor, Christ, Antichrist" is particularly important and indicative of the close link between the thinking of Dostoevsky and Berdyaev for whom "the 'Legend of the Grand Inquisitor' represents the summit of Dostoevsky's oeuvre, the crowning height of his dialectic. It is there that one must seek out his constructive views on religion. All the threads become clear there, and the essential problem, the problem of human freedom, is resolved … Also, the Legend's theme is freedom and must be addressed to freedom. It is in darkness that the light must emerge."[239]

For Berdyaev and his presentation of Dostoevsky's thinking, this problem of human and notably Christian freedom is derived as follows:

> The mystery of Christian freedom is in fact that of Golgotha, the mystery of the crucifixion. The Truth, put on the cross, constrains no one, weighs on no one. It cannot be confessed and embraced other than freely. Truth crucified addresses the freedom of the human spirit. The Crucified did not descend from the cross as the unbelievers demanded, and as is demanded down to the present day, because he was thirsty for free love, and not the servile transports of a slave before a power that once and for all terrorized him … It is therein that the mystery of Golgotha is the mystery of the freedom of spirit.[240]

According to Berdyaev, for Dostoevsky the mystery of Golgotha, in which the core of divine love is made manifest, does not allow, and would be betrayed and trampled if it did, any assimilation within a system or organization that would exert pressure on man or his freedom. For Dostoevsky, the authoritarian figure of the Church – notably his thoughts on the Catholic church that he compared to a theocracy – was becoming a counterfeit of the mystery of Golgotha, and to that extent a figure of the Antichrist.

Berdyaev continues:

> Every time in the history of Christianity that people have tried to convert the Truth Crucified, which addresses the freedom of spirit, into Truth exerting pressure on this spirit, they have betrayed the fundamental secret of Christianity. Acting in this way, the Church has always adopted the mask of sovereignty, it has seized Caesar's sword. First, the organization of the Church takes on a juridical character, the Church submits to the rules of judicial constraint. Second, the dogmatic system of the Church takes on a rationalist character, the Truth of Christ submits to rules of logical constraint. Does that not mean that it was necessary for Christ to descend from the Cross for us to believe in him? In the entirely spontaneous act of the Cross, in the mystery of Truth Crucified, there is no trace of affirmation nor of logical or juridical necessity. Turning the Truth of Christ into something juridical and rational is turning away from the path of freedom toward that of constraint. Dostoevsky remains convinced of the Truth Crucified, of the religion of Golgotha, in other words of the religion of freedom.[241]

This religion was proper to Dostoevsky, because, as Berdyaev notes, "Dostoevsky was alone in defending his conception of Christian freedom, a great number opposed him. His theories of freedom are close to those of Khomiakov, who always rose above official Orthodox theory. The orthodoxy of Khomiakov and of Dostoevsky is not that of Filaret Drozdov, the Metropolitan of Moscow, or of Theophan the Recluse. The spirit of the Grand Inquisitor can manifest itself both at the far 'right' and the far 'left.'"[242] That said, even if the religion of the freedom of spirit was proper to Dostoevsky in the sense that it was distinct from Orthodox doctrine, it still borrowed from Russian literature, notably from Vladimir Solov'ev's *Short Narrative on the Antichrist* in which the Grand Inquisitor is also a helper of humanity and a socialist openly presenting himself as someone full of goodness.[243]

Despite the criticisms that Berdyaev levelled at Dostoevsky, a largely positive impression comes through in his analysis of "The Legend of the Grand Inquisitor":

> If Dostoevsky cannot be a master of spiritual discipline, if we must conquer in ourselves, first "psychologism" then "Dostoevskyism," there is a point on which his teaching remains very precise: he wants to show that through Christ one rediscovers the light amidst the darkness, that the divine form and resemblance exist still in the most fallen individual, that one must love one's neighbor out of respect for his freedom. Dostoevsky had led us through the darkness, but it is not darkness that will have the last word. His work in no way leaves us with an impression of somber and hopeless pessimism, because this darkness includes the light. Light has conquered the world; it lights every obscure corner. The Christianity of Dostoevsky is not a somber Christianity, it is a luminous Christianity, the Christianity of Saint John. It carries elements of a Christianity of the future, of the triumph of the eternal Holy message, of the religion of liberation and of love.[244]

If Berdyaev's comprehension of Dostoevsky's Christianity revealed the bond between their respective ways of thinking, what did Maritain make of the *Esprit de Dostoïevski*? We have some indication because before their meeting on Tuesday, 21 October 1930, in Clamart, Maritain wrote to Berdyaev on 19 October:

> Pardon me for not thanking you sooner for your *Esprit de Dostoïevski* … It is a strange thing that you and I have very different ideological structures behind our thinking, and yet everything you write is deeply interesting to me and inspires my deepest sympathy even when I oppose your arguments. This book on Dostoevsky strikes me as very important for understanding your conception of the world. It is full of admirable visions and is marvellously stimulating. It is the chapter on freedom that provokes in me the most reservations. This dialectic of Dostoevsky regarding freedom is certainly Christian, but a Christianity that operates thanks to a Hegelian ideology. I believe that if Dostoevsky had had a more explicit conception of a *supernatural* order, he would not have transposed into the weave of nature and, if I can put it this way, *metaphysicalized* the Pauline doctrine of law

and freedom (since it is always to those points that we return). But we will speak more about all that. See you soon. All our friendship to your dear family. With all my heart. Jaq Maritain.

Charles Journet's 1932 Article "La Légende du Grand Inquisiteur" in Nova et Vetera

Maritain and his friend Abbé Journet paid close attention to Berdyaev's reasoning in his analysis of "The Legend of the Grand Inquisitor."[245] Indeed, they were not the only ones who had questions about Berdyaev's thinking.[246] After the publication of *L'Esprit de Dostoïevski* and the likely receipt of a copy sent by Berdyaev himself,[247] Abbé Journet took the time, theologian that he was, to reflect and then formulate certain criticisms of Dostoevsky's "Legend of the Grand Inquisitor" and Berdyaev's interpretation of it. Journet's criticisms were eventually published as an article in a spring 1932 issue of *Nova et Vetera* entitled "La Légende du Grand Inquisiteur."[248]

First Journet analyzes the "Legend," and in a second part he identifies Dostoevsky's doctrinal presuppositions. He describes the latter as a "separatist postulate" which "wants the spiritual order and the temporal order to be separated by a firm barrier. Once these two orders are disjoined and declared antinomic, all that's left is to make a choice."[249] However, for Journet, "there is no more anti-Catholic error than to divide the universe in two, the invisible and the visible, and sacrifice one of them on the altar of Manicheism or the other on the altar of materialism. The Holy Church of Christ believes that it is at the same time transcendent and immanent to the world of culture."[250]

For Journet, Dostoevsky wrote "The Legend of the Grand Inquisitor" under this separatist postulate. The antinomy does not only appear there where it must necessarily be, between Christ and Antichrist, faith and atheism, good and evil. It appears everywhere that the modern world places it: in the first temptation, the economic order is opposed to interior freedom; in the second, law is opposed to conscience; in the third, politics is opposed to religion. Dostoevsky agreed, as had Luther and Marx, to separate the spiritual and the temporal, and oppose them like good and evil, the true and the false. It is these two halves of reality, declared antinomic, incompatible, and tragically standing one against the other that forms the representation of Christ and Antichrist in 'The Legend of the Grand Inquisitor.'"[251]

Journet then identifies several consequences that follow from Dostoevsky's doctrinal presupposition. First, he notes, "it is because he fully adopts the separatist postulate, which is the foundation of Marxism, that Dostoevsky, despite having no knowledge of Marxism, was able to so astonishingly predict the advent of socialism in its most 'pure' form, the 'limit' case, namely materialist and atheist communism."[252] In sum, the hypothesis of a separatist postulate is confirmed by the surprising prediction Dostoevsky was able to make, and Journet recognizes in passing the pertinence of certain remarks in Berdyaev's *Esprit de Dostoïevski*.[253]

Secondly, states Journet, "It is also because Dostoevsky adopts the separatist postulate that Christ and Christianity in "The Legend of the Grand Inquisitor" are neither the true Christ nor true Christianity."[254] Journet remarks that

> this opposition between Christ in the "Legend" and Christ in Scripture and the Christian Tradition was sensed by Nikolai Berdyaev who praises Dostoevsky for it here: "It is in 'The Legend of the Grand Inquisitor' that one must seek the constructive part of the religious ideas of Dostoevsky … The veiled image of Christ is related to that of Nietzsche's Zarathustra. It is the same spirit of august freedom, the same dizzying height, the same aristocratic spirit. And this is an original feature of Dostoevsky's understanding of Christ, and one that we have not yet developed. Never before Dostoevsky has there been such a close association made between the image of Christ and the freedom of spirit accessible only to a small number. This freedom of spirit is possible only because Christ renounced all temporal power.'" (*ED*, 243)[255]

Journet's third point identifies another consequence: "A third consequence of the separatist postulate is that the Roman Church, which refuses to conflate (as paganism does) or oppose (as the modern world does) the spiritual and the temporal, and instead distinguishes them and unites them through subordination from inferior to superiority, will be incapable of joining either Dostoevsky's Christ or his Antichrist. It remains outside the dilemma."[256] Journet next denounces the misprision of the author of "The Legend of the Grand Inquisitor":

> Dostoevsky saw the superhuman grandeur of the juridical power of the Pope. But because this power, which in our view is formally spiritual, dared proclaim and defend, as a temporal condition of its full normal exercise, its right to civil authority over the papal state, Dostoevsky, who held that the spiritual must remain absolutely separate from the temporal, concluded that the Pope's power is a formally political power, and that it is superhuman in political and corporeal magnitude. All that remained at that point was to see the Pope as the one who accepts the kingdoms of this world formerly rejected by Jesus, and to assimilate the Pope to the beast of the Apocalypse who receives from the demon authority over all nations.[257]

To pursue his demonstration of Dostoevsky's misunderstanding about the Catholic church, Journet quotes from the Russian novelist's nonfiction work *A Writer's Diary* and concludes thus: "Therefore, after accepting the separatist postulate and consequently being mistaken from the start on the significance of the papal state, and then after having assessed the more than human size of the papacy, Dostoevsky arrives at giving us a representation of the Pope and of Catholicism in the features of the Antichrist and his realm. The consequence is, it would seem, rather extravagant and may serve to open our eyes to the error that occurred from the start."[258]

Journet pursues his presentation by examining "Berdyaev's interpretation" as it appears in *L'Esprit de Dostoïevski* and cites several passages from it to support his criticisms. For example, Journet was aware that for Berdyaev: "In the 'Legend of the Grand Inquisitor' it is socialism that Dostoevsky has in mind, more than Catholicism, which he only knew superficially and from the outside. And the future realm of the Grand Inquisitor accords less with Catholicism than with atheist and materialist socialism [*ED*, 328]."[259] Journet is equally conscious that Berdyaev had noted a "striking coincidence between the description of anti-Christian spirit in Dostoevsky, in the 'Legend of the Grand Inquisitor' and elsewhere, and in Vladimir Soloviev's *De l'Antichrist*[260] [ED, 420]."[261] Journet also remarks that Berdyaev knew that "an analogous description of the spirit of the Antichrist had been given by the English Catholic writer [Robert Hugh] Benson in his remarkable [1907] novel entitled *Lord of the World* [ED, 240]."[262] But on account of these analogies between diverse authors (Dostoevsky, Solov'ev, Benson), Journet was unable to accept that Dostoevsky could be pardoned, nor, as Berdyaev had done, say that "Benson's novel, at the very least, ought to have proved to Dostoevsky that all Catholics are not contaminated by the spirit of the Grand Inquisitor."[263] Having read carefully Dostoevsky's notes in his *Writer's Diary*, and his judgement that "the principal source of Catholicism had been troubled and poisoned by Pope Pius IX proclaiming his right over the states of the church"[264] without being able to "see all the consequences of this 'important decision'"[265] for all Catholics, it is unacceptable for Journet that Berdyaev excuses Dostoevsky for an error that in truth did not concern the extent of the contamination of all Catholics by the spirit of the Grand Inquisitor.

Journet's criticism rests on this "all," which could lead readers to understand that certain Catholics might personally escape the grip of Catholic doctrine, but only on an individual basis, whereas Catholic doctrine in itself, in the eyes of Dostoevsky, carries the germ of contamination. Indeed, for Journet, Dostoevsky's error derives from the principle and not the extent of its consequences for all Catholics: "No, the error of Dostoevsky is not to deny the existence of Catholics uncontaminated by the spirit of the Grand Inquisitor. It is about the very essence of Catholicism. Dostoevsky confused the religion of the Incarnation with the religion of the material."[266] Moreover, Journet declares also on this point that Dostoevsky "misunderstood … the traditional Russian church."[267]

What's more, according to Journet, once Dostoevsky's mistake has been exposed, "one must add that it is the same confusion one finds in Berdyaev. He recognizes without difficulty among many Catholics the existence of an authentic Christian life. But he considers as fundamentally anti-Christian certain theses that traditional Christianity has always considered essential and that are professed not only within Catholicism but also partly in the dissident oriental Churches."[268]

After carrying out these analyses, Journet concludes that "as a consequence, Berdyaev will see in traditional Christianity, especially the Catholic church, the accomplishment of the realm of the Antichrist: 'The spirit of the Grand Inquisitor can manifest itself as much on the far *right* as on the far *left* [ED, 237].' Here we are back at Dostoevsky. Berdyaev took leave of him only in appearance. Where does such a tenacious aberration come from?"[269]

For Journet,

> Berdyaev, along with a crowd of modern philosophers, remains imprisoned within an immanentist philosophy. Consequently, it is impossible for him to distinguish between the natural order and the supernatural order. As a result, spiritual life can only consist in the blossoming of the pure interior freedom of man who will spontaneously have to decide between what is good and what is evil. They practically deny the Holy Spirit the right to manifest itself to men through exterior, public revelation that would be for all a shared rule of truth and common rule for action. Such an intervention, one regulating faith and morals, appears right away in their hypothesis, as a constraint imposed from outside on the spontaneous development of human spirit. Interior freedom, [they say], that is the spirit of Christ; constraint, that is the spirit of the Antichrist.[270]

To illustrate his point, Journet reproaches Berdyaev for these statements (cited earlier) taken from the *Esprit de Dostoïevski*: "First, the organization of the Church takes on a juridical character, the Church submits to the rules of judicial constraint. Second, the dogmatic system of the Church takes on a rationalist character, the Truth of Christ submits to rules of logical constraint [*ED*, 236]."[271] Journet's rejoinder: "We are familiar with these objections. They are the commonplaces of immanentist agnosticism."[272] Journet thus rejects Dostoevsky's new Christianity because "at the base of this new religion it is not difficult to recognize an error and a refusal. The error is that of a spiritualism bothered by the religion of the Incarnation and that therefore seeks salvation in the pure immanence of the human soul. The refusal is that of naturalism that turns away from the supernatural revelation whereby God seeks to break the chains of our created nature and to call us to participate in his intimate life."[273]

In short, for Journet, one ought to deny "against Berdyaev, that constraint is always bad. There are cases where it is not."[274] But above all, "claiming that all constraint is bad … would lead, on a natural level, to adopting the anarchic theories of Tolstoy and demanding, for example, the radical suppression of the penal code."[275] And yet Journet notes that Berdyaev himself, following Dostoevsky's lead, was opposed to doctrines considering criminals as unresponsible, noting that Dostoevsky was "ready to defend the severest punishments because they were ones appropriate for responsible and free beings [ED, 103]"[276] – which amounts to "admitting at the same time that coercive power does not go away when punishing the crime; or put another way, it is an avowal that all constraint is not in itself bad."[277]

Finally, according to Journet, "Berdyaev forces himself to identify liberty with Christianity and constraint, no matter of what kind, with the Antichrist. As a result, every Church that claims some coercive power – moreover … every Church that claims any juridical power, that thinks it can exert obligations, and that wishes along with Saint Paul 'to subordinate all thinking to obedience to Christ' – appears to him for this alone as the work of the spirit of the Antichrist."[278] Journet's conclusion is rather severe:

> The false definition of freedom of spirit that [Berdyaev] adopts, the new Christianity he announces, pushes him by a logical constraint that he cannot escape, despite all that he knows about Catholics, to confuse along with Dostoevsky Catholicism and communism, the holy Church and atheist Bolshevism. He recognized on occasion the presence of an external rule, of an authority. In addition, he ruled out discerning between the exterior authority of Christ and the exterior authority of the Antichrist, between a just constraint and an unjust constraint. And that is why he repeats the confusion of blurring the image of Christ with that of the Antichrist.[279]

At the end of his argument, after refuting Dostoevsky's separatist postulate from which Berdyaev did not really free himself, Journet makes an affirming synthesis of his position: "the power exercised in the name of God may be spiritual and temporal. Spiritual power became visible when God gave omnipotence to Christ who in turn sent his apostles to all nations and to all centuries. Temporal power is represented visibly by the state to the extent that the latter is, in the words of Saint Paul, the minister of God for the good. But it is spiritual power that has primacy."[280]

An Exchange of Viewpoints Between Jacques Maritain and Charles Journet

After the publication of his article about Dostoevsky in the spring of 1932, Journet asked Maritain to send him Berdyaev's address so that he could offer Berdyaev a copy of the issue of *Nova et Vetera* that contained his analysis of "The Legend of the Grand Inquisitor."[281] A dialogue followed between Maritain and Journet about Berdyaev in their correspondence over the two months of March and April 1932.

In a letter dated 26 March 1932, Maritain wrote to Journet:

> I read with great interest and joy your "Grand Inquisitor." You demonstrate very well that Dostoevsky's Christ is not the true Christ. Where I find you too severe is about Berdyaev (p. 92 especially. No matter what one thinks of his philosophy, one cannot say that it is bothered by the Incarnation; it seeks, on the contrary, to center everything on the Incarnation. And when he says that the Great Inquisitor can manifest himself on the far right and the far left, he is not targeting the Catholic church, no! Far less than Dostoevsky. It is Catholics of the A.F. [Action Française] type that he's calling out, or the Billot type. His mistakes lie elsewhere.) Moreover, what I want to ask you is if, not in the church, but in the Christian world there have not been traces of the spirit of the Grand Inquisitor … Where you triumph is with your criticism of the "logical constraint" and rationalism you impute to Catholic theology.[282]

In a letter dated 30 March 1932, Journet replied to Maritain:

Regarding Berdyaev, I must first thank you for having the kindness to read my "La Légende" … I will try to correct as best I can the passages you have indicated. Will I succeed? When I accuse him of not accepting the Incarnation, it is because I believe that as soon as someone denies one of the essential theses of the Church, it is because he has misunderstood, virtually at least, the Incarnation. In the name of freedom as understood by Dostoevsky which is "not only a Christian manifestation, but the manifestation of a new spirit" and which belongs "to a new phase of Christianity itself, which is passing from an essentially transcendent period to a period of more interior penetration," Berdyaev is rising up against not only the abuses of coercive power, nor simply against an erroneous way to understand Catholicism (that of A.F.) but against the thesis of coercive power itself, and against the thesis of a juridical power having the quality of obliging consciences. (I am speaking of Berdyaev as he appears in the *Esprit de Dostoïevski* and in other short passages of his that I have read.) "The obligatory good is already no longer the good, it sinks into evil." I seem to see in Berdyaev an immanentism that considers as violent any obligation that comes from outside. Which amounts to not understanding the teaching of authority given by Christ as Word made flesh.[283]

On 24 April 1932, Maritain wrote again to Journet:

I would like to write to you at length about Berdyaev and the Grand Inquisitor (you are very kind to take note of the impromptu remarks I sent you). Yes, Berdyaev is full of errors. But 1) a statement, a proposition by him does not have the same value that it has for us because philosophy remains for him enveloped in the shrouds of a sort of prophetic poetry. Therefore, there is often a vigorous opinion putting into relief an aspect of things, where we feel we are seeing a thesis determining in an absolute manner what is; 2) his errors come from his Christianity and in no way derive from a hidden repugnance for the mysteries of the Incarnation. On the contrary, it is to save the affirmations of his Christian faith that he squirms every which way in concepts and has reason say all manner of things – in that he is very Russian.[284]

On 26 April 1932, Journet replied again to Maritain:

> You are so kind to write to me again about Berdyaev. I know that you are right. I am profoundly grateful to you, even and especially when you prod me a bit. For a moment, I am only a bit upset, because the criticisms of others do not bother me when I know that I am in accord with you. Since the other day I have been thinking that I would arrange things such that I could simply delete the portions about Berdyaev and focus only on what relates to Dostoevsky. I see Berdyaev only through our French Protestant and pan-Christian context. Therefore, while I sense him to be very dangerous and capable of diverting others, or of worse, rather than being enlightening, you judge him more as angels would judge him.[285]

In the end, Maritain played a mediating role when it came to understanding Berdyaev's thought, since Journet would considerably modify his statements when he revised his "Légende" article for republication in his book *L'Église du Verbe incarné* (Church of the word incarnate, 1941). Finally, Journet only reproached Dostoevsky for misunderstanding the spiritual and apostolic power of the Pope and he set against "these divergences the simple remark of Berdyaev: 'in the Legend of the Grand Inquisitor, it is socialism that Dostoevsky has more in mind than Catholicism which he only knew superficially and from the outside' [ED, 238, cf. 168]."[286]

1932–1933: Founding the Review *Esprit*; The Problem of Communism; The Question of Freedom

Founding the Review Esprit: *Two Publications from 1932*

Bernard Marchadier writes, "It was under the eye of Berdyaev and the patronage of Maritain that [Emmanuel] Mounier founded the review *Esprit*, such a Berdyaevian choice of name, in 1932."[287] Maritain and Berdyaev were linked, each in his own way, to *Esprit* – supporting the journal with their intuitions, advice, and written contributions, while also keeping their distance from Mounier himself.[288]

Berdyaev met Emmanuel Mounier for the first time in the winter of 1928–29 in Meudon at the home of Jacques and Raïssa Maritain.[289] Mounier also participated in the intimate Tuesday meetings in Clamart starting on 16 April 1929.[290] It was during an intense dialogue with Maritain that Mounier contemplated the project over many months, from February 1931 to August 1932,[291] before publishing the first issue of *Esprit* in October 1932. "From June 1931 to January 1933, a set of cordial exchanges between Mounier and Berdyaev occurred alongside the collaborative projects they envisioned."[292]

It is also thanks to an important article by Berdyaev, "Vérité et mensonge du communisme" (The truth and lie of communism), published in the first issue, that the orientation of *Esprit* would become established thanks to the text's clairvoyant analysis of communism based on observations of its principles – something Maritain would congratulate Mounier for undertaking.[293] Later, after some reservations expressed by Maritain following the sixth issue of *Esprit*, Mounier called on Berdyaev to help mollify concerns that the journal was taking an overly accommodating position toward the Communist world, thus giving the Russian thinker the opportunity to publish "Le christianisme russe et le monde bourgeois" (Russian Christianity and the bourgeois world) in the March 1933 issue of *Esprit*.

As two vigilant and established figures, Maritain and Berdyaev were present at early founding events, notably the launching of the review on 24 June 1931 for "the first meeting of the elders and the younger members of the future review *Esprit* with Jacques Maritain and Nikolai Berdyaev participating";[294] and at the Paris "Communauté" Congress of Raymond de Becker in April 1935 where Emmanuel Mounier noted that "among forty or so young attendees, it was touching to see Maritain and Berdyaev come sit and listen like schoolchildren."[295] In April 1931, Maritain invited Berdyaev to Meudon for "a study meeting with the young people whom I spoke to you about at Clamart (most of whom work for the review *Esprit*)."[296] Maritain's exchanges with the journal's editor would end with the start of World War II, while Berdyaev "preferred to step away from writing for *Esprit*,"[297] as he would say to Mounier on 24 February 1948.

Mounier, for his part, wrote little about Berdyaev's thinking,[298] but he paid him sincere tribute, recalling that "personalists recognize in him one of their sources of inspiration, both for his philosophical perspectives and for his attention to distinguishing the meaning and direction of communism within universal history from partisan politics."[299]

During the year 1932, Maritain sent a copy of his masterwork, *Distinguer pour unir ou Les Degrés du savoir* (*Distinguish to Unite, or, The Degrees of Knowledge*, 1959) to the Berdyaevs with a handwritten dedication which translates as "To Mr and Mrs Nikolai Berdyaev, with affection from their friend, Jacques Maritain." All 920 pages of the book, published in French in 1932 by Desclée de Brouwer, were annotated by Berdyaev, especially the chapters on critical realism and metaphysical knowledge, with many passages underlined in pencil. As for Berdyaev, in 1932 the Paris publisher Éditions Demain brought out a Russian translation of Berdyaev's *Le Christianisme et la lutte des classes* (*Christianity and Class War*), and Berdyaev dedicated a copy "To my dear Jacques and Raïssa Maritain, from Nikolai Berdyaev." This copy is annotated by the Meudon philosopher on page 101, where Berdyaev is criticizing the Vatican for opposing the right to strike – a claim which is factually incorrect since the cyclical *Quadragesimo Anno*, which condemns the class struggle, "does not deny this right," as Maritain would note in the margin.[300]

On 12 September 1932, Maritain and Berdyaev would participate in the conference "Journée Phénoménologique" at Juvisy.[301] Also for 1932, a last "visit at Berdyaev's with Raïa"[302] is recorded in Maritain's notebook dated Wednesday afternoon, 7 December.

The Problem of Communism

In November 1932, the series Questions disputées, directed by Maritain and Journet, had published a book by Eugène Dévaud entitled *La Pédagogie scolaire en Russie soviétique*.[303] In that context, Monsignor Michel d'Herbigny, the president of the pontiff's Commission for Russia, in an acknowledgement of receiving a copy, expressed "all the good" that the commission "thinks of the intellectual and charitable work undertaken by Monsieur Maritain to enlighten the most open Russian minds and to have them taste Catholic sympathy at such a high level."[304]

In 1933, the same series, Questions disputées,[305] published Berdyaev's *Problème du communisme* (The problem of communism).[306] In three parts, the book expanded on an article by Berdyaev published shortly before in *Esprit*[307] that Maritain "much enjoyed and admired."[308] The two new parts added in the book were entitled "Psychology of Russian Nihilism and Atheism"[309] and "The General Line of Soviet Philosophy."[310]

In fact, the position of the Russian philosopher of Clamart regarding Soviet Communism was more or less in accord – in practical terms if not necessarily theoretically – with the positions of the Thomists, Maritain and Journet, who therefore readily welcomed this book in their collection. As an experienced witness of Marxist thinking,[311] Berdyaev's statements about Soviet philosophy served the cause of Maritain, who was able to make use of the Russian philosopher's criticisms that were consistent with his own reflections about the errors of Soviet communist doctrine.

As for Charles Journet, who had proven to have a discerning eye when it came to Berdyaev's writings, he criticized some texts while praising others, notably those about Russian Communism. Thus, he played a role in alerting Maritain while allaying the concerns of those who reproached Maritain for his ties to Berdyaev. For example, in March 1933, Journet conveyed to Maritain the fears of Father Garrigou-Lagrange, who worried that "the review *Esprit*, with its articles by Berdyaev, was deviating."[312]

Regarding concerns within the Catholic hierarchy, in his notebook for 15 November 1933 Maritain briefly recorded an interview with the Rector of the Institut Catholique de Paris: "Monsignor Baudrillart informs me that the meetings in Meudon were brought up at a meeting of the Vigilance Counsel, in addition to infiltrations by a Slavic mystic for which Raïssa is responsible! Droll indeed!"[313]

In any event, Maritain became rather cautious about certain publications by Berdyaev, as one can tell from observations he made in 1935 to Yves Simon, then secretary of the *Revue de philosophie*, edited by the philosophy faculty of the Institut Catholique de Paris: "I forgot to tell you this: ask B[erdyaev] for an article on social questions, sure. But watch out for his metaphysics! And keep an eye on the detractors and those jealous of the *Revue* who would be only too happy to see us compromise ourselves over B's philosophy."[314]

Maritain's On the Temporal Regime and Freedom *versus Berdyaev's* Freedom and the Spirit

When Berdyaev published his book *Esprit et liberté* (*Freedom and the Spirit*), he sent a copy with dedication to Jacques Maritain, who acknowledged its arrival in a letter dated 2 May 1933: "Thank you for sending your two books (*Problème du communisme* and *Esprit et Liberté*) with the kind dedications. I will take *Esprit et Liberté* with me and will read the book with great interest while in the south. Like you, I suppose we will disagree, but I know that our amicable relations will not be affected."

On 18 December 1933, Berdyaev took up his pen to thank Maritain for sending his book *Du Régime temporal et de la liberté*, which was dedicated "To Nikolai Berdyaev, to Madame Berdyaev, with faithful affection from Jacques Maritain."

My dear friend!

Thank you very much for sending your book.[315] Your dedication was deeply touching. I have already finished reading it. The study of the philosophy of freedom is very well written, as is everything else you've expressed, and with exemplary clarity. But you have once again proved to me that the Thomist philosophy is not a philosophy of freedom. If nature prevails over freedom, the latter cannot exist but is instead determined. And the resulting position is no better if you speak of metaphysical nature instead of physical nature. In Greek there is one word for both nature and the physical. For me, free will is not the same thing as freedom. Our philosophies are of two different types: one, the primacy of freedom over being, the other the primacy of being over freedom. The second type is always intellectualist and freedom, for it, is not mysterious but grounded in reason. Nonetheless, I greatly sympathize with the second half of your book where you speak of temporal relations. In those pages I am often in total agreement with you. What separates us is a primordial feeling about life and the world. You are much more optimistic. Intellectualist and teleological philosophies are always optimistic.

I am much more pessimistic and my philosophy is a tragic one (the result of the primacy of freedom over being and of the fundamental irrationality of the world). I do not find intellectualism in the Old Testament, nor the New, nor in the Apostolic Epistles. I only find it in Greek philosophy, in the writings of the pagan Aristotle. But we must talk about these questions when we see each other again, which I hope will be soon.

Friendly regards to you all.
Affectionately,
N. Berdyaev

Very soon after receiving Berdyaev's letter, on 24 December 1933, Maritain commented in his reply on the question of freedom:

My dear friend,

I received your letter at the very moment I was planning to write you. It has been too long since we saw each other last. Since my return from Canada I have been very tired, and the summer months were very difficult for Raïssa and myself. I was hoping to read thoroughly your *Esprit et Liberté* so as to be able to talk about it with you. So far I have only been able to skim it – but enough to measure the importance of this work and to deplore the metaphysical dimension, which in my view is a destruction of metaphysics, generous and stimulating like everything from you, but a destruction all the same and a "catastrophe." I intend to take up your book again when I have more free time, study it in detail, and write an article about it in which I shall try to reduce certain misunderstandings. It will stand as both a marker of our philosophical differences and of the deep friendship that unites us. At the moment, however, I must prepare three talks that I am giving in Rome in March. After that *Esprit et Liberté* will be my top priority.

I thank you for what you've written concerning my last book. But I see there once again several misunderstandings, and an overly summary use of general ideas such as "primacy" of nature over freedom or freedom over being, "intellectualism," and so forth. I am fighting precisely against such simplifications.

If freedom necessarily presupposes spirit, and spirit presupposes being (and I too do not think that freedom is the same as free will, far from it! But if one denies free will one ruins freedom), a philosophy that affirms a primary, ontological absolute of freedom over being will not be a philosophy of freedom, but a destruction of freedom. In my view, there is a primacy of freedom over being in the sense that freedom – what I call the freedom of exultation and freedom of autonomy – is at the highest level of spiritual being, which is the highest degree of being, and this freedom may be considered a fruit of being, of intelligence, and of love. But being is always the primordial root and *in this sense* there is a primacy of being; and there is also – and this is above all what I wished to underscore in the passages you are alluding to – a primacy of nature over freedom understood *in the sense of free will*. One cannot say things all at once in a book … As for the optimism that you attribute to me (while ordinarily I am accused of pessimism), it amounts to affirming that God is Love and will triumph in the end, and that has nothing to do with Greek "intellectualism." It is the "optimism" of the Apocalypse, and I do not see how one can be a Christian if one does not have that conception of reality and of history. The Bible is far above philosophy and all philosophical systems, but there is definitely a certain *intellectualism* in the Bible, of course! The Bible places intelligence as the principal foundation of things, "in the beginning was the Word," it believes in the principle of contradiction, in the irreducible opposition of Yes and No, it believes in the reality of things, it tells us that if our eye is bad then our whole body will be in darkness. It is because it presupposes an intact reason that the madness of the Cross is the Divine Paradox in all its sublimity and divinely triumphs over reason. Our friendly regards to you and yours and best wishes over the Christmas holidays. I hope we shall meet again soon. Let's try for early January.

Affectionately,
Jacques Maritain[316]

In chapter 2 of *Du régime temporal et de la liberté*, Maritain marks his agreement with Berdyaev's views by quoting a long passage from *Problème du communisme*: "The guilty are the Christians themselves; it is the old Christian world. Not the Christian religion, certainly, but its members who, most often, have proven to be false Christians. The good which, instead of taking place in life, changes into a conventional rhetoric and hides itself behind true evil and effective injustice, that good can only be responded to with revolt … The position of the Christian world faced with communism is not only the position of the one who carries inside the eternal and absolute truth, it is also the position of the guilty one who has not been able to realize this truth, and who has betrayed it."[317] After citing this passage about the faltering of Christians, Maritain follows up: "Nikolai Berdyaev, whose metaphysics seem unacceptable to us but whose views about the human and history are often so profound, has said important truths here that require no alteration."[318]

Berdyaev's book, *Esprit et Liberté: Essai de philosophie chrétienne*,[319] is present in the Maritain archive of the BNU with the inscription "To my dear friend Jacques Maritain with no hope that this book will please him. N. Berdyaev." It can be noted that this volume, which cites Maritain's *Réflexions sur l'intelligence* (Reflections about intelligence) in its first chapter (page 31) and also quotes *Le Sens commun* by Réginald Garrigou-Lagrange and Étienne Gilson's *Le Thomisme*, was only lightly annotated by Maritain, and only in chapter VII: "La mystique et la voie spirituelle" (Mysticism and the spiritual voice, 255–84). This is hardly surprising. One of the annotations specifies that instead of writing "'to make oneself insensible [*se rendre insensible*] toward all creatures so as to love God with all one's heart,' it would have been better to write 'se detacher' [to detach oneself from creatures] (276)." A similar remark notes that it is not correct to speak of "indifference" toward all men and toward all that is human (277). Elsewhere, in a passage that mentions Saint Francis of Assisi alongside Plato, "la Cabale," Dante, Jakob Böhme, Baader, and Solov'ev as part of a tradition of erotic mysticism, Maritain's annotation states: "Yes but that is to misunderstand the other Catholic saints" (278).

Maritain did not address publicly the arguments of *Esprit et Liberté* that he disagreed with.[320] The article on Berdyaev's thought that Maritain planned to write never happened, despite the encouragement of Journet who prodded Maritain about the matter on 19 March 1937, after the publication of Berdyaev's book *Cinq Méditations sur l'existence* that had not pleased him: "I nearly regret that you did not write the article on him that we had spoken about once."[321] Maritain replied on 22 March 1937: "Yes, he needs to be written about. I like him very much personally, but his mind is deaf. Could you do it? I think I'll never have the time."[322]

That said, Maurice de Gandillac, who was often present at the Meudon gatherings and whom Maritain met with on 21 December 1933,[323] published an article, "Lignes de partages et points de convergence," in the May 1935 issue of *Esprit*,[324] the journal Berdyaev so admired. It compared the thinking of Maritain and Berdyaev, and de Gandillac specifically placed side by side Maritain's *Les Degrés du savoir* and Berdyaev's *Esprit et Liberté*. The opposing views of the two thinkers were clearly delineated by de Gandillac[325] while he also underscored points of overlap, notably their "fraternité veritable" (true brotherhood), "le front commun" (shared front), "un important bastion commun" (large common domain), and "si souvent d'accord" (so often in agreement).

Maurice de Gandillac develops his thoughts around three trouble spots. First, a disagreement about metaphysics: the one distinguishing in order to unite, the other positing "the coincidence of opposites." Second, discord about mysticism: the one, "a strict theologian on divine perfection and who excludes the power of being itself," the other "an intemperate mystic, one who lowers God to his own finitude." And third, an incompatibility between their epistemologies despite a shared rejection of positivism: for one there is "an organic unity of zones of knowledge traversed by spirit"; for the other "all 'objective' knowledge of nature is a betrayal, because it cuts up bits of reality to place them outside consciousness like jigsaw puzzle pieces." And yet, despite these divergences, de Gandillac insists that on both sides there remains a fundamental agreement about "freedom as the original source of all disorder, which also forms the first condition of a true order" as preliminary to "the welcoming of the lights of grace." In short, "between Berdyaev and Maritain, what a moving dialogue!" to quote once more the words of de Gandillac who attempts to save that "large common domain" "between the positions of fraternal enemies."

Roughly two years later, in December 1936, Father Raymond Bruckberger, then editorial secretary of the *Revue thomiste*, sent Maritain a typed note of three pages about *Esprit et Liberté* titled "Berdyaev and Catholicism." He noted that Berdyaev "seems not to have grasped the nature and significance, obviously very complex and always changing, of the juridical life of Catholicism," hoping all the while "that Berdyaev's intellectual loyalty would lead him one day to experience, in personal spirit and freely, the truth of the juridical order, an essentially relative and symbolic order."[326] Moreover, in *L'Église du verbe incarné* (1941), Charles Journet criticizes certain conceptions in *Esprit et Liberté*, notably "the error of prophetism, as it appears in the modernists, or in the Russian philosopher Nikolai Berdyaev, who today adopts the point of view of earlier Gnostics attacked by Saint Irenaeus, which consists essentially in confusing primary inspirations, which are in the domain of prophecy, with the second type which are in the domain of faith and charity."[327]

Later, when Maritain publishes *De Bergson à Thomas d'Acquin* in 1944, in a chapter entitled "Contemporary Aspects of Religious Thinking," a paragraph is devoted to Berdyaev and to Lev Shestov. Maritain makes several observations:

> Regarding Orthodox thought, in which the most recent developments had begun before the October revolution and have since continued in exile, the work of Nikolai Berdyaev should be mentioned above all, as it is highly significant at the present time. In Berdyaev's writings, the mystery of faith, but this time faith operating through reason, occupies a central place. Berdyaev is not a theologian like Karl Barth, he is a philosopher, and his entire oeuvre is to be viewed as Christian philosophy, but a Christian philosophy that he conceives of rather differently than I do. He is also a prophetic philosopher, or rather, for him, philosophy inspired by faith normally has a prophetic function. Being very familiar with Jakob Böhme, Schelling, Franz von Baader, as well as with Catholic spiritual authors, Berdyaev pursues his speculative inquiry in existential philosophy,[328] as one says today, and his central concern is the problem of spirit and freedom. I know that his judgments of Thomism are often unjust, and I do not

> think that he and I will ever agree on the first principles of metaphysics. However, even when disputing with him, one experiences the precious stimulation that comes from the absolute sincerity of spirit in search of being. And on the subject of moral and social philosophy, and especially history, or as he says "historiosophy,"[329] which is his favorite subject of contemplation, he brings us many concrete and productive intuitions that illuminate to a great extent the most urgent practical problems of our time, thanks to an ethical system rich in profound moral experiences and inflected with an irritating irrationalism. He is among those who still think with their heart as a witness of Christian freedom.[330]

This statement by Maritain summarizes well the dividing lines and points of convergence of the Thomist philosopher of Meudon and the Russian philosopher of Clamart.

1934–1936: Jacques Pavlovitch, Nicolas Alexandrovitch, and Raïssa Maritain

In early January 1934, Berdyaev sent a short note to thank Maritain for the invitation extended on 9 January to Nikolai and Lydia Berdyaev and her sister. On 1 February 1934, Maritain recorded, "The Berdyaevs dine. Moving conversation. It is a human problem that plagues him and commands his entire philosophy. And we understand a bit what it means, Raïa is quite shaken up over having been able to make this connection."[331]

Shortly thereafter, on 12 February 1934, the Clamart philosopher wrote to Maritain inviting them to dinner. Some weeks later, on 19 April, Berdyaev apologized for not being able to hear Maritain at a "Union for Truth" meeting because he was "completely exhausted" with "arthritic pains" that were "killing" him. In the same letter he asked Maritain for a favour: "Father Florovsky asks that you recommend him to Father Lebreton, he wants to have a scientific conversation with him, and also a recommendation letter for the Jesuit library in the rue Monsieur." Berdyaev ended his letter with a sentence about wanting to talk with Maritain about the latter's impressions of Karl Barth. Maritain replied on 25 April, regretting Berdyaev's absence at "the meeting in rue Visconti," and he appended to his letter "two cards for Father Florovsky," adding that he knew "no one at rue Monsieur besides Father Doncoeur." On the subject of Karl Barth, Maritain wrote, "The tragedy seems to me to be this: he is a man who wishes that we listen to God alone, yet it is Barth and his personality that one is forced to listen to."

On Friday 1 June 1934, Berdyaev was present at Meudon with other members of the review *Esprit*.[332] The following week, on Thursday 7 June, Maritain dined "at Berdyaev's with Raïa."[333] Six months later, on Sunday, 9 December, in Meudon: "study meeting. Simon speaks of Proudhon. Berdyaev and Landsberg come."[334] And on Thursday, 20 December, "evening meeting of *Esprit* in Paris. Berdyaev speaks of persons and Marxism."[335]

On 24 February 1935, Berdyaev requested another favour of Maritain, asking that he solicit Madame Ocampo for advice on behalf of a Spanish friend, a Monsieur Xirau, who plans to become a professor in Argentina.

The Friendship of "Jacques Pavlovitch" and "Nicolas Alexandrovitch"

During 1935, Maritain recorded several meetings with Berdyaev. On the evening of 1 January Berdyaev was in Meudon.[336] On 13 February, Maritain probably crossed paths with Berdyaev at "a small meeting of Catholics and Russian Orthodox."[337] On 28 February, Maritain spent "the afternoon at Berdyaev's" where he "met Lieb, a Protestant theologian and disciple of Barth."[338] In May 1935, Maritain recorded "visit of Berdyaev" in Meudon.[339] On 8 October "Berdyaev dines [in Meudon]. What an admirable man and so rich in humanity,"[340] noted Maritain who, that same evening, wrote out the project for the manifesto "Pour la justice et la paix" (For justice and peace)[341] that was published on 18 October by *Sept* and by *L'Aube*, and the next day in *La Vie catholique* and *La Croix*.

Starting in December 1934 and for the next three years (December 1934 to April 1938), the pattern of correspondence between Berdyaev and Maritain took a somewhat Russian turn. A letter from Berdyaev dated 7 January 1935 began with the words "My dear friend Jakov Pavlovitch" before informing Maritain that he will not be able to attend the Sunday meeting scheduled for 13 January 1935. On 29 April 1935, Maritain signs off with "Yours, Jacques Pavlovitch." On 3 June 1935, Berdyaev writes "My dear friend Jacques Pavlovitch" on a notecard inviting Maritain to meet with him in Clamart on Monday, 10 June – a meeting impossible for Maritain, who replies on 9 June to "My dear Nicolas Alexandrovitch": "It's impossible for me to come see you tomorrow. I am travelling to Portugal."

The inscription "For Nicolas Alexandrovitch with profound friendship from Jacques Pavlovitch," written in calligraphy on the first page of *Science et sagesse, suivi d'éclaircissements sur la philosophie morale* (1935), confirms the habit of warm salutations and mutual esteem between the two friends. Berdyaev would later write annotations on several pages of each chapter of this personal copy. A similar expression is used in the dedicatory inscription dated 5 July 1935 of *Frontières de la poésie et autres essais*: "For Nicolas Alexandrovitch with the faithful affection of his friend Jacques Pavlovitch." In this volume it is the "other essays" that Berdyaev took notes on, because *Frontières de la poésie* itself was first published in a volume of Roseau d'or in 1927 and had been annotated by Berdyaev at that time.

The affectionate form of address between the two thinkers continued in a letter from 23 October 1936 written "off the coast of Bahia" that begins "Dear Nicolas Alexandrovitch" and an inscription for a copy of Maritain's *Humanisme intégral* that reads, "For Nicolas Alexandrovitch with the deep friendship of Jacques Pavlovitch." Berdyaev also annotated many pages of this volume. The third edition of *Art et scholastique* (*Art and Scholasticism*) published in 1936 and which references Berdyaev in footnote number 144[342] does not repeat the warm salutations between Jakov Pavlovitch and Nicolas Alexandrovitch, and is dedicated instead to "Madame Nicolas Berdyaev, homage très amical, Jacques Maritain."

The first documented occurrence of the signature "Jacques Maritain Pavlovitch" is in a letter from Jacques and Raïssa Maritain to the Berdyaevs dated 1 December 1934, to which Berdyaev responded on 7 January 1935 beginning "Bien cher ami Jakov Pavlovitch." Sometime later, on 25 March 1935, Maritain repeated his greeting to "Bien cher Nicolas Alexandrovitch" and sent a "letter of recommendation for the Jesuit Father Rouët de Journel, director of aid to Russian refugees."

In addition to two quick messages from Maritain addressed to "Bien cher Nicolas Alexandrovitch" dated 7 December 1936 (inviting "all three of you" to dinner at Meudon) and 5 January 1937 (inviting Berdyaev to Meudon on 10 January to listen to Bergamin with "a few Spanish friends, Catholics, who have taken the Republican side against Franco"), there is also a note from Maritain dated 3 February 1937 to "Cher Nicolas Alexandrovitch" and one in the other direction to "Cher Jakov Pavlovitch" dated 27 February 1937 with an invitation to come to Clamart on 4 or 11 March: "We can talk about our impressions of Vienna and many other topics." But "Alas, dear Nicolas Alexandrovitch," Maritain replies on Tuesday 2 March, "I brought a bronchial virus back from Austria." Also, in March 1937, another note is addressed on the 16th to "cher ami Jakov Pavlovitch" with an invitation to Clamart on 22 or 29 March because "We must finally see each other." On 19 March, Maritain sent his reply to "Bien cher Nicolas Alexandrovitch" confirming he shall come on 29 March.

These warm salutations did not occur in every epistolary exchange, however, because on 7 December 1937, shortly before a trip to the Netherlands, Berdyaev asked his "Bien cher ami" to "tell me the days that you would be available to come to our place, all three of you … It's been a long time since we saw you and we would so like to see you again." Maritain wrote back to his "Bien cher ami" that meeting in Clamart on Wednesday, 15 December would be possible.

Maritain reverted to addressing "Bien cher Nicolas Alexandrovitch" on 5 April 1938 to put in a good word to Berdyaev about the poet Jean Le Louët, the director of the short-lived journal *Les Nouvelles Lettres* (1938–39), who wished to have the collaboration of the Clamart philosopher.

The Place of Raïssa Maritain in the Relations between the Maritains and the Berdyaevs

In 1925, Raïssa, who was fluent in Russian, sight-translated for Jacques the original Russian text of *Un Nouveau Moyen Âge*. But the three extant letters from Raïssa to her Clamart friends are completely in French – the first one, an invitation to Meudon dated 1 December 1934, began "Bien chers amis."[343] Likewise, Berdyaev always used French with his Meudon friends, including Raïssa.

On 16 August 1935, Maritain recorded in a notebook: Raïssa "is beginning to read Berdyaev's book on morality [*De la destination de l'homme* (*Destiny of Man*)],[344] she is taking notes, I've advised her to write down all her thoughts about it."[345] A few days later he added, "Raïa speaks to me often about Berdyaev's book in which she finds many of his problems and cares expressed and admires the force and freedom."[346]

On 26 August 1935, Raïssa wrote to "bien cher ami" Nikolai Berdyaev: "I am reading your book, *La Destination de l'Homme*, passionately and enthusiastically! I have almost finished and have been speaking about it with Jacques (who will read it a bit later), and he shares my admiration for your work. We will probably not always be in complete agreement with all of your critical observations, but it is difficult to not feel at one with you regarding the positive and experimental aspects."[347] Berdyaev replied to Raïssa on 28 August: "Your remarks about my book are all the more special because certainly there are some pages that may displease you and Jakov Pavlovitch."

Raïssa felt strongly about *De la destination de l'homme* and made her own annotations in the book.[348] The twenty or so comments in pencil are certainly by Raïssa, since one of them reads "see Jacques" (page 12) and another "this has already been established by Father G[arrigou]-L[agrange] and by Jacques" (page 79). Her comments are either questions, exclamations, affirmations, or negations.[349] The longest comment is a remark on the human creature for whom Berdyaev cannot conceive of a created freedom, whereas for Raïssa, as she writes in the margin, "there are two freedoms: one with its origin in nothing and which bends toward nothing, and the other created by God at the same time as reason and which bends toward the good. It is only of this one that Thomist philosophy and theology speak."

Six months later, Raïssa received a card dated 8 February 1936 and addressed to her – Jacques Maritain was away in America from 3 January to 10 April 1936 teaching courses and giving talks.[350] The card invited her and her sister Véra and the Van der Meers to Clamart on Thursday, 20 February 1936. A few weeks later, a short letter dated 8 March 1936 arrived announcing that Berdyaev could come to Meudon on 12 March 1936, alone without

Lydia, and not for dinner but at 4:30 p.m. for "a philosophical conversation" with Raïssa, since Jacques was still in the United States.[351]

The following year, on 25 May 1937, Berdyaev wrote to Raïssa Maritain to inform her – because "Jakov Pavlovitch" had told him she understood Russian – about an upcoming talk by Father Bulgakov on "Thomism and Sophiology" at 77, rue de Lourmel in Paris.[352]

Based on the few letters exchanged between Nikolai Berdyaev and Raïssa Maritain, as well as her careful reading and annotating of *Destination de l'homme*, it is clear that Raïssa was a full participant in the relations between Berdyaev and the Maritains, notably on subjects that related to morals and mysticism. As a full-fledged interlocutor of Berdyaev, Raïssa, a Russian-speaking Jewish convert, played a discreet but significant role in the friendly yet paradoxical relationship between the Thomist philosopher and the Russian thinker.

1936: *Humanisme intégral* versus *Cinq méditations sur l'existence*

Humanisme intégral

Maritain's *Humanisme intégral* was published in 1936, and he sent a copy to his Russian friend with a kind inscription: "pour Nicolas Alexandrovitch avec la profonde amitié de Jacques Pavlovitch."

The second chapter of the book, "A New Humanism,"[353] analyzes Marxist atheism and criticizes Soviet humanism. On the topic of the actual situation in Soviet Russia, Maritain relies regularly on "the excellent little book" of Hélène Iswolsky, *L'Homme 1936 en Russie soviétique*,[354] and on *Soviet Communism: A New Civilisation?* by Sydney and Beatrice Webb, while also pointing out their limitations.[355] The analysis of Marxist doctrine is largely based on the categories of Thomist philosophy, with no hesitation about resorting to the "lexical notions of Aristotle"[356] but with some concern about "aberrant religious developments that had occurred across vast regions of Russian people and thinking [where] the rational has always been viewed with suspicion."[357] Over the course of his analyses of the situation in Russia, Maritain underscores "the postrevolutionary viewpoint"[358] held by Berdyaev, who is the focus of a paragraph in which Maritain adopts a prudent stance: "One can understand the 'postrevolutionary' viewpoint which is now held by a number of Russian Christians – those who take as their starting point the historical fact of the October revolution, and who think that entirely new developments will come out of that revolution, and they even sometimes hope (it is good to hope against all hope) that having thus rushed forward, Russia will perhaps see the outlines of a new Christianity emerge more quickly than other countries. In any case, what we can believe with greater certainty is that unexpected possibilities for expansion and heroic spiritual struggle will open there for a Christian renaissance, one conscious of its human and divine integration, if there are representatives sufficiently enlightened, and free of everything but God."[359]

One also finds in this second chapter some ideas that Berdyaev certainly did not deny, as when Maritain writes, "Russia had neither a Middle Ages nor a Renaissance."[360] One can also note several statements by Maritain that are completely consistent with Berdyaev's ideas, such as: "Among the founding elements of communism there are also Christian elements. Saint Thomas More had communist ideas. Communism, in its early stages, was not always atheist. The very idea of communion, that which gives it spiritual force, and what it wants to achieve in social life on earth … is an idea of Christian origin."[361] Also this: communism is "a religion, and a most imperious one, and surely will be called upon to replace all other religions; [it is] an atheist religion whose dialectal materialism constitutes its dogma and for which communism, as its life regime, is its ethical and social expression."[362] And finally this: communism is "a religion entirely and exclusively ordered for earthly ends, and the least divergence or opposition regarding the 'general line' defined in relation to those ends immediately wounds itself and awakens among its faithful a sense of the sacred."[363]

Partly indebted to certain analyses of Berdyaev,[364] Maritain cites him twice in this second chapter of *Humanisme intégral*. First, Maritain agrees with Berdyaev's judgement of Marx, who "is right when he says that capitalist society is an anarchical society where life is defined exclusively as a game of particular interests."[365] In similar fashion, on the subject of the proletariat, Maritain notes that "Berdyaev likes to point out the presence of this eschatological element in revolutionary thinking."[366] Thus, there is definitely a convergence between Berdyaev and Maritain around certain regular criticisms in their analysis of Soviet communism, but this chapter, "A New Humanism," demonstrates above all Maritain's own philosophy, whose analyses and sources really have only tangential points of contact with Berdyaev's thinking.

About Berdyaev's statements, Father Raymond Bruckberger wrote the following to Maritain on 18 June 1937: "Besides the fact that Berdyaev likes *Humanisme intégral* very much, he said something to me that I find quite accurate, 'Maritain brought Thomism into the culture.' I believe that says quite a lot coming from him."[367]

Five Meditations on Existence

In 1936 Berdyaev sent Maritain a copy of his book *Cinq méditations sur l'existence: Solitude, société, communauté* with the inscription "To my dear friends Jacques and Raïssa Maritain, affectionately, N. Berdyaev."[368] This volume, found in the Maritain archive, is annotated in the margins on many pages. It also contains an evaluation of the entire work on one of the first blank pages after the cover page that reads as follows: "In sum, a philosopher like Berdyaev does not have the right to speak about theories of knowledge. He must give the results of his existential reflections that are of an entirely different order. If that were all he did, he would be unassailable, but if he refuses to do only that, if he feels obliged to position himself in opposition to Thomist philosophy, for example, it is because he is in fact a theoretician of knowledge and in that area he is very vulnerable."

The Russian title of the book, if it had been translated literally, would have been "The self and the world of objects" – a title announcing more clearly a work of metaphysics or criteriology on the nature of knowledge. In fact, Berdyaev cites Maritain's *The Degrees of Knowledge* (1932), calling it "the definitive word in modern Thomism."[369] However, he is opposed to the Thomist theory of knowledge because he considered it abstract, and faults it for "subtracting the philosopher and philosophy from all forms of tragedy, because all conflict between philosophical knowledge and faith is avoided."[370]

Maritain did not reply point by point to the *Cinq méditations*, which contradicted rather directly the Thomist theory of knowledge that Berdyaev had examined closely through Maritain's *Distinguer pour unir ou Les Degrés du savoir* (*Degrees of Knowledge*), and also through Étienne Gilson's *Le Réalisme méthodique*, which he carefully read and annotated.[371] Here one finds a crucial point of divergence between the Thomist philosopher and the Russian philosopher. It is clearly a noetic divergence, and yet a convergence in the pursuit of a moral fulfilment of the human person, as is underlined in Father Raymond M. Bruckberger's review of *Cinq méditations* published by the *Revue thomiste* in 1937.[372] Charles Journet, however, did not appreciate the way Berdyaev's *Cinq méditations* discusses Maritain's *Distinguer pour unir*.[373]

Nonetheless, the friendly meetings of the Maritain and Berdyaev households continued, as one can see from Raïssa's note in her *Journal* for 14 December 1936: "An extremely difficult day for me. All the same, I get up in the evening to receive the Berdyaevs, who come to dinner. Berdyaev explains to me the theogony of Shestov."[374] The co-operation between Maritain and Berdyaev also continued, since in 1937 Maritain agreed to publish Berdyaev's *Constantin Léontieff, un penseur religieux russe du dix-neuvième siècle* (*Konstantin Leontev: Essay from the History of Russian Religious Thought*) in his series Les Îles.[375] This work, translated by Hélène Iswolsky, was the third book by Berdyaev published in a series directed by Maritain.[376]

1938–1939: The Question of Antisemitism and the Last Exchange of Letters

In a two-page letter written by Berdyaev on 23 March 1938 on the recommendation of Brunschvicg, Maritain was asked to recommend the Russian philosopher Simeon Frank for a subvention provided by the Caisse nationale des recherches scientifiques. This letter would be added to those prepared by "Le Senne, Lavelle, Jean Wahl, Gabriel Marcel, and Gouhier."[377]

The Question of Antisemitism

In 1938, Maritain sent Berdyaev the slim volume *Les Juifs parmi les nations* (The Jews among the nations), published by Éditions du Cerf, with the inscription, "To Nikolai Berdyaev, with friendly regards, Jacques Maritain."

Berdyaev found this study "accurate," and Maritain follows up by promising, on 9 March 1939, to send a copy of his talk on the same subject from February 1939 at the Marigny Theater in Paris.

Berdyaev also speaks on the question of antisemitism in his book *Destin de l'homme dans le monde actuel* (*The Fate of Man in the Modern World*)[378] and in his article "Le christianisme et l'antisémitisme."[379] The question of antisemitism, about which the two thinkers agreed, was also taken up by Abbé Journet, who borrows from both Berdyaev's book and Maritain's article in an editorial of his own published in *Nova et Vetera* in 1941.[380] Journet quotes the following passage from Berdyaev's *Destin de l'homme*:

> The communist doctrine of class hatred is fundamentally antichristian. The doctrine of race hatred is no less so. On this, Berdyaev made the following correct observation: "From both the Christian and the human points of view, race theory is simply much more harmful than the theory of class conflict; the dehumanization [of the former] is much deeper. In truth, in Marxist doctrine, the man who belongs to the bourgeois classes that are destined to disappear may nonetheless obtain salvation through the transformation of his consciousness; he can welcome the Marxist ideology, become communist, and even a commissar of the people. But in race theory, there is no salvation. If you are Jewish or Black, no spiritual transformation is possible, no newly acquired convictions can save you. You are irremediably condemned."[381]

By citing both Maritain and Berdyaev in his *Nova et Vetera* editorial on antisemitism, Journet associates the two thinkers, who were in agreement on this question.

Last Exchanges

In the summer of 1938, the Berdyaevs moved to their new house in Clamart at 83, rue Moulin des Pierres, and Berdyaev hastened to write to his "dear friend" on 9 August 1938 and extend an invitation: "We so want to see you at our new house."

Also in 1938, Berdyaev, the "great solitary thinker, relentlessly linked to the Christian spirit,"[382] as Maritain noted, published *Les sources et les sens du communisme russe* (*The Origin of Russian Communism*)[383] that was admired by Charles Journet in a note to Maritain: "I am struck by the agreement of our positions with those of Berdyaev."[384]

In the spring of 1939, Maritain sent Berdyaev a copy of his *Le crépuscule de la civilization* (*The Twilight of Civilization*) with the inscription, "To Nikolai Berdyaev with the deep friendship of Jacques Maritain." In the summer of the same year, Raïssa Maritain had a volume of her poetry published by Desclée de Brouwer, and she dedicated a copy "For Lydia Berdyaev, for Nikolai Berdyaev, with my deepest affection, Raïssa Maritain." Shortly thereafter, on 10 September 1939, during the "phony war," Berdyaev sent a postcard (without knowing if the Maritains were still in Meudon) in which he asked for news and a chance to see them. The card was forwarded to the Maritains at their new address, Le Chalet at Fontgombault (Indre department). In December 1939, having heard that the Maritains were back in Meudon, Berdyaev sent another postcard "to know if it's true." Maritain replied on 10 December: "We did not go back to Meudon so as to avoid unnecessarily moving … For I am going to America … In any case, we are absolutely determined to see you before going."

Near the end of World War II, in December 1944, during his passage through Paris between New York and Rome,[385] Maritain saw Berdyaev and his wife Lydia, who was "already very sick." In 1945 Maritain also received news of Berdyaev from Charles Journet, who was in contact with Marie-Madeleine Davy.[386] Troubled by the news of Lydia's death, Maritain wrote to his "very dear friend" to express "the immense pain of all three" – Raïssa, Véra, and Jacques.

A letter from Berdyaev dated 28 August 1946 broke the silence between the two friends with the acknowledgment of "two packages you sent from America," later commented on by Marie-Madeleine Davy.[387] Berdyaev wrote, "I am greatly touched that you thought of me. Food supplies in Paris are still in a chaotic state which is why your packages were greeted with such pleasure." Berdyaev added, "I am crushed by the amount of work and meetings I have. I would be happy to see you when you come to Paris and to discuss with you some worrisome matters." In 1946

Berdyaev was working a lot and published two books with Aubier: *Essai de métaphysique eschatologique: Acte créateur et objectivation* (*The Beginning and the End*), translated from the Russian by Maxime Herman, and *De l'esclavage et de la liberté de l'homme* (*Slavery and Freedom*), translated by S. Jankélévitch.[388] Both books, without dedications or annotations, are present in the Maritain archive.

After the war, Maritain sent Berdyaev his *Court traité de l'existence et de l'existant* (*Existence and the Existent*), published by Paul Hartmann in 1947, and included a small card "with compliments of the author, absent from Paris." Judging from the pencil marks in the margins, Berdyaev seems to have read this book. In January 1948, Maritain had his publisher Elgoff send Berdyaev a copy of his *Raison et raisons* (Reason and reasons) with a similar card, "Hommage de l'auteur, absent de Paris." This was the last book of Maritain's that Berdyaev would receive shortly before his death, and it contains no annotations.

Berdyaev died on 24 March 1948. Father Evgraf Kovalevskii, who had been present at the Meudon meetings "with the Russians" from the beginning in 1928, officiated at the funeral.[389]

In 1965, when he published his *Carnet de notes*, Maritain made an accurate observation about Dostoevsky and Bloy, classifying them as among "certain poets and certain great writers" who were "voices who manifest to the world a type of prophetic meaning, a meaning at work in a people of faith, of which Berdyaev was so deeply conscious."[390]

Following Maritain, one can apply to Berdyaev the declaration the Meudon philosopher made about Dostoevsky, Léon Bloy, Charles Péguy, and Georges Bernanos: "One ought not forget that these disorganized and unorganizable lay people did more for Christian faith, in individual souls and in the culture as a whole, than many pious associations and battalions of 'Christian shock troops.'"[391]

Concluding Remarks

The first phase, and the best known, of the dialogue between Maritain and Berdyaev took place between 1925 and 1931. Their first meeting in 1925 under the auspices of Léon Bloy led fairly quickly to the reciprocal publication of articles in journals that they each directed. Shortly after, the publication in 1927 of *Un Nouveau Moyen Âge* and *Primauté du spiritual* gave considerable visibility to their thinking about the necessity of a spiritual renewal after the errors of the modern world. Next, their collaboration in organizing interfaith meetings in Paris from 1926 to 1928, and later the more intimate meetings in Clamart with the participation of Raïssa between 1929 and 1931, as well as the public debate on Descartes at the Studio franco-russe on 27 January 1931, all together made Maritain and Berdyaev stand out as noteworthy witnesses and engaged thinkers representing different types of Christian philosophy during the interwar period.

In a second phase, especially in 1933, their respective publications, *Du régime temporal et de la liberté* (Maritain) and *Esprit et Liberté* (Berdyaev), revealed with increasing clarity the dividing lines of their thinking. Indeed, both were perfectly aware of their differences, such as when Maritain wrote to Berdyaev, "It is a strange thing that you and I have very different ideological structures behind our thinking, and yet everything you write is deeply interesting to me and evokes my deepest sympathy even when I oppose your arguments." And Berdyaev would say to Maritain, "Our philosophies are of two different types." Nevertheless, their dividing lines did not become fault lines because between them there remained points of convergence, among which were a shared interest in Dostoevsky, their vigilant support for the journal *Esprit*, and their criticisms of Soviet communism.

Accustomed to solitary combat, Maritain and Berdyaev both took pains, each in his own way, to inscribe the presence of Christian thinking into the culture of their day, and to pursue and preserve their research into the philosophy of history (*Humanisme intégral*, 1936) or historiosophy (*Les sources et le sens du communisme russe*, 1938). And far from considering their "philosophical dissentiment" as an obstacle to their collaboration, these two thinkers managed to co-operate and lead, each with his own rhetorical tools, the fight against antisemitism.

Just as Plato and Aristotle were close while each pursued his own intellectual itinerary for more than twenty years, these two twentieth-century philosophers conducted a co-operative dialogue without choosing truth over their friendship nor their friendship over the truth. While each was faithful to his own intellectual universe and sphere of preoccupation, a shared space in the field of philosophy of modern history and social questions genuinely united them and nourished their friendship. There is no doubt that, on the one hand, Jacques Pavlovitch "personally very much loved" the philosopher of Clamart, and, on the other, that Nicolas Alexandrovitch really "developed affection for" the philosopher of Meudon. In truth, their friendship, which also extended to their respective families, revealed their openness of spirit, their indignation when confronting the turbulent tragedies of the modern world, and their investigation of the unsayable. Their hearts were bigger than their respective philosophies.

Notes

1 All translations from the French are C. Jon Delogu's unless otherwise noted. Eugène-Melchior de Vogüé, *Le roman russe* (Paris: Backès, 1886).

2 Léonid Livak, "L'émigration russe et les élites culturelles françaises 1920–1925," *Cahiers du monde russe* 48, no. 1 (2007): 23–43.

3 Ralph Schor, "Solidarité chrétienne? Orthodoxes russes et catholiques français dans les années 1920," *Cahier de la Méditerranée* 63 (2001): 157–67.

4 Nicolas Berdiaev, *Essai d'autobiographie spirituelle* [1940], French translation from Russian by E. Belenson (Paris: Buchet/Castel, 1992), 330: "I grew to like him [Maritain], which does not happen to me often, and I think that Maritain likes me as well. Our relations are rather unique. He pardons my unorthodox ideas he disagrees with and that he would not accept from others. Perhaps it is in part because I belong to a different world that is neither Catholic nor French."

5 Anto Gravic and Nicola Bolsec, "Attitude de N. Berdiaev envers J. Maritain et le thomisme," *Život* (Revue de philosophie et de sciences religieuses de la Compagnie de Jésus à Zagreb) 69, no. 3 (2014): 291–300, 294 and 300.

6 Maurice de Gandillac, "Lignes de partage et points de convergence," *Esprit*, no. 20 (May 1934): 311–16.

7 Bernard Marchadier, "Berdiaev, Les Maritain, Mounier: Un modernisme russe dans la France de la première moitié du XXe siècle," *Cahiers de l'émigration russe*, no. 8 (2004) (*Nicolas Berdiaev*): 44: "Even when criticizing Marx, Maritain and Berdyaev wish to be no less revolutionary, and both make use

of Proudhon." See also Berdyaev, *Essai d'autobiographie*, 345: "These young people took an interest in the personalist philosophy that I most uncompromisingly advocated, defending its social vision that was close to the socialism more inspired by Proudhon than by Marx. This point of view was called communitarian personalism."

8 Berdiaev, *Essai d'autobiographie*, 330.

9 Ibid., 331.

10 Michel Fourcade, "De Soloviev à Boulgakov: la reception catholique de l'orthodoxie russe en France," *Contacts, Revue française de l'orthodoxie* no. 238 (April-June 2012): 118–45, 135–6.

11 Berdiaev, *Essai d'autobiographie*, 331. Stanislas Fumet, *Histoire de Dieu dans ma vie: Souvenirs choisis* (Paris: Fayard-Mame, 1978), 292: "Berdyaev got Maritain interested in the social problems that the critical realism of the disciple of Saint Thomas had until then not yet taken the time to fully examine. But he himself had been an anarchist, before his conversion, and the injustices of the world would always call him into combat."

12 Fumet, *Histoire de Dieu*, 292: "Maritain liked the Russians and was more and more attracted by the Jews for whom Berdyaev felt an equally real sympathy that was rare among his compatriots whether aristocrats or not."

13 Marchadier, "Berdiaev, les Maritain, Mounier," 42.

14 De Gandillac, "Lignes de partage et points de convergence," 311–16.

15 Nicole Rolland, "Philosophie de l'histoire selon Nicolas Berdiaev et Jacques Maritain: prophétisme ou prospective?," *Contacts, Revue française de l'orthodoxie*, no. 238 (April–June 2012): 146–63. See also Boris L. Goubman, "J. Maritain and N. Berdiaev on the Meaning of History," Tver State University, Russia, http://seekingwisdom.com/goubman.htm (accessed 27 June 2023).

16 Hélène Iswolsky, *Au temps de la lumière* (Montreal: Éditions de l'Arbre, 1945), chapter VI, "La Maison de Meudon," and chapter VII, "La Maison de Clamart," 83–117, especially 100–13. This book was recently republished as *Au temps de la lumière: Une catholique russe au coeur du renouveau spirituel français*, preface by Jacques Maritain, foreword by Florian Michel, epilogue by Baudouin de Guillebon (Paris: Éditions Salvator, 2021).

17 Marchadier, "Berdiaev, les Maritain, Mounier," 37–48. See also Gérard Lurol, "Berdiaev, Mounier, Maritain: des 'dimanches de Meudon; aux 'dimanches de Clamart,'" in *Nicolas Berdiaev, 1874–1948: Un philosophe russe à Clamart. Colloque Clamart, 24 and 25 November 2018* (Grenoble, FR: Éditions Le Mercure Dauphinois, 2018), 95–113. See also Gonzalo Ibanez, *Persona y derecho en el pensamiento de Berdiaev, Mounier y Maritain* (Santiago de Chile: Ediciones Universidad Católica de Chile, 1984).

18 Patrick de Laubier, "Le courant personnaliste au XXe siècle: Max Scheler (1874–1928), Nicolas Berdiaev (1874–1948), Jacques Maritain (1882–1973)," *Roczniki Nauk Spolecznych* [Annales des sciences sociales, Université

Jean-Paul II, Lublin] XVIII, no. 1 (1990). See also Olivier Clément, *Berdiaev, un philosophe russe en France* (Paris: Desclée de Brouwer, 1991), 108.

19 Iswolsky, *Au temps*, 100.

20 Bressolette, "Jacques Maritain," 291–7.

21 Pierre Pascal, "Les grands courants de la pensée russe contemporaine," *Cahiers du monde russe et soviétique* 3, no. 1 (January–March 1962): 5–89, 35: "On 15 August 1909 Berdiaev sent Archbishop Antonii an 'Open Letter' in which he wrote, 'By complicated and circuitous paths I have come to faith and the Church of Christ which I now consider to be my spiritual mother.'" In 1917, however, Berdiaev would retreat some distance from the Holy Synod; see Pascal, 48. See also Stanislas Fumet, "Un exégète de l'histoire: Nicolas Berdiaev et le procès de l'humanisme," *Revue hébdomadaire* II (February 1927): 227, "Berdiaev criticized the Synod with good reason for not being a faithful representation of Christian spirit, but instead a political organization taking orders from a temporal power. Against the Synod, he held up the Patriarchal Church. This earned him a mandate of expulsion made moot by the sudden eruption of the Russian revolution."

22 Of the authors who were Maritain's contemporaries, the number of times Berdyaev is mentioned is quite high, with a total of forty-six occurrences across all of Maritain's publications, particularly during the period 1932–35.

23 Pascal, "Les grands courants," 5.

24 De Vogüé, *Le roman russe*, chapter IV, "les années quarantes: Tourguénef." In 1918, Berdyaev published a collection of articles entitled *La destinée de la Russie* where, according to Pierre Pascal, he "expressed views similar to Slavophiles while also distancing himself from them on many points." See Pascal, "Les grands courants," 47.

25 Pascal, "Les grands courants," 17.

26 Ibid., 22.

27 Clément, *Berdiaev*, 18.

28 Ibid., 87.

29 Ibid., chapter 5, "Une rencontre: Nicolas Berdiaev et Léon Bloy," 125–40, especially 125–6.

30 Ibid., 137.

31 Marchadier, "Les Maritain, Mounier," 44.

32 Nicolas Berdiaev, "Le destin de la culture," Roseau d'or no. 2 (Paris: Plon, 1926), 91: "The bourgeois spirit dominates the civilized regime of this world. This spirit believes only in the visible and no longer believes in invisible things. This spirit of civilization is attached to perishable and ephemeral things … It is also a spiritual phenomenon, the phenomenon of the extermination of spirituality."

33 Clément, *Berdiaev*, 129.

34 Ibid., 131, and also 89 and 134.

35 Fumet, "Un exgégète," 226: "This great Christian thinker was a Marxist in his early youth. In 1900 he broke with communist socialism." In Berdyaev's library in Clamart is a copy of a book by Georges Sorel, *D'Aristote à Marx: L'ancienne et la nouvelle métaphysique*, foreword by Édouard Berth (Paris: Marcel Rivière Éditeur, 1935), with an inscription which translates as "To the former Marxist, Nikolai Berdyaev, with the compliments of the author, E.B. 18-12-35." See also Clément, *Berdiaev*, 14: "1894 to 1901 is Berdiaev's Marxist period"; Pascal, "Les grands courants," 12: "Marxism had been adopted by a few superior minds – economists, philosophers, Peter Struve, Sergei Bulgakov, Nikolai Berdyaev, Simeon Frank. For them it was a precious doctrine, but with aspects to be kept or dropped … While accepting the political goals of social democracy, or even collaborating with it, they could yet not adhere to the discipline of a political party. Thus they were called 'legal Marxists.'" Also Pierre Pascal, "Les grands courants," 17: "He himself had been seduced by Marxism's economic doctrine, and to a certain extent by its explanation of history, and by the figure of Marx. But nourished on Ibsen, Dostoevsky, and Tolstoy, he experienced a sharp feeling of personal destiny. He could not accept the determinism of Marxism."

36 Iswolsky, *Au temps de la lumière*, 103.

37 Pascal, "Les grands courants," 17: "With his deep knowledge of European culture, natural nobility, love of beauty, audacious thinking, flair for writing, and sensitivity about current events, he was one of the typical figures of this new twentieth century."

38 Marchadier, *Berdiaev*, 39–40; also Pascal, "Les grands courants," 82: "At the end of 1922, Berlin prospered from the arrival of the best of Russian intellectualism. It was not just the twenty-five philosophers, historians, and writers banished as idealists in September, but also Struve, Gorky … Along with literature, philosophy flourished under the leadership of Berdyaev, Frank, and Vysheslavtsev. The Academy of Religious Philosophy was inaugurated on 22 November 1922. The idea of its founders was for it to be a renewal of the Societies for Religious Philosophy."

39 Catherine Gousseff, "Une intelligentsia en exil: Les orthodoxes russes dans la France des années 20," *Intellectuels chrétiens et esprit des années 20*, Actes du colloque de l'Institut Catholique de Paris, 23–24 September 1993, ed. Pierre Collin (Paris: Éditions du Cerf, 1997), 116.

40 Ralph Schor, "Les écrivains russes blancs en France: Un entre-deux identitaire (1919–1939)," *Revue européenne des migrations internationals* 33, no. 1 (2017): 11–16 §14. See also Stanislas Fumet, *Histoire de Dieu*, 291: "[Berdyaev] himself did not flee the country, but Bolshevism imprisoned him and then Lenin exiled him."

41 Kevin Bonvin, "La World's Christian Federation et l'orthodoxie: Son action en faveur des étudiants russes exilés (1918–1935)," master's thesis in

Russie-Europe médiane, September 2019, Global Studies Institute, Université de Genève, Collection "Mémoires éléctroniques," vol. 106 (2020): 43: "1924 marks the start of RSCM [the Russian Student Christian Movement] … one observes a correlation between the two organizations of Russian students and the traditional poles of intelligentsia emigration … This intellectual proximity led Father Bulgakov to consider 1924 as "the time of religious creation." Note also that for Russian émigrés in France, "the situation changes in 1924–25 with the start of diplomatic recognition of the URSS by the *radical* government of Édouard Herriot" (69). From that moment, Russian émigrés are in danger, as they depend administratively on the very state they wished to flee.

42 Schor, "Les écrivains russes," 11–16, §1: "The Bolshevik revolution of 1917 pushed many Russians onto the road of exile. In France their numbers reached 32,247 in 1921 and 67,219 in 1926. Subsequently the numbers stabilized at around 70,000 to 80,000 individuals. See Nikita Struve, *Soixante-dix ans d'émigration russe, 1919–1989* (Paris: Fayard, 1996).

43 Cyrille Sollogoub, "Berdiaev, un philosophe russe à Clamart," *Colloque Clamart*, 39.

44 Fumet, *Histoire de Dieu*, 287: "When Nikolai Berdyaev arrived in France, I was the first writer to invite him over." "On the first visit of Nikolai Berdyaev to our home in Paris in 1924, we gave him the address of Madame Léon Bloy. His wife, Lydia Trushev, wanted to write to her. The widow of Léon Bloy put Berdyaev in touch with Jacques Maritain. I did not dare advise Berdyaev to go see him, since I saw so few intellectual affinities between them" (292).

45 With the posthumous publication of Léon Bloy's book *Le PAL, suivi des nouveaux propos d'un entrepreneur de démolitions* (Paris: Stock, 1925), Jeanne Bloy dedicates a copy "To Monsieur Nikolai Berdyaev, this book which ought to please you. Jeanne Léon Bloy."

46 Schor, "Les écrivains russes," §11: "The Russians, well-known intellectuals and often French-speaking, kept up regular relations with their French counterparts. In their memoirs they listed the names of the many writers they met over the years, such as Maurice Barrès, Paul Valéry, André Gide, André Malraux, Jean Cocteau, Jacques Maritain, Charles Vildrac, Jean Giraudoux, Sacha Guitry, Anna de Noailles, Henri de Montherlant, Marcel Aymé, André Maurois, Gabriel Marcel, as well as many politicians."

47 Iswolsky, *Au temps*, 102; Clément, *Berdiaev*, 82; Fumet, *Histoire de Dieu*, 288: "[Berdyaev] spoke correct, simple, direct French without the least artifice."

48 Gousseff, "Une intelligentsia," 115: "The configuration of the Christian [Orthodox] intelligentsia established in France in the 1920s can be traced through the places they occupied and from which they served as guides to Russian emigration. These included the journal *Put'*, an important periodical of religious thinkers in exile, the Christian Association of Russian Students (ACER), the leading Orthodox movement of Russian émigrés, and the

Saint-Photius fraternity, a student circle of the Institut de théologie orthodoxe de Paris." About the Saint-Photius "confrerie," founded in 1925 with Evgraf Kovalevskii as participant, see Élie de Foucauld, *Évêque Jean de Saint-Denis (Eugraph Kovalevsky)*, chapter 4, "La confrerie Saint-Photius," 61–70. Its goal was to "restore to the Church the universal spirit," "open borders," "make a passage for the 'catholic' value of the Orthodox Church," "not limit the Church to one spirit, one psychology, one culture," "wishing to not be more Platonic than Aristotelian, and to pursue in theology that something which surpasses both Orient and Occident" (62). "The fraternity is called to break the iron curtain between the isolated sister Churches, between Slavs and Greeks, between Orient and Occident. It opposes any and all spirit of domination of one part of the Church against others" (67).

49 Bonvin, "La World's Student Christian Federation," 38: "The establishment of Monsignor Evlogii in Paris roughly coincides with the early stages of the gathering of the Russian émigré intelligentsia in the same city. Before, its members were mostly in Berlin and Prague, but the hyperinflation that wracked the Weimar Republic reached its peak in 1923 and provoked the departure of a number of Russian émigrés who again escaped from poverty and took refuge in Paris, which was already a haven for several members of the Russian aristocracy … With this new influx of émigrés, Paris became a mirror or copy of the entire Russian society and the capital of the Russian diaspora in Europe."

50 Charles Du Bos made early contact with the Russian émigré writers in France and tried to open doors to have their work published. See Livak, "L'émigration russe," 23–43, §14: "Boris de Schloezer, an émigré himself and a literary critic of foreign literature at the *Nouvelle Revue française*, initiated an advertising campaign to introduce the thinker Lev Shestov and get his foot in the door at the publishers Plon and Grasset with the assistance of Charles Du Bos and Daniel Halévy."

51 Tamara Klépinine, *Bibliographie des oeuvres de Nicolas Berdiaev*, introduction by Pierre Pascal (Paris: Institut d'études slaves, 1978), "Résumé chronologique de la vie," 17. See also Igor Sollogoub, "De Kiev à Clamart: La vie de Nicolas Berdiaev (1874–1948)," in *Colloque Clamart*, 28; Cyrille Sollogoub, "Berdiaev," *Colloque Clamart*, 38. On the spread of the YMCA (Young Men's Christian Association) founded in London in 1844 with an interfaith agenda, as well as the World Student Christian Federation (WSCF), founded in 1895 on the model of the YMCA, and later the Russian branch RSCM that all supported Orthodoxy, see Bonvin, "La World's Student Christian Federation," 1–90. See also Matthew Lee Miller, *The American YMCA and Russian Culture: The Preservation and Expansion of Orthodox Christianity, 1900–1940* (Lanham, MD: Lexington Books, 2013).

52 Igor Sollogoub, "De Kiev," 30–1.

53 The first card sent by Jacques and Raïssa Maritain to Monsieur and Madame Berdyaev is from 1925: “We are thinking affectionately of you, Jacq and Raïssa Maritain.”

54 Berdiaev, *Essai d’autobiographie*, 329–30. Pierre Pascal claims the *Essai d’autobiographie spirituelle* was “mostly completed by 1940.” Bernard Marchadier says that Lydia Berdyaev is the one who wished to meet Jeanne Bloy. See Marchadier, “Berdiaev,” 42.

55 Jacques Maritain, “Carnets de 1925–1927,” *Cahiers Jacques Maritain* no. 67 (December 2013): 6. Berdyaev makes a passing allusion to the poet Alexandre Blok in his book *Un Nouveau Moyen Âge* (Paris: Plon, 1927), 94. On Blok, see Jacques Maritain, *Humanisme integral* in *Oeuvres Complètes* (OC), vol. VI, 365. The seventeen volumes of the *Oeuvres complètes* of Jacques and Raïssa Maritain were published by Éditions Saint-Paul (Paris) and Éditions universitaires de Fribourg (Switzerland), 1986–2007.

56 The journal *Put’* (The way) was published in Paris from 1925 to 1940 in three phases: a modernist phase (1925–29), a non-conformist phase (1930–35), and a spiritual phase (1935–40). See Antoine Arjakovsky, “Les intellectuels russes en France: la revue *La Voie* (*Put’*), revue de la pensée religieuse russe (1925–1940),” *Revue des études slaves* LXXII, no. 2–3 (Paris, 2001): 461–4. The review borrowed its name from the Russian publishing house Put’ founded by the donor Margarita Morozova. Its directors proposed to serve “the vocation of Russia to contribute, in thinking and in life, to the achievement of a universal Christian ideal” (Pascal, “Les grands courants,” 33).

57 Antoine Arjakovsky, *La génération des penseurs religieux de l’émigration russe en France,* La revue *La Voie (Put’), 1925–1940* (Kiev-Paris: L’Esprit et la Lettre, 2002), 176. “In September 1925, in his review of the books by Maritain, *Réflexions sur l’intelligence et sur sa vie propre* and by Father Réginald Garrigou-Lagrange, *Le sens commun: La philosophie de l’être et les formules dogmatiques,* Berdyaev characterizes the neo-Thomist movement as a renewal of classic Catholicism.” Note that in the Berdyaev library in Clamart are two books by Garrigou-Lagrange: *Le sens commun* (Paris: Nouvelle Librairie nationale, 1922) and *Perfection chrétienne et contemplation selon S. Thomas d’Aquin et S. Jean de la Croix,* Saint-Maximin, I et II, quatrième edition, 1927 (London: Forgotten Books, 2018). For Berdyaev’s review, see *Put’* no. 1 (September 1925), “Neotomizm”: 169–71. A Berdyaev review of another book by Father Garrigou-Lagrange, *La providence et la confiance en Dieu,* was published in *Put’* no. 35 (September 1932): 97–9.

58 In Berdyaev’s Clamart library, which I visited two times, in December 2019 and February 2020, thanks to the welcome extended by the hieromonk Father Joseph, there are many volumes by French writers, philosophers, and theologians: Emmanuel Mounier (4), Stanislas Fumet (3), Charles Journet (2), Réginald Garrigou-Lagrange (2), Étienne Gilson (2), Henri de

Lubac (2), Gabriel Marcel (1), Gaston Fessard (1), Georges Sorel (1), Vladimir Jankélévitch (1). Many of the volumes have dedicatory inscriptions. For example, Henri de Lebac, *Le drame de l'humanisme athée* (Paris: Éditions Spes, 1944) with the inscription "To Nikolai Berdyaev, this work which owes him much, in respectful homage, Henri de Lubac s.j."; Henri de Lubac, *Proudhon et le christianisme* (Paris: Seuil, 1945) with an accompanying card that reads "From the author, absent from Paris, and the Éditions du Seuil"; Gaston Fessard, *Autorité et bien commun* (Paris: Aubier, 1944) with the inscription "To Nikolai Berdyaev, in respectful homage, G. Fessard."

59 Berdiaev, *Essai d'autobiographie*, 330.

60 Lurol, "Berdiaev," 107.

61 Fumet, *Histoire de Dieu*, 292: "I detected few intellectual affinities between them. But it turned out that this difference in their points of view was so great that it did not encumber them. Maritain and Berdyaev operated on different planes that did not touch, but this allowed them to make a free attachment with each other. Maritain listened to Berdyaev with close attention, but I think that Berdyaev only vaguely understood Maritain's thinking … They were in agreement about action."

62 The sixty-seven letters from Jacques Maritain (1925–1945) and the three from Raïssa Maritain (1934–1936) addressed to Nikolai and Lydia Berdyaev are kept at the Russian State Archive of Literature and Art (RGALI), archive number 1496-1, unit 605 and RGALI, archive 1496-1, unit 606.

63 Gousseff, "Une intelligentsia," 118–20.

64 Igor Sollogoub, "De Kiev," 27; Cyrille Sollogoub, "Berdiaev," 37.

65 Gousseff, "Une intelligentsia," 125: "The project around the journal *Put'* was initiated with the YMCA and received significant financial backing from it. The participation of the American organization was formalized by having one of its representatives, Gustave Kullmann, named co-director of *Put'* alongside Vysheslavtsev and Berdyaev. This collaboration conferred an international status on the journal, though it was in fact mostly a voice piece for the Russian diaspora in Europe with authors stretching from the Baltic Sea to Great Britain and circulation within all the Russian communities in the West." Gousseff, 135: "At the crossroads of the 1930s … the powerful YMCA, which up until then had financed at least in part a large number of Christian intellectual activities, began to considerably reduce its level of aid."

66 Fourcade, "De Soloviev à Boulgakov," 133–4. Maritain took up "a small discussion conducted with Berdyaev and Laberthonnière" that had originated at one of the interfaith meetings in Paris. This talk became an article, "Pie XI et le Christ-Roi," *Revue des Jeunes* 10–29 March 1927, vol. 1 (see Journet-Maritain, *Correspondance, Vol. 1*, 404–5 and 452, note 2). The Russian philosopher Lev Alexandrovich Zander (1893–1964) founded an Orthodox centre during his time in France in February 1924 (see Bonvin, "La World's Student

Christian Federation," 43). Zander was professor of philosophy at the Institut orthodoxe Saint-Serge.

67 Maritain realized already in 1925 (19 October 1925) that it would be "difficult to attend all the meetings," and suggested that Berdyaev "find another philosopher who represents the same way of thinking" for the times when he would be absent. He would also apologize to Berdyaev for not being able to attend a meeting (see letter of 18 December 1926).

68 Jacques Maritain, "Metafizika I mistika," *Put'* no. 2 (January 1926): 88–100.

69 This article later became the first chapter of Maritain's book *Degrés du savoir* (1932).

70 Berdiaev, "Le destin de la culture," 73–100. The original Russian text was not published, but a German translation appeared in *Europäeische Revue* (1 April 1926): 6–18.

71 On the composition of this volume, see Michel Bressolette, "Jacques Maritain et 'Le Roseau d'or,'" *Littératures* no. 9 (1984): 295.

72 Berdiaev, "Le destin," 74–5.

73 Ibid., 76.

74 Nicolas Berdiaev, *Essai d'autobiographie*, 331: "Maritain is a mystic and our spiritual exchanges were very interesting."

75 Jacques Maritain, "Expérience mystique et philosophie," *Revue de philosophie* 26e année, t. XXXIII, no. 6 (November–December 1926): 571–618.

76 Fumet, *Histoire de Dieu*, 289: "Berdyaev had just written [in Russian and published in Berlin] while in Germany *Un Nouveau Moyen Âge* which my wife immediately wanted to translate … It is in our 'Roseau d'or,' which is just now getting started, that we hope to publish this translation of *Un Nouveau Moyen Âge*. The work of A.-M. F. took longer than Berdyaev would have liked, but the book did finally appear in early 1927."

77 Letter from Maritain to Berdyaev, 2 November 1926.

78 Letter from Maritain to Berdyaev, 6 November 1926.

79 Jacques Maritain, "Avons-nous une culture international?," in *Les Chroniques du jour* (August 1926), OC, III, 1304.

80 Nicolas Berdiaev, *Un Nouveau Moyen Âge: Réflexions sur les destinées de la Russie et de l'Europe*, translated from the Russian by Aniouta Fumet, Le Roseau d'or, no. 13 (Paris: Plon, 1927), viii–296. The first Russian edition was published in 1924. Other translations appeared in German (1927), Spanish (1932), English (1933), Dutch (1935), Danish (1936), Hungarian (1935), Polish (1936), and Japanese (1953, 1958).

81 Aniouta Fumet, "Introduction," II–III in Berdyaev, *Un Nouveau Moyen Âge*.

> Berdyaev suffered under the former tsarist regime. At the age of twenty-five he was exiled from Kiev to Vologda in northern Russia. Later, on the eve of the 1917 revolution, he was punished with an order of exclusion for having criticized the Synod which, as he saw it, did not

> faithfully represent the Christian spirit but was above all a political organization obeying a temporal power. When the revolution erupted, Berdyaev continued with his customary frankness to speak what he considered to be the truth. A free philosopher and writer, he was later named professor of philosophy at the University of Moscow by the Faculty of Philology and History. He was imprisoned two times. Then in 1922 he was expelled from Russia, along with other notable writers and academics, for having affirmed his religious convictions under the Bolshevik regime … As an ex-pat, Berdyaev lived first in Germany then France. He founded in Germany and later in France an Academy of Religious Philosophy. In Paris he currently directs the journal *Put'* [*La Voie*, The Way].

In 1909, Berdyaev had already founded in Russia a Society for Religious Philosophy dedicated to Vladimir Solov'ev that brought together major figures of Russian thinking. See Pierre Pascal, "Les grands courants," 31–2. These biographical details are also related by Stanislas Fumet in "Un exégète," 226–8.

82 Berdiaev, *Un Nouveau Moyen Âge*, 105: "Léon Bloy used to say, 'Suffering passes, having suffered never passes.'" See also A.-M. Fumet, "Introduction," IV: "The first part was written in 1919, the others in 1923."

83 Nicolas Berdiaev, *L'Esprit de Dostoïevski* (Prague: YMCA Press, 1923; Munich, 1925; Paris: Éditions Saint-Michel, 1929; London, 1934; Barcelona, 1935; Turin, 1942; New York, 1957).

84 Nicolas Berdiaev, *Le sens de l'histoire: Essai d'une philosophie de la destinée humaine* (Paris: Aubier, 1948; Berlin: Obelisk, 1923 in Russian); Darmstadt, 1925; London, 1936; Santiago de Chile, 1938; Tokyo, 1960.

85 Nicolas Berdiaev, *Le sens de la creation: Un essai de justification de l'homme* (Paris: Desclée de Brouwer, 1955; Moscow: G. Leman and S. Sakharov, 1916 in Russian); Tübingen, 1927; London, 1955. The French translation included a long preface by Stanislas Fumet (13–29) that helped establish Berdyaev on the French intellectual scene.

86 Klépinine, *Bibliographie*.

87 Marchadier, "Berdiaev," 41; Clément, *Berdiaev*, 106.

88 Pascal, "Les grands courants," 82.

89 Clément, *Berdiaev*, 90–1: "In 1927 the huge success of *Un Nouveau Moyen Âge* made Berdyaev into a source of inspiration for the younger generation that would engage in the Personalism movement, in other words in the direction of *Esprit*."

90 Fumet, "Un exégète," 227.

91 In the Berdyaev library in Clamart there are two books by Charles Journet, *L'Union des Églises et le christianisme pratique* (Paris: Grasset, 1927) and *La Juridiction de l'Église sur la cité*, Questions disputées (Paris: Desclée de Brouwer 1931).

92 Card from Maritain to Berdyaev, 17 March 1927: "We'll be happy to come to Clamart next Tuesday 22 March around 4:30. Our best regards to Madame Berdiaev. Affectionately, Jaq Maritain."

93 Pascal, "Les grands courants," 86: "One can say that Berdyaev inserted himself within the current of thinking that was postrevolutionary, existentialist, personalist, and progressive – and powerfully added to it. It was in the Russian milieu that he received less credit."

94 Berdiaev, *Un Nouveau Moyen Âge*, 236.

95 Jacques Maritain, *Primauté du spirituel*, Le Roseau d'or no. 19 (Paris: Plon, 1927). A copy of *Primauté* from a special printing from 1927 (one of sixteen thousand copies) and with no annotations or inscription is in the Berdyaev library in Clamart.

96 Maritain, *Primauté*, 132; OC, III, 872.

97 Muriel Guitat-Naudin, "La reception de Vladimir Soloviev en France," *Vladimir Soloviev, Jacques Maritain et le personnalisme chrétien*, ed. P. de Laubier (Paris: Parole et Silence, 2008), 75–98, 85:

> Considered as the first Russian philosopher, the first to have constructed a coherent philosophical system, Solov'ev became one of the principal authorities for an entire generation of intellectuals including Nikolai Berdyaev, Nikolai Lossky, Lev Shestov, Simeon Frank, and Sergei Bulgakov who were the most well-known figures in France … Nikolai Berdyaev was definitely the one who did the most to introduce Soloviev's philosophy into France. And yet he was not Soloviev's closest follower, and rather openly disagreed with his conception of freedom and his sophiology. However, Berdyaev did take up and develop in his own writings a certain number of intuitions, notably about the preeminence of man in the historical process founded on the notion of the "divine-humanity" of Christ, a true man and true God, a notion present among the Church Fathers and taken up again by Solov'ev in his anthropology.

98 Maritain, *Primauté*, 267; OC III, 940.

99 Jacques Maritain, *Le Docteur angelique*, 1929, OC IV, 91: "Modern history seems to be entering, in the words of Berdyaev, a new Middle Ages where the unity and universality of Christian culture will be revived and extended this time to the entire universe." Maritain would write roughly the same thing in "Les lettres catholiques hongroises et l'unité de la culture chrétienne," *Élet* XXX (7 July 1929): 13; OC XVI, 405: "Some months ago, three philosophers had a conversation about modern history: the Russian Nikolai Berdyaev, the German Peter Wust, and myself a Frenchman. We share the same opinion on two points: the first is that modern history seems to be entering a new Middle Ages where the unity and university of Christian culture will be revived, but this time extended to the four corners of the world; the second is that for the

moment the general movement of modern civilization seems to be taking it toward the universalism of the Antichrist rather than toward Christ." There is also the final note that mentions *Un Nouveau Moyen Âge* in *Théonas* (second edition, 1925, with a text revised after 1927 in view of a new edition that was not published but with a preface dated 1932); OC II, 921: "We may quote again the Russian philosopher Nikolai Berdyaev, who in his suggestive reflections about *Un Nouveau Moyen Âge* demonstrates the now archaic and 'reactionary' character of the myth of progress."

100 Maritain, *Primauté*, 264–72; OC III, 939-43.

101 Maritain, *Primauté*, 265; OC III, 939.

102 Maritain, *Primauté*, 265–6; OC III, 939.

103 Élie de Foucauld, *Évêque Jean de Saint-Denis (Eugraph Kovalevsky), Biographie 1905–1945* (n.p.: Les Éditions de Forgeville, 2020), 58: during his "early years in France, 1920–1925" one sees Kovalevskii "begin to participate in the circle organized by the Maritains who open for him a door to a France passionate about the search for the truth of Christianity." A few early letters (1928–30) from Kovalevskii to Maritain are present in the Maritain archive of the national university library of Strasbourg (BNU), as well as one dated 1960, when he was passing through New York, in which he writes, "I would be pleased to meet with you."

104 Jacques Maritain, "Carnet de Jacques Maritain: Journal 1937," annotated by Michel Fourcade, *Cahiers Jacques Maritain*, no. 80 (June 2020): 28, note 38: "This 'Russian group' (distinct from the interfaith meetings organized by Maritain and Berdiaev) met regularly at Maritain's home starting in the late 1920s. It was led by two young Orthodox theologians, Evgraf Kovalevskii (1905–1970) and Vladimir Lossky (1903–1983), co-founders in 1925 of the 'Confrérie Saint-Photius' dedicated to a renaissance of Orthodoxy in the West. The two worked to found a 'Catholic Orthodox Church in France.' Lossky, a student of Gilson, would also introduce to France oriental mystic theology."

105 Marlène Laruelle, "Les ideologies de la 'troisième voie' dans les années vingt: Le movement eurasiste russe," *Vingtième siècle, revue d'histoire*, no. 70 (2001/2): 31–46, §11: "The Eurasian movement was born from the need to find some compensation when faced with an insolvable problem, one intolerable in the eyes of a young, cultivated, and impatient elite that refuses the decadence of the homeland, namely the humiliation of the Soviet peace deal with Germany, and that accuses the West for the difficult historical development of Russia." §54: "Eurasianism inherits the ambiguity of a discourse marked by religious and national traits but also one sensitive to the social question. Its extremism and maximalism may be interpreted as a fundamentalism that is both of the 'right' and the 'left' as was noted by the philosopher Nikolai Berdyaev in one of his major texts on Eurasianism." Berdyaev gave his analysis of the form of Eurasianism he called "the most subtle

articulated by some contemporaries," in the journal *Put'* (September 1925): 134–9. See also Marlène Laruelle, "Politique et culture dans l'émigration russe: les débats entre l'eurasisme et ses opposants," *La revue russe* (2000): 35–46, 35: "Eurasianism was born amidst the Russian exodus during the interwar years to Belgrade, Prague, and then Paris … It was the most original type of thinking among Russian émigrés, a combination of philosophy, meditations on identity, and politics. It was extremely productive in the 1920s, but the movement weakened in the 1930s and disappeared due to internal disputes, notably at the moment of a rallying of a certain number of its partisans ('the Clamart schism') to the Soviet Union and its infiltration by the GPU [Soviet secret police]." Starting in November 1928, Clamart was the location for the weekly publication of *Evrazija* [Eurasia] that promoted a political line close to Maxim Gorkii. At the start, the Eurasian movement interested many Russian intellectuals, including Trubetskoi, Florovsky, and Fedotov, who later distanced themselves from it. This movement was particularly lively during the 1920s and declined in the 1930s following the "Clamart schism," §19–26.

106 Maritain, *Primauté*, 266; OC III, 939–40.

107 Maritain, *Primauté*, 267; OC III, 940.

108 Maritain, *Primauté*, 268; OC III, 940–1.

109 Berdiaev, *Essai d'autobiographie*, 332.

110 Ibid., 326.

111 Ibid.

112 Pius XI, *Mortalium Animos*: "nor is it anyway lawful for Catholics either to support or to work for such enterprises; for if they do so they will be giving countenance to a false Christianity, quite alien to the one Church of Christ." https://www.vatican.va/content/pius-xi/en/encyclicals/documents/hf_p-xi_enc_19280106_mortalium-animos.html (accessed 29 June 2023). On the impact of this encyclical on religious unity, see Arjakovsky, *La Génération*, 188. See also Laura Pettinaroli, *La politique russe du Saint-Serge (1905–1939)* (Rome: École Française de Rome, 2015; OpenEdition Books accessed 22 March 2016), chapter 9, § "Une remise en ordre: *Mortalium Animos* (1928)": "The encyclical *Mortalium Animos* by Piux XI seizes the opportunity of the condemnation of all Catholic participation in 'pan-Christian' congresses (aiming to effect a rapprochement between different Churches through the bond of charity and to agree on a minimal *credo*) to underscore the Catholic vision of the unity of Christians. The latter holds that this unity already exists – it resides in the Catholic church and to retrieve it, dissidents have only to return to the 'one Church of Christ.'"

113 Fourcade, "De Soloviev à Boulgakov," 136: "With the aim of restoring some vital circulation within Christian thinking, these innovative interfaith meetings were held until 1928. They would have been interrupted more quickly if they had been only a cacophonous dialogue of the deaf. The encyclical

Mortalium Animos (6 January 1928) put an end to them since it was swiftly followed by the withdrawal of all the invited Catholic theologians who feared 'overly engaging' by their presence or possibly sometimes leaving too much to chance in discussions of 'all who stray' and 'the unity of the Church.'"

114 Letter from Maritain to Berdyaev, 5 March 1928, in which Maritain invites him "to Meudon on Sunday 18 March around 4 o'clock."

115 Letter from Berdiaev to Maritain, 22 February 1928, in which Berdiaev expresses his wish to see him very soon "at the interfaith meeting." During the summer of 1928, Maritain noted for 25 July: "At 4 o'clock visit to Berdiaevs in Clamart." See Jacques Maritain, "Carnets de 1928," *Cahiers Jacques Maritain* no. 68 (June 2014): 17.

116 After consultations with Maritain about how to proceed, Monsignor Emmanuel Chaptal, the auxiliary bishop of Paris in charge of foreigners, clearly stated his position in a letter dated 28 March 1928:

> I feel less and less favourable toward confrontations with the Russians, especially in public discussions – all the more since we find ourselves exposed to canonical decisions that will certainly be severe. I would be much more inclined to the method that was used in Boulevard Montparnasse for the meetings that were held under the direction of Prince Trubetskoi. There it was Russian professors who wished to hear a presentation of Church doctrine on a series of different points. After the lecture, the Russian listeners asked for further explanations about points that seemed to them obscure or debatable. There were no spectators. The sincere desire to instruct appeared to be the dominant feature.

Mgr Chaptal ended his letter to Maritain by stating "I would very much like to speak with you." In another letter to Maritain dated 4 April 1928, Mgr Chaptal proposes they meet on Thursday, 18 April 1928, at 1:30 p.m. (see the letters from Mgr Chaptal to Maritain in the Maritain archive, BNU).

117 Pettinaroli, *La politique*, chapter 9, § "Vers de Nouvelles voies de rencontres avec les orthodoxes":

> Certain direct exchanges between Orthodox and Catholic intellectuals took place on the margins of Church hierarchies. In 1928, just a few weeks after *Mortalium Animos*, Mgr Chaptal signaled two "hints of rapprochement" with the Orthodox of Paris. First, on the request of several Orthodox professors, lectures are organized by Mgr Beaupin and the group French Friendships Abroad … Second, the French prelate evoked the "conversations" about philosophical and historical topics organized by Jacques Maritain at the request of the "Russian professor" Berdyaev … The idea is the same as for the meetings organized by Mgr Beaupin: "no spectators" are to be admitted to "these meetings" that must be "interviews between philosophers clarifying their respective metaphysical and religious positions." Chaptal ex-

pressed confidence because Maritain's personality guaranteed "that the interviews would not degenerate into dangerous or pointless controversies."

118 On the Maritain-Berdyaev meetings between Orthodox and Catholics, see Philippe Chenaux, *Entre Maurras et Maritain: Une génération intellectuelle catholique (1920–1930)* (Paris: Éditions du Cerf, 1999), 171–4. See also Fourcade, "De Soloviev," 136–7; Marchadier, "Berdiaev," 42–3.

119 Berdiaev, *Essai d'autobiographie*, 333: "I have a consoling memory of these exchanges and a regret about their interruption after three years. The participants also expressed to me their regret at the time."

120 Pierre Van der Meer, *Dieu et les hommes* (Paris: Desclée de Brouwer, 1949), 319.

121 Berdiaev, *Essai d'autobiographie*, 329.

122 Fumet, *Histoire de Dieu*, 292: "Maritain liked the Russians." See also Raïssa Maritain, *Les grandes amitiés*, OC XIV, 662. Note also that one of Jacques Maritain's first texts from 1905 was "Tolstoï et Le Matin," published in the *Tribune russe* (OC XVI, 674–81). The Maritains also had relations with Russian musicians (Nabokov starting in 1924, Igor Stravinsky in 1926 and later, through him, Arthur Lourié). See Olesya Bobbrik, "La famille de Jacques Maritain et les musiciens russes," *Cahiers Jacques Maritain* no. 64 (June 2012): 46–58. Jacques et Raïssa Maritain were also acquainted with the Russian painter Marc Chagall starting in 1928. See Piero Viotto, "Marc Chagall et Jacques Maritain," *Cahiers Jacques Maritain*, no. 58 (July 2009): 4–24.

123 Berdiaev, *Essai d'autobiographie*, 331. See also Marchadier, "Berdiaev," 43. A list of the participants at these meetings is given by Arjakovsky, *La génération*, 193–4: Charles Du Bos, Olivier Lacombe, Émile Dermenghen, Étienne Gilson, Louis Massignon, Emmanuel Mounier, Gabriel Marcel, Jeah Wahl, Jules Lebreton, Charles Journet, Jean de Pange.

124 Jean de Pange, *Journal (1927–1930)* (Paris: Grasset, 1964), 147.

125 In Berdyaev's Clamart library there is a copy of Gabriel Marcel's *Être et avoir* (Paris: Aubier, 1935).

126 In Berdyaev's Clamart library there are two books by Étienne Gilson: *Saint Thomas d'Aquin*, ed. J. Gabalda, Les moralistes chrétiens (Paris: Librairie Victor Lecoffre, 4th edition, 1925); *Le réalisme méthodique* (Paris: Pierre Téqui, 1935). The first contains annotations, the second numerous underlined passages.

127 Berdiaev, *Essai d'autobiographie*, 332.

128 Iswolsky, *Au temps*, 99.

129 Arjakovsky, *La Génération*, 193.

130 Maritain, "Carnets de 1928," *Cahiers Jacques Maritain*, no. 68 (June 2014): 48: entry for 17 December 1928, "Evening meeting with the Russians." Present at that meeting were Olivier Lacombe, Jean de Menasce, Jean Daniélou

(president) Kerdov, Emmanuel Mounier, and several young women in the company of Schevitch, Karpov, and Florovsky.

131 Iswolsky, *Au temps*, 98–9, 181–2: "A group of young Russians often visited Jacques Maritain whom they regarded with great admiration and deep respect. One of them, Eugraph K[ovalevsky, whose parents, exiled from Russia, had moved to Meudon in 1920] was later ordained. He organized a small circle of particularly fervent Orthodox. They had their own chapel in the Latin Quarter that was under the patronage of Sainte Geneviève." Maritain records in his notebook for 25 July 1928 (*Cahiers Jacques Maritain*, no. 68 [June 2014]: 15) that he met Evgraf Kovalevskii. Father Evgraf Kovalevskii (1905–1970) would officiate at the funeral of Nikolai Berdyaev in 1948. See Olivier Clément, *Berdiaev*, 231.

132 Maritain, "Carnets de 1929," *Cahiers Jacques Maritain*, no. 69 (February 2015): 34: "Monday 18 February. Berdyaev meeting Boulevard Montparnasse … Dinner with the Barthes. Meeting with the Russians. Evgraf [Kovalevskii] talks about the Orthodox missions established in Russia; M. Guyon, a friend of Yves Simon, speaks about Catholic missions and Pius XI." See also Jacques Maritain, *Carnet de notes*, 1929: "Monday 18 February, Berdiaev meeting, Boulevard Montparnasse. Pastor Lecerf, Abbé Simeterre" (OC XII, 327).

133 Maritain, "Carnets de 1929," *Cahiers Jacques Maritain* no. 69 (February 2015): 31: "Tuesday 29 January. Russian meeting at Berdyaev's. (Massignon, Fumet, Olivier, Jean-Pierre [Altermann], Raïa and myself for the French side. Du Bos sick), Florovsky, Kadechoft, Fedotov, Vysheslavtsev, Jakubisiak, etc. … Excellent presentation by Berdiaev." See also Jacques Maritain, *Carnet de notes* (OC XII, 327).

134 Maritain, "Carnets de 1929," *Cahiers Jacques Maritain* no. 69 (February 2015): 36: "Tuesday 5 March. 4 p.m. meeting at Berdyaev's, Massignon presentation on Christina the Astonishing. Discussion with Florovsky and the others about reparative suffering. With a few quick and incisive words Raïa halts the further remarks of Florovsky who imputes to Catholics doctrines they have never held." See also Maritain, *Carnet de notes* (OC XII, 327). Also "Carnets de 1929," 37: "Monday 11 March. Evening Russian meeting. Eugraph speaks about the Orthodox missions in Russia."

135 An *agrégé* is a person in the French educational system who has passed a state exam.

136 Maritain, "Carnets de 1929," *Cahiers Jacques Maritain*, no. 69 (February 2015): 42: "Tuesday 16 April. Meeting at Berdyaev's. Florovsky speaks about Byzantine mysticism and Gregory Palamas." See de Pange, *Journal*, 155: "I go to Berdiaev's in Clamart. Small house in the suburbs. A meeting is held there in which people compare the mystics of the Orthodox church and the Roman church. A Russian professor, M. Florovsky, speaks today about Byzantine mystics."

137 Maritain, "Carnets de 1929," 51: "Tuesday 4 June. Discussion about Saint John of the Cross at Berdyaev's. Evening, Russian ballet. (*Le fils prodigue*, music by Prokofiev, sets by Rouault)."

138 Letter from Maritain to Berdyaev, 18 November 1929: "I have now reached out to Plon three times, and I've been promised that they're sending you the volumes of the *Roseau d'or* that you're missing. I am very annoyed by their negligence, and especially eager for you to receive my preface on Bergson."

139 Maritain, "Carnets de 1929," *Cahiers Jacques Maritain* no. 69 (February 2015): 66. In a fall entry Maritain records a meeting "with the Russians" for 10 November; 71: "Sunday 10 November. Russians. Schevitch, Arseniev, Evgraf, Godmé, Phangiado."

140 Jacques Maritain, *Clairvoyance de Rome*, 1929, OC III, 1217.

141 Maritain, "Carnets de 1929," *Cahiers Jacques Maritain* no. 69 (February 2015): 75: "Tuesday 10 December. 4 p.m. at Berdiaev's, Orthodox-Catholic meeting. Ilyin speaks about sophiology."

142 Maritain, "Carnets de 1929," *Cahiers Jacques Maritain* no. 70 (November 2014): 35.

143 Ibid., 36.

144 Ibid., 37: "Sunday 26 January. Mass (P. Bruno). Garin, Berdyaev, Fou Nouen, young Polish person, the Colums."

145 Letter from Maritain to Berdyaev, 30 January 1930: "We would like to have his opinion on the double question: What is the relationship between Pseudo-Dionysus and properly Neo-Platonic mysticism, and what is his relation with Christian mysticism (not the kind that followed him but with that of Saint Paul, for example). In short, to what extent is Pseudo-Dionysus Neo-Platonic and to what extent is he Christian?"

146 Letter from Maritain to Berdyaev, 21 February 1930.

147 Maritain, "Carnets de 1930," *Cahiers Jacques Maritain* no. 70 (November 2015): 54: "Tuesday 25 March. Meeting at Berdyaev's. [Henri-Charles] Puech on Dionysus."

148 Letter from Maritain to Berdyaev, 27 March 1930. Some time later, in a letter from mid-April 1930, Maritain tells Berdyaev that he has received a reply from Father Théry that requires "finding another evaluator."

149 Sergei Bulgakov (1872–1944) was an early friend of Berdyaev. See Clément, *Berdiaev*, 16–17, 52–4. Bulgakov was an important figure in the Russian Student Christian Movement, within liberal Orthodoxy, and at the Institut Saint-Serge that offered its courses in Russian. The Russian Student Christian Movement welcomed three types of gatherings: "completely interfaith circles, majority Orthodox circles that remained open to other faiths, and exclusively Orthodox circles." See Bonvin, "La World's," 44.

150 Maritain, "Carnets de 1930," *Cahiers Jacques Maritain*, no. 70 (November 2015): 54. See de Pange, *Journal*, 288–9. Maritain even asked Berdyaev in a

letter dated 27 March 1930 if he wished to have a meeting with Cardinal Jean Verdier in Paris. Then in a letter from mid-April 1930, Maritain adds in a postscript: "I went to see the Cardinal of Paris and told him what I thought of M. Quénet's report."

151 Maritain, "Carnets de 1930," *Cahiers Jacques Maritain*, no. 70 (November 2015: 67: "Tuesday 15 May. Wrote to Berdyaev."

152 Ibid., 66. Böhme's *Ungrund* (sometimes translated as "groundlessness") is the nothingness, or abyss, that Böhme believes to be the source out of which God or the Trinity arises.

153 Berdiaev, *Essai d'autobiographie*, 332.

154 De Pange, *Journal*, 297–8: "13 May 1930." See also Marie-Madeleine Davy, *Nicolas Berdiaev, l'homme du huitième jour* (Paris, 1964; Paris: Éditions du Félin, 1991), 75: "Nikolai Berdyaev debated passionately. When the opposition became a bit too lively, the French words would not come to him and he would speak in Russian. Sometimes his Russian friends were so eager to speak that they would not take turns and wait for the other person to complete his sentence. Words would jumble together and the voice of Nikolai Berdyaev would impose itself over the tumult."

155 Fedor Dostoïevski, *Les frères Karamazov* (Paris: Gallimard Bibliothèque de la Pléiade, 1952), 77. The passage in an English translation of *The Brothers Karamazov* can be found by searching an online edition for the word *starets* (elder).

156 Letter from Maritain to Berdyaev, 14 May 1930 (RGALI, dossier 1496-1, unit 605, folios 33 and 34).

157 Maritain, "Carnets de 1930," *Cahiers Jacques Maritain*, no. 70 (November 2015): 68: "Sunday 18 May … After dinner, the Russians."

158 Jacques and Raïssa Maritain would understand later, in 1934, that it was a human problem that was torturing him. Jacques Maritain, "Carnets de 1934," *Cahiers Jacques Maritain*, no. 77 (December 2018): 26. On Berdyaev's conversion and its relation to the event he suffered from, see Olivier Clément, *Berdiaev*, 17–18.

159 Jacques Maritain, *La philosophie bergsonienne* (2nd edition, 1930), OC I, 511. See also Jacques Maritain, *Court traité de l'existence et de l'existant* (1947), OC IX, 14: "Many philosophers, from Jaspers and Gabriel Marcel to Berdyaev and Shestov, called themselves 'existentiels' philosophers." And in *La personne et le bien commun* (1947), Maritain specified that "the distinction between individuality and personality" is "invoked by schools as different as the Thomists, certain disciples of Proudhon, by Nikolai Berdyaev, and by philosophers who, before the invasion by a young group of existentialists, were already calling themselves 'existentiels'" (*La personne et le bien commun*, OC IX, 187). On the misunderstanding of Berdyaev's use of the term "existentiel," see Clément, *Berdiaev*, 106–7.

160 Maritain, "Carnets de 1930," *Cahiers Jacques Maritain*, no. 70 (November 2015): 102.

161 Letter from Berdyaev to Maritain. The preceding letter, presumably dated 20 October 1930, has not been found. Maritain, "Carnets de 1930," *Cahiers Jacques Maritain*, no. 70 (November 2015): 101: "Wrote to Berdyaev."

162 Letter from Maritain to Hélène Iswolsky dated 17 December 1930. Maritain archive BNU: "The first Sunday in December [7 December], 3 p.m., Olivier Lacombe will present to us a report on the Upanishads. We would be very pleased that you attend." The first exchange of letters between Iswolsky and Maritain began in early November 1930. It was around then that Maritain accompanied Iswolsky, a young Catholic Russian émigré, to Berdyaev's. See Hélène Iswolsky, *Au temps*, 99.

163 Maritain, "Carnets de 1930," *Cahiers Jacques Maritain* no. 70 (November 2015): 110: "Thursday 4 December. Raïa and I go to Berdyaev's. He speaks to us about the tragic condition of China. It is decided that we will resume the Tuesday meetings at his place."

164 Ibid., 111; Jean de Pange, *Journal*, 356.

165 Maritain, "Carnets de 1930," *Cahiers Jacques Maritain*, no. 70 (November 2015): 112: "Sunday 21 December … Berdyaev after dinner." De Pange, *Journal*, 356, entry for Tuesday, 16 December: "At 4 p.m. at Berdiaev's, presentation by Olivier Lacombe on intelligence and the principle of identity. Lacombe's face becomes somewhat transformed when he's speaking about divine truths. An expression of mystic fervor. It shows that neither the heart nor the intellect experience peace if they have not met God."

166 The letters from Maritain and Berdyaev to Gilson are published in Étienne Gilson, Jacques Maritain, *Deux approches de l'être: Correspondance (1923–1971)*, ed. Géry Prouvost (Paris: Vrin, 1991), 42–3.

167 Maritain, "Carnets de 1931," *Cahiers Jacques Maritain*, no. 73 (April 2017): 32: "Tuesday 20 January. Prepared Berdyaev meeting. At 4 p.m. meeting at his place. Gilson comes and supports me. I speak on 'Philosophy, Theology, Mysticism.' My little Raïa is very happy, she gives me so much comfort." Jean de Pange, *Journal*, 364.

168 Maritain, *Carnets de notes*, OC XII, 330–1.

169 Maritain, "Carnets de 1931," *Cahiers Jacques Maritain*, no. 73 (April 2017): 38. Maritain does not specify the topic at this meeting. It could be the meeting mentioned by Jean de Pange in his *Journal* (364) as being on 20 January, and that he perhaps confused with that of 24 February 1931. De Pange writes, "Afternoon at Berdyaev's. He speaks about the book by Jouhandeau, *Monsieur Godeau intime* (N.R.F.) where he finds pages on the problem of evil that remind him of Dostoevsky. This Catholic professor has an almost satanic spiritual experience that troubles Maritain."

170 De Pange, *Journal*, 44. See also Jean de Pange, *Journal (1931–1933)* (Paris: Grasset, 1967), 21.

171 Maritain, "Carnets de 1931," *Cahiers Jacques Maritain* no. 73 (April 2017): 51. See also de Pange, *Journal (1931–1933)*, 29–30, that specifies the respective positions of Berdyaev and Maritain.

172 Iswolsky, *Au temps*, 99–100. On Iswolsky, see Florian Michel, "Jacques Maritain et Hélène Iswolsky: Les enjeux politiques d'une amitié franco-russe," *Nova et Vetera* 2 (2012): 167–92.

173 Maritain, "Carnets de 1932," *Cahiers Jacques Maritain* no. 74 (November 2017): 36. See also de Pange, *Journal* (1931–1933), 87: "19 January. Afternoon National Library (Goethe translation) then at Berdiaev's where I find Maritain, Marcel, and Van der Meer. I ask for information about the Eurasian movement."

174 Maritain, "Carnets de 1932," *Cahiers Jacques Maritain*, no. 74 (November 2017): 46. For Sunday, 19 April, Maritain notes "Berdiaev at 5 p.m. I speak on *factible* and *usus*. He says remarkable things about the current state of Soviet philosophy." See also Maritain, *Carnets de notes*, OC XII, 333.

175 Berdiaev, *Essai d'autobiographie*, 333.

176 de Foucauld, *Évêque*, chapter 6, "Le schism de l'émigration russe, 1931," 97–114, 109: "The year 1931 is a sad display of the situation of the Orthodox in France and offers a picture that contrasts sharply with the preceding years: a dismembered ecclesiastic hierarchy, a missionary project, the Confrérie Saint-Photius, removed, and young French Christian communities left more or less to fend for themselves."

177 Gousseff, "Une intelligentsia," 136: "In 1931 at the time of the rupture between Evlogii and Moscow, this decision which had been generally well received by the faithful was, on the contrary, met with sharp opposition among the intelligentsia. Only a minority decided to remain aligned with Moscow, but it was composed of figures such as Berdyaev who were very influential. The consequences of this division were decisive for precipitating the disintegration of the original French Orthodox community and the deterioration of bonds between the different protagonists of the religious renaissance."

178 Emilio Britto, "La 'philosophie chrétienne' a-t-elle un avenir?," *Revue théologique de Louvain* 36, no. 4 (2005): 508–35; "La querelle de la philosophie chrétienne," 513–20.

179 Chenaux, *Entre Maurras et Maritain*, 171. For a history of the stakes surrounding the meeting of "Orient" and "Occident" by Catholic intellectuals in the 1920s (Stanislas Fumet, Léopold Levaux, Henri Massis, Jacques Maritain …), see "La Russie et l'Église universelle" in the chapter "L'Orient et l'Occident" (163–74).

180 Leonid Livak, "Le Studio franco-russe (1929–1931)," *Revue d'études slaves* LXXV, no. 1 (2004): 109–23; the quotation is from Wsevolod de Vogt's "Soirées de Paris," *France et monde*, no. 135 (1929): 62.

181 Livak, "Le Studio," 114: "If we compare the subjects debated during the Studio franco-russe meetings to those discussed at the Décades de Pontigny gatherings, one notices a certain thematic continuity that links the two enterprises: the Studio was aiming to deepen the major themes treated at Pontigny, situating them in relation to Russian experience of the revolution and exile, and within the dynamic Franco-Russian cultural context." Also 115, "It is thus hardly surprising that most of the regulars at Pontigny would turn up at the Musée social hall [rented by the Studio franco-russe]."

182 Ibid., 109–10.

183 On the Studio franco-russe, see also Arjakovsky, *La génération*, 195.

184 Livak, "Le Studio," 110, 119: "The quick departure of the lead organizer of the Studio franco-russe and the financial difficulties that swept through contemporary humanities studies in 1931 … would seem to explain its abrupt end."

185 Ibid., 112. On the subject of a publishing job for Robert Sébastien, Maritain replied to Charles Du Bos's letter of 1 March 1929, "I think that Robert Sébastien would be suited to the job and I hope very much that you will be able to take him on. He is young, intelligent, Catholic, and capable of devoting himself to this sort of work that he will enjoy. In addition, his presence at De Brouwer offers many advantages, I think." Robert Sébastien and his friend André Verdier were present several times in Meudon; for example, on Monday, 18 June 1928; see "Carnets de 1928," *Cahiers Jacques Maritain*, no. 68 (June 2014): 10, and on Sunday, 6 January 1929; see "Carnets de 1929," *Cahiers Jacques Maritain*, no. 69 (February 2015): 29.

186 Livak, "Le Studio," 110.

187 Ibid., 112.

188 In a letter from 25 May 1930, Berdyaev asks Maritain: "Will you come to our discussion [at the Studio] with Massis about the Orient and Occident?" but on 21 May 1930, Maritain had written to Robert Sébastien apologizing for his absence at "a session of the Studio franco-russe where Berdyaev and Massis spoke" (OC IV, 1135).

189 Michel Aucouturier, "Recension de: Leonid Livak, Gervaise Tassis, éds., *Le Studio franco-russe, textes réunis et présentés par Leonid Livak sous la direction de Gervaise Tassis* (Toronto: Slavic Library, 2005, 621 p.)," *Cahier du monde russe* 46, no. 4 (2005). "The topics, proposed each time to a Russian speaker and a French speaker, were to be in the following order: concerns about literature, the mutual influence of Russian and French literature, the work of Dostoevsky, Tolstoy, Proust, Gide, the novel (French and Russian), Descartes, Péguy, the spiritual renewal (in France and Russia). Among the speakers on the French side: René Lalou, Stanislas Fumet, Louis Martin-Chauffier, Benjamin Crémieux, Jacques Maritain; on the Russian side, Nikolai Berdyaev, Georgii Adamovich, Vladimir Weidlé, Nina Berberova, Georgii Fedotov, Boris Vysheslavtsev."

190 Livak, "Le Studio," 112; Van Der Meer, *Dieu*, 318–19.
191 Livak, "Le Studio," 118.
192 Van Der Meer, *Dieu*, 319.
193 Maritain, "Carnet 1930," *Cahiers Jacques Maritain*, no. 70 (November 2015): 70.
194 Maritain, "Carnet 1931," *Cahiers Jacques Maritain*, no. 73 (April 2017): 32.
195 Fourcade, "De Soloviev," 136.
196 Maritain, "Carnet 1931," *Cahiers Jacques Maritain*, no. 73 (April 2017): 33. See also Raïssa Maritain, *Journal de Raïssa*, OC XV, 358: "I see Jacques … at the Studio franco-russe, such as last Tuesday, exposed to the contradictions between Russian philosophers and French academics."
197 Jacques Maritain, *Le songe de Descartes* (Paris: Éditions Corréa, 1932 – OC V). Reviewed by Zen'kovskij, *Put'* 4, no. 32 (1934): 76–7.
198 Jacques Maritain, "Descartes et l'esprit cartésien," in *Descartes, textes suivis de débats au Studio franco-russe* (Douzième reunion, 27 January 1931) (Paris: Cahiers de la quinzaine, February 1931), 31 (*Le songe de Descartes*, OC V, 173).
199 Maritain, "Descartes," 33–4; Maritain, *Le songe*, OC V, 175.
200 Maritain, "Descartes," 34; Maritain, *Le songe*, OC V, 175–6.
201 Maritain, "Descartes," 35; Maritain, *Le songe*, OC V, 176.
202 On Boris Vysheslavtsev (1877–1954), see Clément, *Berdiaev*, 55–6: "This law professor was exiled from Russia in 1922, just like Berdiaev, with whom he collaborated in Berlin and then in Paris, where he taught moral theology at the Institut orthodoxe Saint-Serge. In his important work, *L'Éthique de l'Éros transfiguré*, he developed an anthropological meditation, in the Orthodox tradition, on the play of the unconscious as revealed by psychoanalysis."
203 Boris Vysheslavtsev, "Descartes et la philosophie moderne," in *Descartes, textes suivis*, 39: "There are two points where this Hindu reduction approximates Descartes," these two points being dream and the true self, the *ego cogitans* or "Atman."
204 Vysheslavtsev, "Descartes," 41–2.
205 Ibid., 44–5.
206 Ibid., 48.
207 Ibid., 47.
208 Ibid., 48–9.
209 Ibid., 49.
210 Ibid., 52–3.
211 See Berdiaev, *Un Nouveau Moyen Âge*, 117: "What is rational philosophy if not complete confidence in individual reason, fallen from the throne of truth, separated from the sources of being; if not also the affirmation of the right of thought not to wish to choose the Truth nor to expect from it the power to know?"
212 Berdiaev, "Les débats," in *Descartes, textes suivis*, 58–9.
213 Ibid., 59.

214 Ibid., 60.
215 Ibid., 61
216 Ibid., 61–2.
217 Ibid., 61.
218 Maritain, "Réponse de M. Jacques Maritain," in *Descartes, textes suivis*, 65–7; OC V, 214–15.
219 On "the surprising evening at the Studio franco-russe where Maritain was to speak on Descartes" and on the verbal sparring between Maritain and the Sorbonne professor Désiré Roustan "that the audience, transfixed, applauded uproariously," see Fumet, *Histoire de Dieu*, 232–4.
220 Léonid Gabrilovitch, "Suite des débats," *Descartes, textes suivis*, 75.
221 Ibid., 76–7.
222 Iswolsky, *Au temps*, 106: "Another element of the religious thinking of Berdyaev is his conception of knowledge as a mystic gnosis that does not require the light of human reason. Not only does this conception contradict the Catholic interpretation of the word 'knowledge' (and it is on this point that Berdyaev most often was in disagreement with Maritain) but it is also opposed to the interpretation given by certain schools of Protestant thinking."
223 Clément, *Berdiaev*, 219: "In the chapter 'Foi et connaissance' within his *Philosophie de la liberté*, Berdyaev writes: 'sin is the ontological foundation of the limitations of our knowledge. It is the sin of intelligent will that has broken the roots of being, brought into the world separation and inimical exteriority, subordinated the universe to laws of space and time, enclosed the knowing subject in the prison of logical categories.'" See also 233–4: "In the domain of *ecclésiologique*, Berdyaev, following his essay on Khomiakov, in 1912, elaborated a sort of generalized *sobornost* [sometimes translated as 'conciliarity'] which is no doubt the key to his theory of knowledge. Man knows, with an integral knowledge that transcends objectification, to the extent of his free love. There is no other criteria of truth than its evidence, but this evidence is only given to man in communion. Berdyaev's theory of knowledge is in sum the philosophical expression and like a generalization of the communion of *ecclésiologie* that is traditional within Orthodoxy."
224 Letter from Berdyaev to Maritain, 22 February 1928, Clamart (Seine) 2 rue Martial Grandchamp:

> My dear friend! Gabriel Marcel wrote me to say that you spoke of the possibility of publishing my book on Dostoevsky in the Roseau d'or, and that he considers the publisher Plon to be the best solution. But it is important to know if this book suits you. It is likely that you will not agree with many of my ideas. But perhaps, on principle, the Roseau d'or could publish a book which is very representative of Russian religious thinking and that might even aid in understanding the idea of the Russian revolution. The editorial board of the Roseau d'or could

> add a preface along those lines. I would like to explore the question with Plon, and I would be very grateful to you if you could help me do so.

Berdyaev published his *Esprit de Dostoïevski* in 1929 with Éditions Saint-Michel and sent a copy to Maritain on 25 May 1930.

225 Jacques Maritain, "Dialogues" (*Chroniques*, 1928), in *Frontières de la Poésie* (1935); OC V, 745.

226 Vogüé, *Le roman russe*, chapter V, "La religion de la souffrance. Dostoïevski."

227 Maritain, "Dialogues," 745.

228 In a 22 October 1930 letter, Maritain gives some advice to Berdyaev about his relations with the publisher Éditions Saint-Michel: "I've thought about what you said to me yesterday concerning the publisher Saint-Michel. Here is what I advise – say you will give your manuscript to them on the following conditions: 1) the contract shall be signed within eight days; 2) in the contract the publisher shall agree to pay you an indemnity (2000 francs, for example) if the work is not published within six months. They have acted on this matter in a way that is sufficiently bizarre as to warrant you taking certain precautions."

229 F. Dostoïevski, *La légende du Grand Inquisiteur*, translated from the Russian, Introduction Luba Jurgenson (Lausanne: Éditions L'Age d'Homme, 2004), 374; Marchadier, "Berdiaev," 41–2: "It was Berdyaev in particular who made Dostoevsky into the leading Christian thinker, notably through his reflections on the theme of the Grand Inquisitor. This character, imagined by Ivan Karamazov, is not only at the center of Berdyaev's *Esprit de Dostoïevski* (1929) but of his entire philosophy of freedom. Berdyaev would say that his whole life was a fight against the Grand Inquisitor, who had become a stock type among the stock thinkers of Christian inspiration who were fascinated by the opposition between authority and freedom."

230 Marchadier, "Berdiaev," 41.

231 Letter from Berdyaev to Maritain, 25 May 1930: "I am sending you my *Dostoïevski*. Our friendly wishes to you all. Affectionately, N. Berdyaev." Maritain had written to Berdyaev on 14 May 1930: "Do not forget to have a copy of your *Dostoïevski* sent to me."

232 Maritain, "Carnet 1930," *Cahiers Jacques Maritain*, no. 70 (November 2015): 101: "Friday 17 October … Read Berdyaev's *L'Esprit de Dostoïevski*"; on Tuesday, 21 October, Maritain records, "Berdyaev at 4:30 p.m" (102).

233 Klépinine, *Bibliographie*, 16; Pascal, "Les grands courants," 64.

234 Clément, *Berdiaev*, 81.

235 Nicolas Berdiaev, *L'Esprit de Dostoïevski*, trans. Lucienne Julien Cain (Paris: Éditions Saint-Michel, 1929), 7.

236 Ibid., 73.

237 For an analysis of "La légende du Grand Inquisiteur de Dostoïevski comme paradigme critique," see Jean-Marie Gourvil, "État et société dans la pensée

de Berdiaev: Contribution à une réflexion sociétale et spirituelle alternative," in *Colloque Clamart*, 172–86.

238 Berdiaev, *L'Esprit*, 7.

239 Ibid., 223.

240 Ibid., 234–5.

241 Ibid., 236.

242 Ibid., 237. See Clément, *Berdiaev*, 42: "The Metropolitan Filaret Drozdov (1782–1867), a central figure of the Russian Orthodox Episcopate ... reacted against the uprooted spiritualism of the 'Holy Alliance' by relying on the grand tradition of the Fathers, especially Gregory of Nazianzus. He underlines that man is in the image of the Triune God."

243 On Dostoevsky's "Legend of the Grand Inquisitor," Berdyaev notes that "the Grand Inquisitor is full of compassion towards men, he is a democrat and socialist" (*L'Esprit*, 239).

244 Ibid., 270.

245 Letter from Charles Journet to Jacques Maritain, 22 April 1929 (Journet-Maritain *Correspondance* I, 695): "You are very kind to send me these pages of guidance. I have developed an outline of sorts in which I try to respond to Dostoevsky and also to Berdyaev (namely his study on the *Russian religious idea*) but I have still not started writing." Journet specifies in a note that he is referring to Berdyaev's text "L'idée religieuse russe," *Cahiers de la Nouvelle Journée* no. 8 (Paris: Bloud et Gay, 1927), 9–32 (an issue devoted to the Russian soul). In a letter from Journet to Maritain dated 17 January 1930 (Journet-Maritain *Correspondance* II, 33) he writes, "I was able to speak with someone who knows oriental theology well and who, moreover, considers the Khomiakov-Berdyaev-Bulgakov movement as a form of modernism compared to the true Russian tradition."

246 Letter from Maritain to Journet, 29 October 1929 (*Correspondance* I, 730): "Have you read the article by P. Omez on Berdyaev in the *Documents*? I am very eager that you deal with all that!" In a note is the reference for H.-J. Omez of the Russian Seminar in Lille, "L'Église et le problème de l'unité chrétienne d'après M. N. Berdiaev," *Documents de la vie intellectuelle*, no. 1 (20 October 1929). Letter from Journet to Maritain, 8 November 1929 (*Correspondance* I, 732): "I did not like the *Documents*, it is only good for upsetting minds. There are only objections and few replies. The first two articles are typical in that regard. The one by Omez is so insufficient! He has seen the great danger of Berdyaev, but that's all. Because he was Russian, he saw a piece of interesting work to do: show how Berdyaev is on the margin of all that the Russian church has always considered to be the true Church."

247 Letter from Maritain to Berdyaev, 14 May 1930: "Don't forget to send me a copy of your *Dostoïevski*. It would also be good, I think, to send a copy to

Abbé Journet at the Grand Séminaire de Fribourg in Switzerland. He can talk about it in *Nova et Vetera*."

248 Charles Journet, "La Légende du Grand Inquisiteur," *Nova et Vetera* (1932), 77–100.

249 Ibid., 79

250 Ibid., 80.

251 Ibid., 81.

252 Ibid.

253 Henceforth abbreviated to *ED*.

254 Journet, "La légende du Grand Inquisiteur," 83.

255 Ibid., 84: "To these last words of Berdyaev, one must quickly reply that the true Christ would have kept his freedom of spirit even if he had exercised the temporal royalty of the universe, which he radically possessed, since it is a power 'given from on high' (John, XIX:11) and that all power was given to him on earth and in heaven (Matthew, XXVIII:18); and that as soon as one rejects the separatist postulate, there is no essential incompatibility between the notion of saintliness and the notion of political power; and that saints have been kings."

256 Ibid., 85.

257 Ibid., 85–6.

258 Ibid., 87.

259 Ibid., 88.

260 The title is *Court récit sur l'Antéchrist* (A short narrative on the Antichrist).

261 Journet, "La Légende du Grand Inquisiteur," 88.

262 Ibid.

263 Ibid.

264 Ibid., 89.

265 Ibid.

266 Ibid.

267 Ibid.

268 Ibid.

269 Ibid.

270 Ibid., 90–1.

271 Ibid., 91.

272 Ibid.

273 Ibid., 92.

274 Ibid., 93.

275 Ibid. "Saying that all constraint is bad proceeds from imperfect knowledge of human nature which is not pure spirit, but a substantial composition of soul and body, destined for a life in society, and where the soul is profoundly influenced, especially among the weak and among beginners, by pleasure and pain."

276 Ibid.

277 Ibid.
278 Ibid., 94.
279 Ibid., 94–5.
280 Ibid., 95.
281 Letter from Journet to Maritain, 8 February 1932 (*Correspondance* II, 204): "I would be pleased to have Berdyaev's address because in the same issue of *Nova et Vetera* I returned to the question of 'The Legend of the Grand Inquisitor.'"
282 Journet-Maritain *Correspondance* II, 218.
283 Ibid., 221–2.
284 Ibid., 225.
285 Ibid., 230. The discussion continued in a letter from Journet to Maritain dated 28 February 1935: "A) to not confuse the positions of Berdyaev and Dostoevsky. B) Dostoevsky was oriented to a conquering millenarianism where the Church absorbed the State. Berdyaev described what I am calling 'millenarianism' as 'theocratism.' Berdyaev rejects the 'theocratism' of Dostoevsky." Journet-Maritain *Correspondance* II, 444.
286 Charles Journet, *L'Église du Verbe incarné*, Essai de théologie speculative, I. La hiérarchie apostolique (Paris: Desclée de Brouwer, 1941), 564–5n1.
287 Marchadier, "Berdiaev," 45.
288 Berdiaev, *Essai d'autobiographie*, 344–6.
289 Emmanuel Mounier is in Meudon with the Russians on Sunday, 19 December 1928. He would be in Clamart on Tuesday, 16 April 1929. Mounier and Berdyaev probably met in Meudon some time between these two dates. For Bernard Marchadier, Berdyaev met Mounier in Meudon ("Berdiaev," 43).
290 Emmanuel Mounier, *Entretiens: 1926–1944* (Rennes, FR: Presses Universitaires de Rennes, 2017), 88–9: "At Berdiaev's with Maritain, Gabriel Marcel, Du Bos, 16 April 1929."
291 Jacques Maritain – Emmanuel Mounier, *Correspondance 1929–1949* (Paris: Desclée de Brouwer, 2016): "Autour de la naissance d'une revue: février 1931–août 1932," 73–140; "Les débuts d'Esprit: entre complicités et désaccords: septembre 1932–juillet 1933," 141–227.
292 Lurol, "Berdiaev," 105. See *Bulletin des amis d'Emmanuel Mounier*, no. 33. (1969).
293 Maritain-Mounier *Correspondance*, 136. Letter from Maritain to Mounier, 3 August 1932: "I am particularly happy that the publication of Berdyaev's text has been decided. In my view it has great importance, and on many points will immediately 'situate' the journal clearly and correctly. We could not have wished for more with this first issue."
294 Lurol, "Berdiaev," 104.
295 Mounier, *Entretiens*, 525.
296 Letter from Maritain to Berdyaev, 13 April 1932.

297 Letter from Berdyaev to Mounier, 24 February 1948, quoted in Gérard Lurol, "Berdiaev," 105.

298 Marchadier, "Berdiaev," 45: "Mounier gave space to Berdyaev in his *Introduction aux existentialismes* (Paris: Gallimard, 1946), 12, 77, 141, 179."

299 Emmanuel Mounier, "Nicolas Berdiaev, premier humaniste de l'Europe nouvelle," *Combat*, Paris, 26 March 1948, quoted by Gérard Lurol, "Berdiaev," 108.

300 In his presentation of the collection "Les Îles," Jacques Maritain quotes Berdyaev's *Le Christianisme et la lutte des classes* in a note about dialectial materialism (OC V 1077).

301 Maritain, "Carnets de 1932," *Cahiers Jacques Maritain*, no. 74 (November 2017): 61: "Monday 12 September. Phenomenology day in Juvisy. Raïssa comes in the afternoon with Véra. Return with Berdyaev. I am broken."

302 Maritain, "Carnets de 1932," 76.

303 Eugène Dévaud, *La pédagogie scolaire en Russie soviétique* (Paris: Desclée se Brouwer, 1932).

304 Letter from Mgr Michel d'Herbigny to Maritain, November 1932 (Maritain archive, BNU).

305 Maritain and Journet shared their views with each other about Berdyaev's book. Letter from Maritain to Journet, 2 July 1932 (Journet – Maritain *Correspondance* II, 248): "Chapter on 'Questions disputées': I think that in November we could have three beautiful and important studies by Berdyaev on Russian communism and Soviet philosophy. I hope I am not forgetting anything." 19 July 1932, Journet to Maritain, (*Correspondance* II, 252): "OK for … Berdyaev whose studies of communism would, I agree, be of prime importance. We should almost begin from there."

306 Nicolas Berdiaev, *Problème du communisme*, Questions disputées (Paris: Desclée de Brouwer, 1933).

307 Nicolas Berdiaev, "Vérité et mensonge du communisme," *Esprit*, no. 31 (October 1932): 104–28.

308 A letter from Maritain to Berdyaev, 11 October 1932, addresses the progress of Madame Cain's translation because Maritain is "eager to see this volume appear."

309 Chapter 2 of *Problème du communisme* is the French translation of a study published in Russian (Paris: YMCA Press, 1931).

310 "'La ligne générale' de la philosophie soviétique" is the French translation of a study published in *Put'*, no. 34 (July 1932): 1–28.

311 In 1960, in *La philosophie Morale* (OC XI, 680) and specifically in the chapter on Marx, Maritain quotes Berdyaev's *Royaume de l'esprit et royaume de César* (Neuchâtel-Paris: Delachaix et Niestlé, 1951), 82: "Marxism is a philosophy of happiness and not a philosophy of values. With Marxists it is not even possible to speak of a hierarchy of values, because they do not allow posing the

problem of values for themselves. All that exists for them is necessity, utility, and happiness."

312 Letter from Journet to Maritain, 24 March 1933 (*Correspondance* II, 295):

> I received a card from Father Garrigou-Lagrange that surprised me: "From various quarters, I am being told that the journal *Esprit* is deviating." I replied to him that I found more truth than errors in Berdyaev's writing, and that if *Esprit* was deviating it was on account of other texts, and that it was improper to ask this journal to obey an overly severe orthodoxy, and that if Berdyaev defended errors they appeared elsewhere besides in the articles published in *Esprit*. I do not know what Father Garrigou-Lagrange has against Berdyaev: is it his type of spiritual millenarianism? Or the way he speaks about property, offensive for the bourgeois spirit but in close conformity to Saint Thomas? I am saying this to you on account of Berdyaev's book that will appear in "Questions disputées." Let's hope it will be understood.

The *Esprit* articles of Berdyaev in question are "Vérité et mensonge du communisme," *Esprit* (October 1932), 104–28, and "Le Christianisme russe et le monde bourgeois," *Esprit* (March 1933): 933–41. Later, in 1940, the concerns of Father Garrigou-Lagrange were still alive: letter from Garrigou-Lagrange to Journet, 13 March 1940 (Journet–Maritain *Correspondance III*, 54): "I fear that the influence of Mounier and perhaps to some degree that of Berdyaev has moved J. M. away from his first positions that he stood by when we understood each other perfectly." Letter from Journet to Garrigou-Lagrange, 19 March 1940 (58–9): "It is Henri Massis who must be circulating these rumours about the influence of Mounier or Berdyaev on Jacques. All the errors that Mounier might make (while making many profound remarks) or that Berdyaev might make, have to be found in Jacques too. And I know that there are those in Rome who have sworn to make Jacques pay a high price for his non-adherence to a political ideology, condemned with force by Pius XI and since by Pius XII in the encyclical *Summi Pontificatus*."

313 Maritain, "Carnets de 1933," *Cahiers Jacques Maritain*, no. 76 (2018): 69.

314 Letter from Maritain to Simon, 21 March 1935, *Jacques Maritain – Yves Simon Correspondance I, Les années françaises (1927–1940)* (Tours: Éditions CLD, 2008), 205–6.

315 Many passages in Maritain's book are underlined by Berdyaev.

316 RGALI, dossier 1496, unit 605, folios 46 and 47.

317 Jacques Maritain, *Du régime temporal et de la liberté* (1933), OC V, 426. The quotation is in Berdyaev's *Problème du communisme*, 47–8.

318 Maritain, *Du régime*, 426. In Maritain's *L'Homme et L'État*, published after Berdyaev's death, he notes that "men of faith … are the freest for facing up to the faults of their fellow members and to the way in which, in one degree

or another, Christianism, as Berdyaev observed, is ordinarily betrayed by the behavior of Christians" (*L'Homme et L'État*, OC *IX*, 701).

319 Nicolas Berdiaev, *Esprit et Liberté, Essai de philosophie chrétienne*, trans. I.P. and H.M. (Paris: Éditions "Je sers," 1933, original in Russian, Paris: YMCA Press, 1927–28). To specify the perspective of Berdyaev's "essay," we can note that when dealing with the question of Western philosophy, Jacques Maritain observed "that it had never freed itself from Christianity: wherever [Christianity] did not help philosophy construct itself, it was for philosophy a source of scandal. It is in this sense that Nikolai Berdyaev would say that all great modern philosophies (and certainly even that of a Feuerbach) are Christian philosophies – philosophies that without Christianity would not be what they are." *De la philosophie chrétienne*, OC V, 256; this passage is reprinted with slight changes in "About Christian Philosophy," in *The Human Person and the World of Values* (New York: Fordham University Press, 1960); OC XI, 1046.

320 Lurol, "Berdiaev," 108: "During the years 1927–28, Nikolai Berdyaev is immersed in forming his conception of the relations between Being and freedom. His book *Esprit et Liberté* would be published in 1933. His disagreements with Jacques Maritain were often on this issue."

321 Journet–Maritain *Correspondance* II, 644.

322 Ibid., 647.

323 Letter from Maritain to Mounier, *Correspondance*, 240.

324 Maurice de Gandillac, "Lignes de partage et points de convergence," *Esprit*, no. 20 (May 1934): 311–16. Clément, *Berdiaev*, 108: "Almost no properly 'metaphysical' work by Berdyaev was ever reviewed in *Esprit* or elicited a lively reaction. In responding to *Esprit et Liberté*, the only 'theoretical' book by Berdyaev analyzed in the journal, Maurice de Gandilac … sees it in parallel with Maritain's *Degrés du savoir*, which he prefers."

325 De Gandillac, "Lignes," 311–16: "the vocabulary irks them," "the misunderstandings," "strongly opposed philosophical paths," "Berdyaev on the contrary," "we have rarely seen a more distinctive antithesis," "antitheses to this scholastic narrowness that posits God as pure Act," "again the opposition reappears," "Berdyaev opposes on the contrary," "just the opposite … Berdyaev," "at bottom, the misunderstanding is evident," "the positions of enemy brothers," "irreducible misunderstanding."

326 Raymond Bruckberger, "Note sur Nicolas Berdiaev et le catholicisme," accompanied his letter to Jacques Maritain, 10 December 1936: "I am sending you a note about Berdyaev written more than two years ago" (Maritain archive, BNU).

327 Journet, *L'Église*, 151. In several notes (152–4), Journet quotes the passages from *Esprit et Liberté* that illustrate the criticisms he is making about Berdyaev.

328 Clément, *Berdiaev*, 107: "To the very end Berdyaev remained a Russian religious thinker, holding to what he called in his writings from before

the revolution, 'mystical realism' ... Once in France, Berdyaev naively replaced the expression 'mystical realism' with 'existential philosophy,' not thinking that it would be of any consequence. And he was believed. Hence his belated protests, first during the wave of Sartrean existentialism at the end of the Second World War, and then when he was placed within a series of "existentialists," whether Christian or other, notably by Mounier in his *Introduction aux existentialismes*."

329 In his *Pour une philosophie de l'histoire*, Maritain specifies that "the wisdom of history, what Berdyaev called 'historiosophie,' is the focus of Christian theology, but also the concern of Christian moral philosophy" (OC X, 646). Besides history, Maritain also refers to "what Berdyaev called 'meta-history.'" See Jacques Maritain, "La religion et les intellectuels," *Partisan Review* XVII, no. 4 (April 1950): 322–7 (OC IX, 1121–2).

330 Jacques Maritain, *De Bergson à Thomas d'Aquin* (1944) (OC VIII, 25–6). In his preface to Berdyaev's *Sens de la creation* (15), Stanilas Fumet wrote, "Why, one may ask, are Catholics interested in him? It is simple. The spirit of Berdyaev, which I insist is nobility itself, opens passageways through obscurity that make splendid sparkles there where we were used to seeing nothing. And his heart is so forthright that despite making statements that are unacceptable for a Catholic, he gives one a thousand reasons to reaffirm one's faith."

331 Maritain, "Carnet de 1934," *Cahiers Jacques Maritain*, no. 77 (December 2018): 26. Later, in 1944, in *De Bergson à Thomas d'Aquin*, Maritain described Berdyaev as "haunted by the problem of evil" (OC VIII, 26).

332 Maritain, "Carnet de 1934," *Cahiers Jacques Maritain*, no. 77 (December 2018): 59: "Friday 1 June. Yves, Olivier [Lacombe], Becker and Mounier dine. Then Gandillac, Humeau, Touchard, Madaule, Berdyaev. Becker reads his manifesto. It is a bit off."

333 Ibid., 59.

334 Ibid., 77, 71.

335 Ibid., 73. See Arjakovsky (*La génération*, 380), who refers to a meeting in Clamart attended by Raïssa Maritain and her sister Véra Oumansoff on 11 November 1934.

336 Maritain, "Carnets de 1935," *Cahiers Jacques Maritain*, no. 78 (June 2019): 31: Tuesday, 1 January.

337 Ibid., 39: "Wednesday 13 February ... I am going to Paris to see Mgr Paulot, then a friend of Mme Iswolsky at a small Russian-Orthodox-Catholic meeting where the speaker is Mlle Danzaz who spent eight and a half years in prison there – devastating testimony."

338 Maritain, "Carnets de 1935," *Cahiers Jacques Maritain*, no. 78 (June 2019): 41: Thursday, 28 February.

339 Ibid., 53, Wednesday, 8 May.

340 Ibid., 77, Wednesday, 8 October.

341 Jacques Maritain, "Pour la justice et la paix," OC VI, 1040–2.

342 Jacques Maritain, *Art et scholastique* (3rd edition 1935) OC I, 78: "Berdyaev affirms that a perfect classicism, that is, one capable of deriving from nature a completely happy and fulfilling harmony, is impossible after the agony of Christ and the crucifixion. According to him, the classicism of the Renaissance retains unknowingly a Christian wound. I think Berdyaev is right."

343 RGALI, dossier 496-1, unit 606, folio 1.

344 Nicolas Berdiaev, *De la destination de l'homme: Essai d'éthique paradoxale*, trans. I.P. and H.M. (Paris: Éditions "Je sers," 1935). The first edition in Russian was published in 1931; other translations were published in German (1933), English (1937), Spanish (1947), Greek (1950), and Japanese (1966).

345 Maritain, "Carnets de 1935," *Cahiers Jacques Maritain*, no. 78 (Monday, 19 August): 68.

346 Ibid., 69.

347 See RGALI, dossier 1496-1, no. 606, folio 2.

348 *De la destination de l'homme* is one of the books that Raïssa Maritain asked Charles Journet to send to her in New York. In a letter dated 26 August 1940, she asks Journet to send her books by Bloy, Garrigou-Lagrange, Kierkegaard, Grignon de Montfort, J. Maritain, R. Maritain, Pierre Van der Meer, Henri Ghéon, Henri Massis, and N. Berdyaev (Journet – Maritain *Correspondance* III, 117).

349 The annotations are questions ("why?" 51; "how in this theory?" 178; "and Pushkin?" 181) or exclamations ("obviously," 11; "big debt to Saint Thomas here," 11; "and the fallen angels!" 60; "of course!" 221, on the subject of freedom of conscience) or affirmations ("this freedom is good," 73; "there was a social morality in the state of innocence," 255) or negations ("no, it is the model of the revolted one!" 59, on the subject of the devil; "it is not necessary that it be conscious," 101, on the subject of happiness as a conscious aim; "but it was born from Catholicism," 220, on the subject of freedom of moral consciousness; "that is not the ethic of beatitude as understood by Catholics," 231).

350 Maritain, "Journal de 1936," *Cahiers Jacques Maritain*, no. 79 (December 2019): 75–87.

351 Later, in a letter from Raïssa Maritain to Berdyaev dated 29 November 1936, she tells him of her husband's absence because he is in Rome for the Thomist Conference: RGALI, archive not dossier. 1496-1, no. 606, folio 3.

352 Klépinine, *Bibliographie*, 19: "1937 … The Academy of Religious Philosophy was transferred to the Center for Orthodox Action (77 rue de Lourmel) founded by Mother Maria (Skobtsova)."

353 Jacques Maritain, *Humanisme intégral*, chapter II, "Un nouvel humanisme," OC VI, 335–400: I. The roots of atheism; II. The philosophical problem of atheism; III. The cultural significance of Russian atheism. This chapter returns to the content of the article "Deux essais pour un nouvel humanisme" (*Esprit*,

no. 37 [October 1935]: 88–117), the first part of which is titled "The Meaning of Marxist Atheism," 88–101.

354 Jacques Maritain, *Humanisme*, OC VI, 387, note 28: "The excellent little book by Hélène Iswolsky, *L'Homme 1936 en Russie soviétique*, Les Îles (Paris: Desclée de Brouwer, 1936).

355 Ibid. "Cf. Sydney and Beatrice Webb, *Soviet Communism: A New Civilization?* (London and New York, 1936). The good faith of the authors and their care in providing exact information does not save them from a certain naivety that is easily discernable." Also, 389n32: "While furnishing very objective information, though limited to official sources, about the battle against God, the Webbs seriously minimize the scale and significance of antireligious work."

356 Maritain, *Humanisme*, OC VI, 353.

357 Ibid., 370.

358 Ibid., 372.

359 Ibid., 372–3.

360 Ibid., 370.

361 Ibid., 341.

362 Ibid., 336.

363 Ibid., 340.

364 Philippe Chenaux, "Maritain et le communisme soviétique," *Nova et Vetera* (April–June 2012), 157–8.

365 Maritain, *Humanisme*, OC VI, 344. Maritain says he is quoting Berdyaev though he does not indicate the exact reference, which is *Problème du communisme*, Questions disputées (Paris: Desclée de Brouwer,1933), 11.

366 Maritain, *Humanisme*, OC VI, 354.

367 Letter from Raymond Bruckberger to Jacques Maritain, 18 June 1937, Maritain archive (BNU).

368 Nicolas Berdiaev, *Cinq meditations sur l'existence: Solitude, société et communauté*, trans. Irène Vilde-Lot (Paris: Aubier, 1936). The original version was in Russian (Paris: YMCA Press, 1934). See also the English translation by George Reavey (*Solitude and Society*, London: Centenary Press, 1938) and the German translation by Maximilian Braun (*Das Ich und die Welt der Objekte*, Darmstadt: Holle, 1951).

369 Berdiaev, *Cinq meditations*, 19, note 1: "Cf. Jacques Maritain, *Distinguer pour unir ou Les degrés du savoir*. This is the definitive word on modern Thomism."

370 Ibid., 19.

371 Present in Berdyaev's Clamart library are Étienne Gilson, *Le réalisme méthodique* (with many passages underlined) and Étienne Gilson, *Saint Thomas d'Aquin* (with annotations).

372 Raymond Bruckberger, review of Berdyaev's *Cinq méditations* in *Revue thomiste* (1937), 152–6.

373 Letter from Journet to Maritain, 19 March 1937 (Journet – Maritain *Correspondance* II, 644): "One thing causes me much suffering: Berdyaev. I am quite angry about the way he 'liquidated' the *Degrés du Savoir* in his *Cinq méditations*, and with the way he talks about Saint Thomas! Every time it is to impute to him naïve statements. And then there are all the heresies in his major books *Esprit et Liberté* and *Destination de l'homme*. These books could do a lot of harm later. Who knows? Perhaps a decisive influence on a future Russia. I almost regret that you wrote that article about him that we spoke about once." In a note, Journet quotes statements of Berdyaev to the effect that he considered Maritain's philosophy in *Degrés du savoir* as "a particular variety raised to Dogma."

374 Raïssa Maritain, *Journal de Raïssa*, OC XV, 396.

375 Nicolas Berdiaev, *Constantin Léontieff, un penseur religieux russe du dix-neuvième siècle*, trans. Hélène Iswolsky, Les Îles (Paris: Desclée de Brouwer, 1937). Original Russian version published by YMCA Press, 1926.

376 In a letter to Berdyaev dated 17 February 1931, Maritain mentions the Léontieff book "whose translation is not yet finished": "I am quite annoyed by the delay of *Léontieff* … It will be truly bothersome for me if I cannot publish this work in the *Roseau*. However, it is of some material importance that this volume appear quickly, so it is entirely clear that you are free to propose it to another publisher."

377 To justify making this request to Maritain, Berdyaev reminds him that "there were very favourable reviews of Frank's book *La connaissance de l'être* in the *Revue thomiste* (Étienne Borne) and in *Études*." He adds that "in the *Revue de philosophie*, no. 1, 1938, there is a long article about his book." Berdyaev adds other arguments to support the Russian philosopher and concludes: "It really would be great if you wrote a letter to support Frank, a Christian philosopher … I would be very grateful if you are able to do this. We hope to see you some day at our place. Our friendship to you all. Affectionately, N. Berdyaev."

378 Nicolas Berdiaev, *Destin de l'homme dans le monde actuel: Pour comprendre l'homme* (Paris: Stock, 1939). Original Russian version, YMCA Press, 1934. Berdyaev sent Maritain a copy of this book with the inscription, "To my dear friends Jacques and Raïssa Maritain. Affectionately, N. Berdyaev."

379 Nicolas Berdiaev, "Le Christianisme et l'antisémitisme," French translation, *Le Christianisme social*, no. 9 (1939). Original Russian version in *Put'*, no. 56 (May–June 1938): 3–18.

380 Letter from Journet to Maritain, 7 November 1941 (Journet–Maritain *Correspondance* III, 226): "I would really like to steal from you for my editorial in *Nova*." Journet's editorial in *Nova et Vetera* (July–September 1941, 225–31) quotes a text from Maurice Samuel, a Jew, that also appears in Maritain's article "On Anti-Semitism," *Christianity and Crisis*, 6 October 1941.

381 Charles Journet, "Antisémitisme," *Nova et Vetera*, no. 3 (July–September 1941): 228.

382 Jacques Maritain, "Avant-Propos [Foreword] au livre d'Hélène Iswolsky, *Light before Dark*" (1942), OC VII, 1316–17.

383 Nicolas Berdiaev, *Les sources et le sens du communisme russe*, trans. Alexis Nerville (Paris: Gallimard, 1938; Paris: YMCA Press, 1955).

384 Journet - Maritain *Correspondance* III, 180.

385 Letter from Maritain to Journet, 28 December 1944 (Journet - Maritain *Correspondance* III, 305): "Saw Berdyaev, so moving in his poverty and solitary work."

386 Letter from Journet to Maritain, 9 August 1945 (Journet - Maritain *Correspondance* III, 335): "I was to transmit to you messages from Berdyaev who telephoned the other day to M.-M. Davy where I happened to be and to whom I said I hoped to see you: he asked me if Raïssa had joined you." Davy was a historian of medieval mysticism and a biographer of Berdyaev.

387 Marie-Madeleine Davy, *Nicolas Berdiaev, l'homme du huitième jour* (Paris: Flammarion, 1964; Éditions Félin, 1991, 75): "During the war a friend whose husband is said to be ambassador at the Holy See regularly gave me tea and sweets for Nikolai Berdyaev, whose life at that time was rather difficult. He received an occasional package from America."

388 Vladimir Jankélévitch, the son of Samuel Jankélévitch, sent Berdyaev his book, *La Mauvaise Conscience* (Paris: Librairie Félix Alcan, 1939) with a dedication, "For Mr. Nikolai Berdyaev, with sincere and deep sympathy, Vl Jankélévitch, 1 quai des fleurs."

389 Iswolsky, *Au temps*, 181–2; Clément, *Berdiaev*, 231. The Maritain archive of the BNU contains roughly ten letters from "Eugraph Kovalevsky" to Jacques Maritain.

390 Maritain, *Carnet de notes*, OC XII, 351: "Can one imagine a Dostoevsky, a Léon Bloy, a Péguy or a Bernanos organized into a work community? It is surely difficult to conceive of … It seems that certain poets and great writers are like voices through whom a type of prophetic sense at work in the faithful is made manifest in the world and that Berdyaev was deeply attuned to this."

391 Maritain, *Carnet de notes*, OC XII, 351.

Correspondence between Jacques and Raïssa Maritain and Nikolai Berdyaev

Edited by Bernard Hubert

No. 1, Letter from Jacques Maritain to Nikolai Berdyaev
(RGALI, dossier 1496, unit 605, folio no. 74)
+Pax
Meudon, 10 rue du Parc, 4 March 1925
Dear Monsieur,
My wife and I would be very pleased to come see you in Clamart. Would you and Madame Berdyaev be free next Tuesday around 4 o'clock? That day would be convenient for us.

My wife has begun to read and translate out loud for me your book about the new Middle Ages.[1] It is a great comfort and lively pleasure for me to see

The letters of Nikolai Berdyaev to the Maritains are kept in the Fonds Maritain at the BNU of Strasbourg and published in accord with the Cercle d'études Jacques et Raïssa Maritain. The letters from Jacques and Raïssa Maritain are kept in the "Russian State Archive of Literature and Art" in Moscow (RGALI, dossier 1496, unit 605 for the letters from Jacques Maritain to Nikolai Berdyaev, and unit 606 for the letters from Raïssa Maritain to Nikolai Berdyaev). These letters from the Maritains to Berdyaev are published with the permission of the Russian State Archive of Literature and Art and for each one, the folio number is indicated.

1 Nikolai Berdyaev's *Un Nouveau Moyen Âge* was published in Russian in Berlin in 1924. Maritain would learn of Aniouta Fumet's French translation in August

how on so many essential points, and especially the criticism of the "modern" world, our ways of thinking converge. I would have liked to offer you a copy of my book *Théonas* in which I develop ideas about Progress and Revolution that are similar to your own, but unfortunately it is out of print.[2] In this envelope you'll find an offprint of "Saint Thomas, Apostle of Modern Times,"[3] which I hope you will like.

Pass along our respectful regards to Madame Berdyaev, and rest assured, dear Sir, of my cordial and sincere sympathy in Xto JESU.
Jacq Maritain

No. 2, Postcard from Jacques and Raïssa Maritain to Nikolai and Lydia Berdyaev (RGALI, dossier 1496, unit 605)
18 [summer[4]] 1925
We are thinking of you affectionately.
Jacq and Raïssa Maritain

No. 3, Letter from Nikolai Berdyaev to Jacques Maritain (BNU, Fonds Maritain)
Clamart, 5 October [1925]
Dear Monsieur and friend!
We have been back in Clamart for a few weeks now and would like to see you. Would it suit you if we came to your place this Sunday (11 October) around 4 o'clock?

I await your reply.
Devotedly,
N. Berdyaev

1926. (cf. Infra Letter from Jacques Maritain to Nikolai Berdyaev, 9 August 1926) before its publication in 1927 by Plon in the collection le Roseau d'or.

2 Jacques Maritain, *Théonas, ou les entretiens d'un sage et de deux philosophes sur diverses matières inégalement actuelles*, Bibliothèque Française de Philosophie, no. 1 (Paris: Nouvelle Librairie Nationale, 2nd ed., 1921).

3 Jacques Maritain, "Saint Thomas apôtre des temps modernes," *Revue des jeunes* 14e année, vol. 39, no. 5 (10–25 March 1924): 461–505.

4 Postcard with unreadable postage stamp, addressed to Monsieur et Madame N. Berdiaev, 2 rue Martial Grandchamp, Clamart, Seine.

No. 4, Letter from Jacques Maritain to Nikolai Berdyaev
(RGALI, dossier 1496, unit 605, folio no. 26)
+Pax
Meudon, 10 rue du Parc, 7 October [1925[5]]
Dear Monsieur and friend,
A group of six young people are coming Sunday afternoon, and I cannot refuse to see them because they are only available this Sunday! I fear that with so many youths here we shall not have the luxury of speaking peacefully together. Perhaps, if you are free, it would be better if you could come the following Sunday? Do what suits you best, and rest assured, I beg you, of my affectionate devotion.
Jaq Maritain
[PS:] My respects to Madame Berdyaev

No. 5, Postcard from Nikolai Berdyaev to Jacques Maritain
(BNU, Fonds Maritain)
Clamart, 9 October [1925]
Dear Monsieur and friend!
Agreed. We will come to your place next Sunday (18 October) around 4 o'clock.
With affectionate devotion,
N. Berdyaev

No. 6, Letter from Jacques Maritain to Nikolai Berdyaev
(RGALI, dossier 1496, unit 605, folio no. 5)
+Pax
Meudon, 10 rue du Parc, Monday morning [19 October 1925[6]]
Dear Monsieur and friend,

5 The mention of the year is missing, but the phrases "cher Monsieur et ami" and "votre affectueusement dévoué" are really present in their correspondence. Nikolai Berdyaev's answer on 9 October is confirmation.

6 The date and year are missing, but the greeting "Cher Monsieur et ami" only occurs at the start of their correspondence in 1925 and 1926. The Monday morning in question follows a meeting, probably on Sunday, 18 October 1925. The date of Ghéon's show is also an indication.

I fear I overestimated my capacities when I answered you yesterday. With all my responsibilities, and the unpredictable nature of our lives, I think it will be rather difficult for me to attend *all* of your meetings.[7] Perhaps one solution would be to find a second philosopher whose thinking is similar to mine, such that he could be present at the meetings when I am unable to come? We can speak about that at our next interview, next Friday or the following Thursday.

Yesterday we forgot to give you the tickets to the next performance of Ghéon.[8] I enclose them with this letter.

Our best regards to Madame Berdyaev and you, dear Monsieur and friend.
Very affectionately,
Jaq Maritain

No. 7, Card from Nikolai Berdyaev to Jacques Maritain (BNU, Fonds Maritain)
Clamart, 23 November 1925
Dear Monsieur and friend!
I need to see you and talk over something that is rather urgent. Could you set a day and time for a meeting that will not take long? I would be able to come to your home on Saturday (28 November) in the morning or afternoon, and also Sunday (29 November) around 4 o'clock, if on that day you could give me thirty minutes of your time to talk.

Salutations to Madame Maritain
Cordially,
N. Berdyaev

---

7 These were monthly interfaith meetings on Thursdays uniting Protestants, Orthodox, and Catholics. They were organized by Lev Zander and Nikolai Berdyaev from 1926 to 1929 and took place in the Russian students' house in Paris, first on the rue Dupuytren, then starting in 1928 on the Boulevard Montparnasse. See Michel Fourcade, "De Soloviev à Boulgakov," *Contacts* April–June 2012, 133–4; and Fourcade, *Feu la modernité? Maritain et les maritainismes*, vol. 1, Antimodernes, ultramodernes (1906–1926) (Nancy, FR: Éditions Arbre Bleu, 2021), 422–4.

8 Henri Vangeon (1875–1944), alias Henri Ghéon, converted to Catholicism during World War I. He wrote many plays, including one on the life of Saint Genès, *Le comédien et la grâce*, that was published by Plon in the Roseau d'or no. 2 in 1925.

No. 8, Letter from Jacques Maritain to Nikolai Berdyaev
(RGALI, dossier 1496, unit 605, folio no. 28)
+Pax
Meudon, 10 rue du Parc, 25 November 1925
Dear Monsieur and friend,
Saturday, I have a class at the Institut Catholique and I have a lunch engagement in Paris. (It is true that I do not know if I will be able to go, as I have been rather sick these past days.) Therefore, if it does not bother you to come Sunday (29 November) in the afternoon, that would be better. On that day I will certainly be able to give you all the time we need for our conversation.

See you soon, dear Monsieur and friend, and rest assured of my cordial affection in Xto JESU.

Our best regards to Madame Berdyaev.
Jaq Maritain

No. 9, Letter from Jacques Maritain to Nikolai Berdyaev
(RGALI, dossier 1496, unit 605, folio no. 1A)
+Pax
Meudon, 10 rue du Parc, 4 January 1926
Dear Monsieur and friend,
Our best wishes to Madame Berdyaev and you for the new year. I've taken up recruiting some friends for our monthly Thursday meetings.[9]

Those who are able to come: my wife, who will be happy to accompany me when her health allows it; Stanislas Fumet;[10] Rev. Father Gillet, a Dominican and theology instructor;[11] Abbé Beaussart[12] who, though not a

---

9 Interfaith meetings.

10 Stanislas Fumet (1896–1983) was a writer, art critic, editor, and publisher. He was a close associate of Jacques Maritain, and they codirected the Roseau d'or series. His wife Aniouta Fumet, being of Russian origin, translated Berdyaev's *Un nouveau Moyen Âge* (1927) into French.

11 Martin Stanislas Gillet (1875–1951) was a member of the Dominican Ordre des Prêcheurs and held doctorates in philosophy and theology. He was the leader of the Dominican Order from 1929 to 1946.

12 Roger Beaussart (1879–1952) was a priest at the Collège Stanislas in Paris and its director from 1928 to 1932. He was auxiliary bishop of Paris from 1932 to 1945. Abbé Beaussart would not be invited because some wished to limit the

specialist, pays close attention to philosophical questions; Madame Noële Denis-Boulet (daughter of the painter Maurice Denis), a former student of mine with a doctorate in philosophy and a very good Thomist.

I would also like it if Roland Dalbiez,[13] whom you know already (a professeur agrégé at the Laval high school), could attend these meetings. Unfortunately, however, I do not think he will be free this year.

I am sending the addresses to Monsieur Kullmann.[14]

My respectful salutations to Madame Berdyaev. Rest assured, Monsieur and friend, of my sympathetic devotion.

Jaq Maritain

[Two cards:] 1) an image of Sainte Thérèse de l'Enfant Jésus and the First Communion, 2) a reproduction of a painting of Simone Martini, *S. Martino vede in sogno Gesù Cristo* in the Lower Church of the Basilica of Saint Francis of Assisi (Umbria).

No. 10, Letter from Jacques Maritain to Nikolai Berdyaev
(RGALI, dossier 1496, unit 605, folio no. 3)
+Pax
Meudon, 10 rue du Parc, Easter Tuesday, 6 March 1926
My dear friend,

I am returning your manuscript[15] so that you can look over the corrections (in red ink) that I propose. Generally, they only concern matters of form and style. On three or four points, however, I thought it necessary to explain and specify further the ideas presented. I tried to do so while remaining

---

number of Thomists, as Suzanne de Dietrich explains to Berdyaev in a letter from 24 November 1925 (see Fourcade, *Feu la modernité?*, Tome 1, 422–3.)

13 Rolland Dalbiez (1893–1976) was a navy officer during World War I. He later obtained the *agrégation* in philosophy, was close to Maritain, and became a critic of the works of Sigmund Freud.

14 Gustave Gérard Kullmann (1894–1961) was a lawyer and secretary of the YMCA that assisted Orthodox Russians in exile.

15 The manuscript in question is the one for Berdyaev's article "Le destin de la culture" that was published in the second volume of le Roseau d'or (Paris: Plon, 1926), 73–100.

faithful to your line of thought. I hope I have succeeded, but I prefer that you judge for yourself if all is well here. The points are as follows:

At the very beginning, on page one, a note about the words *culture* and *civilization*.

Page 5. An explanation of the meaning you give to the word "symbolic." This is very important for French readers who otherwise might believe that you are a defender of "religious symbolism" in the modernist sense.

Page 6. I added "in some respects" regarding the seventeenth century. (Because from the point of view of political power, that century was a high point for France.)

Page 12. Don't you think the word *sacrifice* conveys your thought better than *résignation*, which in French has a rather weak and passive connotation?

Page 18. I added "par la disposition de la Providence" so that one does not think that for you Christianity is a matter of pure historical determinism. I also added some details regarding the word "symbolique" – again so as to avoid a confusion with modernism.

Finally, there's the question of the title. "La culture, la civilization et la transfiguration religieuse" strikes me as rather heavy. I offer you two simpler alternatives: "La sagesse de l'histoire" or "Philosophie de la culture." Let me know what you think.

I wrote a long letter to Monsignor Chaptal[16] after seeing you at the Driesch dinner.[17] Here is his reply that I received this morning.[18]

My best regards to Madame Berdyaev and affectionately to you my dear friend.

Jaq Maritain

[PS:] Kindly return your manuscript to me *as soon as possible.*

---

16 Monsignor Emmanuel Chaptal de Chanteloup (1861–1943) was named auxiliary bishop of Paris and known as "the foreigners' bishop" (*évêque des étrangers*).

17 Hans Driesch (1867–1941) was a German biologist and philosopher with whom Maritain studied at Heidelberg from August 1906 to June 1908. In 1927, on the occasion of Driesch's sixtieth birthday, Maritain prepared a short text for a volume in his honour under the title "Hans Driesch restaurateur de la philosophie de la nature," *Oeuvres complètes*, vol. 3, 1334–5.

18 Monsignor Chaptal's letter has not been found.

[On an attached card (RGALI, dossier 1496, unit 605, folio 4):] Title: "La sagesse de l'histoire au point de vue de la pensée russe" [The wisdom of history from the point of view of Russian thinking] or "Philosophie de la culture" [Philosophy of culture].

No. 11, Letter from Jacques Maritain to Nikolai Berdyaev
(RGALI, dossier 1496, unit 605, folio no. 6)
+Pax
St. Jorioz, Haute Savoie, 9 August 1926
My dear friend,
I am as sorry as you about what you have expressed to me about the translation of your book.[19] I think the best thing would be to write to Fumet to say that you find the translation faithful but too literal, and that you believe a total reworking is necessary to make the French, in style and substance, an equivalent of the Russian text. Therefore, either Stanislas Fumet must himself take on the task of rewriting the whole thing, while using the existing translation as a foundation, or, if he does not have the time, the work must be handed over to someone else who would sign the translation along with Madame Fumet. (It is not necessary that this other person know Russian, it is more important that they be familiar with philosophical vocabulary.)

If you prefer, I can say this to Fumet myself in a letter.

But in any case, I think it would be best if I did so before reading the work itself, and in that way reduce the chance of upsetting Madame Fumet who devoted herself so entirely to this translation (and who, moreover, I believe deliberately crafted a literal translation).

So do not send the manuscript here, but do let me know if you approve of my writing to Fumet. You can also lay this all out to him directly and add that you've written to me and that we're in agreement.

19 *Un Nouveau Moyen Âge*, translated from Russian into French by Aniouta Fumet.

I hope the waters at Contents were beneficial and that you were able to rest. We are returning around the 15th or 20th of September (in Meudon, Father Garrigou's retirement begins on the 24th).[20]

Our friendly regards to Madame Berdyaev and to you.

Affectionately,
Jaq Maritain

No. 12, Card from Jacques Maritain to Nikolai Berdyaev
(RGALI, dossier 1496, unit 605, folio no. 7)
+Pax
Meudon, 2 November 1926[21]
My dear friend,
For several days I have been immersed in the translation of your book that I am now rereading carefully. I am taking the time to offer some corrections of style that will make for smoother reading in French. I am also proposing some indentations because reading a mass of several pages without divisions into distinct paragraphs would be very arduous in the French context. This work is unfortunately taking longer than I expected, and yet we must get the manuscript to the printer as soon as possible since we have already lost a lot of time. Would you like me to come see you in Clamart some afternoon as soon as I have finished? Or do you prefer to look it all over once it has been typeset?

In any case I would be happy to see you. I hope you are well. I recently saw a Jesuit priest, Father Vassili Bourgeois[22] who took the Orthodox rites out of love for Russia and recently returned from the Orient. He will be in Paris for a few months. He would very much like to meet you. He strikes me as quite remarkable. If you think it a proper moment, you could perhaps invite him to the rue Dupuytren meetings (if they are expected to continue

20 Réginald Garrigou-Lagrange (1877–1964), theologian and professor at the Angelicum in Rome.

21 A letter with envelope and postage stamp dated "3 nov. 26."

22 Charles Bourgeois (1887–1963) was a Jesuit who lived many years in Estonia and went by the name Father Vassili.

this year). I did not want to mention them to him without speaking to you first. Our best regards to Madame Berdyaev.
Affectionately,
Jaq Maritain

No. 13, Card from Jacques Maritain to Nikolai Berdyaev
(RGALI, dossier 1496, unit 605, folio no. 8)
+Pax
Meudon, Saturday [6 November 1926][23]
My dear friend,
Did you receive my last letter? I would like to see you briefly before handing over the translation of your book, which I just finished reading, to the printer. I made some stylistic changes that I would like to go over with you. Your study is of great importance, and I would like it to appear in a French version that is as readable and as striking as possible.

Our kind regards to Madame Berdyaev.
Affectionately,
Jaq Maritain
[PS:] I just received your letter. Agreed for Wednesday. I will be at your place at 4 o'clock.

No. 14, Letter-card from Jacques Maritain to Nikolai Berdyaev
(RGALI, dossier 1496, unit 605, folio no. 9)
+Pax
Paris, Saturday evening [27 November 1926][24]
Dear friend,
I was very upset about having to leave before the end of the discussion, but I had an appointment (made several days earlier) at 6:30 and I could not stay any later than 7 o'clock!

My warmest congratulations for your rich presentation that was so intelligent, so full of historical sense, and such a powerful synthesis. I was

---

23 The envelope has a postage stamp dated "7 nov. 26."

24 The postage stamp on the card is dated "27-11-26."

embarrassed by the unfortunate objections of Langene,[25] who may be a great doctor but knows nothing about philosophy. I wanted to intervene, but he would not stop talking, and then came your peremptory replies, and I would not have been able to stay as calm as you.

My respectful salutations to Madame Berdyaev.
Rest assured of my admiration and devoted friendship.
Jaq Maritain

No. 15, Postcard[26] from Jacques Maritain to Nikolai Berdyaev
(RGALI, dossier 1496, unit 605, folio no. 10)
18 December 1926
My dear friend,
Pardon me for not coming to the meeting last Thursday.[27] My flu which had made me very sick was over and I hoped to be able to go to Paris. But at the last minute I felt so tired that I feared a relapse, and so with some remorse I decided to stay home. It was too late to alert you. Again, please excuse me and rest assured of my loyal friendship. Our best regards to Madame Berdyaev.
Jaq Maritain

No. 16, Card from Jacques Maritain to Nikolai Berdyaev
(RGALI, dossier 1496, unit 605, folio no. 11)
+Pax
Meudon, 10 rue du Parc, 11 January 1927
My dear friend,
We have been forced to suspend our Sunday meetings due to my state of fatigue, which will also oblige me to go away at the end of the month, and next Sunday we have a meeting with a friend whom we must go see at 4 o'clock. But if you can come by at around 2, that would be fine, unless you prefer to

25 Cornelis Douwe de Langene (1887–1967).

26 Picture postcard of a neighborhood of Meudon-Val-Fleury. The postage stamp is dated "18 décembre 1926."

27 Interfaith meeting of Thursday, 9 or 16 December 1926.

come instead on Tuesday at 3 (we have to go out at 5 that day). Please be so kind as to let me know your chosen day.

In any case I count on seeing you at the meeting on the 20th.[28]

Our best wishes for the new year to you and your family.

Our respectful salutations to Madame Berdyaev.

Cordially,
Jaq Maritain
[PS:] Could I ask you to please invite to the meeting on Thursday the 20th the following two friends: 1) Louis Massignon,[29] 21 rue Monsieur; 2) Nikolai Nabokov,[30] 3 rue de l'Estrapade. Thanks.

No. 17, Card from Jacques Maritain to Nikolai Berdyaev[31]
(RGALI, dossier 1496, unit 605, folio no. 13)
+Pax
Oosterhout, 6 February 1927
My dear friend,
I'm rather bothered by the difficulty of selecting a title for my introduction.[32] I still think the best would be *La nature créée dans ses relations avec Dieu* [Created nature in its relations with God]. What do you think? My respectful salutations to Madame Berdyaev.
Affectionately,
Jaq Maritain

28 Interfaith meeting of Thursday, 20 January 1927

29 Louis Massignon (1883–1962), an Orientalist and professor at the Collège de France from 1926 to 1954.

30 Nikolai Nabokov (1903–1978), a Russian émigré in France, composer, musicologist, and writer.

31 Picture postcard of St Paul's Abbey, Oosterhout (Netherlands). The postage stamp is dated "8, II, 1927."

32 The introductory remarks to open the discussion at an interfaith meeting in February 1927.

No. 18, Card from Jacques Maritain to Nikolai Berdyaev
(RGALI, dossier 1496, unit 605, folio no. 14)
+Pax
Meudon, 17 March 1927
My dear friend,
Thank you for your kind letter. We'll be happy to come to Clamart next Tuesday 22 March around 4:30. Our best regards to Madame Berdyaev.
Affectionately,
Jaq Maritain

No. 19, Letter from Jacques Maritain to Nikolai Berdyaev
(RGALI, dossier 1496, unit 605, folio no. 12)
+Pax
Meudon, 24 April 1927
My dear friend,
Monsieur Florovsky[33] must do the introduction. He was supposed to write you, I do not understand why you have received no word. Given my faulty memory, I fear giving you inexact information. I seem to recall that the date set was Thursday 5 May, because of M. Florovsky being absent during the Easter break (yes, that was definitely the date chosen). As for the subject, I do not recall the exact words, I only remember that it was about the creation. Perhaps you could use "*L'idée de la creation et la conception orthodoxe*," though the formulation that M. Florovsky gave me orally was more explicit. Maybe Monsieur Kartashev[34] remembers better than I? I did not think to write it down because I was expecting M. Florovsky to write you as he told me he would.

I hope you had a good journey. We wish you very pleasant Easter holidays. Our best regards to Madame Berdyaev and her sister.
Affectionately yours,
J. M.

---

33 George Florovsky (1893–1979) was a Russian Orthodox theologian and professor at the Institut Saint-Serge in Paris, and later at Saint Vladimir's Orthodox Theological Seminary in New York.

34 Anton Kartashev, a professor at the Institut Saint-Serge.

[PS:] I would have so liked to see you before your next departure. But I am completely overwhelmed and will not have a free moment this entire week. Have you read the two long articles on *Nouveau Moyen Âge* by M.F. Deschamps[35] in the Brussels publication *Revue catholique des Idées et des Faits*? Your book is being enthusiastically received in Belgium.

No. 20, Letter from Jacques Maritain to Nikolai Berdyaev
(RGALI, dossier 1496, unit 605, folio no. 29)
+Pax
Meudon, Wednesday 30 November [1927[36]]
My dear friend,
Agreed for Wednesday 7 December. We will arrive around 5 o'clock. It will be a joy to see you again – before your departure, which is approaching too soon![37]
Our friendship to you all.
Affectionately,
Jaq Maritain

No. 21, Letter from Nikolai Berdyaev to Jacques Maritain
(BNU, Fonds Maritain)
Clamart (Seine), 2 rue Martial Grandchamp, 22 February 1928
My dear friend!
Gabriel Marcel[38] wrote me to say that you spoke of the possibility of publishing my book on Dostoevsky in the "Roseau d'or," and that he considers the publisher Plon to be the best solution. But it is important to know if this book suits

35 Fernand Deschamps (1868–1957), a Belgian philosopher and sociologist.

36 The year does not appear on the letter, but there was a Wednesday, 30 November and Wednesday, 7 December in 1927. At this time Maritain's letters begin "Bien cher ami" (My dear friend).

37 Between 17–21 December 1927, Jacques Maritain gave a series of four lectures in Berlin, Cologne, and Bonn. See Journet-Maritain *Correspondance, Volume 1, 1920–1929*, published by the Foundation of Cardinal Journet (Fribourg, CH: Éditions universitaires) and (Paris: Éditions Saint-Paul, 1996), 526, note 4.

38 Gabriel Marcel (1889–1973) was a Christian existentialist philosopher, writer, dramaturge, and literary critic.

you. It is likely that you will not agree with many of my ideas. But perhaps on principle the "Roseau d'or" could publish a book which is very representative of Russian religious thinking and that might even aid in understanding the idea of the Russian revolution. The editorial board of the "Roseau d'or" could add a preface along those lines. I would like to explore the question with Plon and I would be very grateful to you if you could help me do so.[39] I hope to see you Monday at the interfaith meeting and we can speak further.
Our friendship to you all.
With great sympathy,
N. Berdyaev

No. 22, Letter from Jacques Maritain to Nikolai Berdyaev
(RGALI, dossier 1496, unit 605, folios no. 15 and 16)
+Pax
Meudon, 5 March 1928
My dear friend,
I am writing to you about our interfaith meetings. I must tell you frankly that I am personally incapable of continuing to put up with the interventions of Father Laberthonnière.[40] They create an abnormal, completely intolerable atmosphere. The respect that I owe the person and priest pre-

39 Berdyaev's book on Dostoevsky was not published in the Roseau d'or collection. In a letter to Gabriel Marcel dated 29 February 1928, Maritain writes, "I have just seen Monsieur Berdyaev and we spoke about the translation of his Dostoevsky book. It is a work that on many counts I would have liked to be able to publish in the Roseau d'or. However, upon reflection, we need to let the idea go because the Roseau d'or, though not exactly without a 'denominational' character, probably has an overly marked intellectual and doctrinal orientation such that the book's publication in this collection would necessarily provoke misunderstandings. I am sending you this letter to keep you informed and in the hope that you will be able to make room for this remarkable work in your collection. I ask you, cher Monsieur, to receive my sincere good wishes." At the time, Gabriel Marcel had recently launched the series Feux-croisés – Âmes et terres étrangères (Crossed fires – Foreign souls and lands) with the publisher Plon, but the Dostoevsky book would eventually be published by Éditions Saint-Michel in 1929. (I thank Michel Fourcade for alerting me to this letter from Maritain to Gabriel Marcel, as well as Claude Lorentz, the head librarian at the BNU, for sharing it with me.)

40 Lucien Laberthonnière (1860–1932) was a modernist philosopher and theologian.

vents me from describing the theories which he defends in the terms they deserve. There is a higher question regarding what we owe to holy truths, which a priest is not permitted to consider simply as he wishes. Life is too short for me to add to ordinary pains the burden of hearing the dogmatic statements of modernism (and of liberal Protestantism).

I am prepared to collaborate actively and with all my heart on anything you might organize between the Orthodox and Catholics, because, however opposed they might be on many points, they at least have a common veneration for the revealed deposit and the holy truths of Faith. Then we can collaborate and do useful work. With the modernists and the Protestants (with the exception of Father Lecerf[41]) it is completely impossible, as experience has made abundantly clear, it seems to me. I understand that it is difficult for you to organize the meetings differently. I therefore ask you to allow me to withdraw from these meetings in their current form, unless I could bring in some theologians who would have the ability to point out, as necessary, the errors of Laberthonnière (I will attend to that in the next days). I am sure, my dear friend, that you understand my reasons.

My respectful salutations to Madame Berdyaev.

Affectionately,
Jaq Maritain
[PS:] I have written to Gabriel Marcel as we agreed. Could you perhaps come to Meudon on Sunday 18 March around 4 o'clock?

No. 23, Letter from Nikolai Berdyaev to Jacques Maritain
(BNU, Fonds Maritain)
Clamart (Seine), 14 rue de Saint-Cloud, 3 July 1928
My dear friend!
We would very much like to see you at our new house. Could you all come to our place on Monday (9 July), Tuesday (10 July), or Thursday (12 July)

41 Auguste Lecerf (1872–1943) was a Protestant minister, Calvin specialist, and professor of dogmatics at the Faculté de théologie protestante.

around 4:30? The best would be Tuesday. On the fifteenth I am going away for one week. I await your reply.[42]

With friendly regards and thanks for the book by Léon Bloy.[43]

Cordially,

N. Berdyaev

No. 24, Letter from Jacques Maritain to Nikolai Berdyaev

(RGALI, dossier 1496, unit 605, folio no. 17)

+Pax

Meudon, 28 November 1928

My dear friend,

For the meetings we have spoken about, I have already secured the participation of Charles Du Bos,[44] Abbé Altermann,[45] and Jean de Menasce.[46] Bremond[47] will not be in Paris until the spring. Massignon is in Syria and will return in three weeks, I believe. The best day for all those I have contacted would be Tuesday afternoon. Does that suit you also? They also say that it would be more convenient for them if the meetings could take place in Paris. Perhaps we could find a friend who would loan us the use of their apartment?

---

42 In his daily planner "Carnet 1928," published in *Cahiers Jacques Maritain*, no. 68 (June 2014): 17, Maritain notes for Wednesday, 25 July, "4 p.m., visit at the Berdiaev home in Clamart."

43 The reference is probably to Léon Bloy's *Lettres à ses filleuls* (Paris: Librarie Stock, 1928), which includes a preface by Maritain.

44 Charles Du Bos (1882–1939) was a literary critic who converted to Catholicism. Near the end of his career, he taught in the United States at the University of Notre Dame.

45 Jean-Pierre Altermann (1892–1959) was a Jewish convert to Catholicism. He was a priest of the Paris diocese and assigned to the foreigners' church. He founded the Maison d'Ananie and co-founded the review *Vigile*.

46 Jean de Menasce (1902–1973), of Egyptian origin, an Orientalist as well as a theologian, became a member of the Ordre des prêcheurs and was ordained in 1934.

47 Henry Bremond (1865–1933) was a priest, literary critic, and historian of religious feeling.

We were very happy to see you the other day. Our affection to you all. Rest assured of my devotion.
Jaq Maritain

No. 25, Letter from Jacques Maritain to Nikolai Berdyaev
(RGALI, dossier 1496, unit 605, folio no. 18)
+Pax
Meudon, 10 rue du Parc, 19 December 1928
My dear friend,
Please excuse my late reply to you. I have been exceedingly tired for the past while and unable to stay current with my correspondence.

Yes, for the meetings at your place, I think it would be advantageous to invite Gilson.[48] Fumet and Dermenghen[49] are obvious. I inform you that not far from your place (93bis route de Clamart in Issy) lives my colleague, Abbé Simeterre,[50] a professor of the history of ancient philosophy at the Institut Catholique. I believe he would find these meetings very interesting if his health allows him to attend. He is very learned and wonderful to speak with.

As for the location, it would probably be best to try first at our place. We'll see if the Parisians find it too difficult to get here. If so, we could perhaps meet in the home of Massignon (who just got back) or else in the home of a friend who would lend us their apartment.

For the other meetings in the Boulevard Montparnasse, I think your idea of three lectures on the nature of the church is very good. We need

48 Étienne Gilson (1884–1978) was a philosophy professor who held the chair in medieval philosophy at the Collège de France from 1932 to 1950 and became a member of the Académie française in 1946.

49 Émile Dermenghen (1892–1971) studied at the École de Chartres and became a journalist and writer. He published several works, notably *La vie admirable et les révélations de Marie des Vallées*, le Roseau d'or (Paris: Plon, 1926), and *La vie de Mahomet* (Paris: Plon, 1929).

50 Abbé Raymond Simeterre (1877–1947) joined the faculty of the Institut Catholique in 1908. In 1921 he was appointed full professor of ancient and medieval philosophy at the Institut Catholique of Paris, where he also served as dean from 1943 to 1946.

only to find a Catholic speaker. If Father Lebreton[51] could do it that would be great. Otherwise, you could ask Father Lathoud.[52] I do not know him myself, but he is interested in the union of the churches, and I am told he is very pleasant. And there is also Abbé Journet.[53] He could come directly from Geneva and would certainly give an excellent lecture (I consider him one of the best theologians of the day). Finally, if you prefer a lay person, you could consider a young *agrégé* among my friends, Olivier Lacombe,[54] who is studying the question at the moment (though it might be improper to turn to such a young lecturer with so little experience).

When you have made a decision, let me know. I probably ought to write to Monsignor Chaptal if we want a priest as lecturer and a sufficiently large Catholic audience. Regarding the audience, I'll furnish you with a list of twenty-five people to invite.

Our friendship to you all.

Affectionately,
Jaq Maritain
[PS:] Lacombe could also be invited to our Clamart meetings.

No. 26, Letter from Nikolai Berdyaev to Jacques Maritain
(BNU, Fonds Maritain)
Clamart (Seine), 14 rue de Saint-Cloud, 27 December [1928]
My dear friend!

---

51 Father Jules Lebreton (1873–1956) was a Jesuit theologian. In 1907 he became chair of the History of Christianity at the Institut Catholique of Paris.

52 Father David Lathoud (1892–1958) was an Assumptionist (a controversial association of priests and brothers that was dedicated to missionary activity and social welfare; they were accused of being royalist and antisemitic). He contributed to the publications *Échos d'Orient*, *Union des Églises*, *Unitas*, and *Revue des études byzantines*, which in 1959 published his obituary (308–9) with a bibliography.

53 Abbé Charles Journet (1891–1975) was a Swiss Catholic theologian and a close friend of Jacques Maritain. He was named cardinal in 1965.

54 Olivier Lacombe (1904–2001) held a doctorate in philosophy. A specialist in Indian culture, he taught comparative philosophy at the University of Lille and later at the Sorbonne.

Thank you very much for your letter. I have the feeling that everything is working out. It would be good to meet a first time at my place, and afterwards we can choose another location in Paris. We still need to decide two things: what topics are we going to discuss (of course it will be Occidental and Oriental mysticism), and we need to choose a theme for the first meeting, decide who will give an introduction, and set a date. Do you have an idea for the first meeting? I think it would be good to discuss the question of mysticism as a principle and its relations with religion. As for a date, I propose Tuesday January 29, at 4 p.m.[55] Can you be in charge of inviting all the French Catholics, or should I also write to some, such as Gilson and Du Bos (what is his address)? As for the Montparnasse meetings, we could begin with a lecture by Father Boegner. Then it would be good to have Abbé Journet give a lecture. I await your reply.

May you have joyous Christmas holidays. Our best wishes to you all.
With all my heart,
N. Berdyaev
P.S. If the small gathering takes place at my home, it needs to be said in the invitation that tramway number 89 comes right to our street, rue de Saint-Cloud, just a few short steps from our door, and that the train from Montparnasse to Clamart takes only ten minutes.[56]

---

55 The meeting on Tuesday, 29 January 1929 took place at the Berdyaev home in Clamart. It was the first "intimate" gathering between Orthodox and Catholics around the themes of mysticism and spirituality. On these "intimate gatherings" initiated by Berdyaev and Jacques Maritain, see Michel Fourcade, *Feu la modernité? Maritain et les maritainismes, vol. 2, Quand prime le spirituel (1925–1929)* (Paris: Éditions Arbre bleu, 2021), 702–6.

56 The letter of invitation for this meeting from Maritain to Charles Du Bos, inscribed Meudon, 10 rue du Parc, 10 January 1929, includes directions for how to get from Paris to Berdyaev's home in Clamart: "Meudon, 10 rue du Parc, 10 January 1929. My dear friend, Monsieur Berdyaev has asked me to invite you to a meeting that will take place at his home on Tuesday 20 January at 4 o'clock. There will be only a small number of Orthodox and Catholics in attendance. M. Berdyaev will speak on mysticism and its relations to religion. I myself will be attending this meeting and would be very happy to see you there. I think of you faithfully, my dear Charlie, and with sincere affection. Jaq – Address of M. Berdyaev: 14 rue Saint Cloud, Clamart. Tram #89 has a stop at rue Saint Cloud. The train from Gare Montparnasse takes ten minutes." (Fonds Maritain at the BNU of Strasbourg, dossier Du Bos.)

No. 27, Letter from Jacques Maritain to Nikolai Berdyaev
(RGALI, dossier 1496, unit 605, folio no. 19)
+Pax
Meudon, 10 rue du Parc, 7 January 1929
My dear friend,
Pardon me for not replying sooner. I was paralyzed by migraines these past few days. Yes, I agree with you on having our first meeting be on Tuesday January 29 at 4 o'clock at your place. I do not recall exactly the list of French people you wished to invite. Here are the names I do remember: Fumet, Abbé Altermann, Charles Du Bos, Jean de Menasce, Dermenghen, Massignon, Gilson. I can take care of inviting the first four. For the three others, I think it would be better if the invitations came from you. I advise you not to invite Dwelshauwers.[57] His views lean quite heavily toward "experimental psychology," and I fear he would not really be in tune with the meeting. If you could get Father LeBreton to come that would be excellent, but is he healthy enough to do so? I also spoke to you, I think, about Abbé Simeterre, my colleague at the Institut Catholique and your neighbor in Clamart. There is also a very intelligent and open young priest at the Institut Catholique named Abbé Cadiou.[58] If you wish, I will invite these two ecclesiastics, but I won't do so before getting confirmation from you.

The title "Mysticism and Its Relations with Religion" strikes me as very suitable for the first meeting. I think the best thing would be for you to do the first introduction yourself.

For the Montparnasse meetings, let me know what I am to do regarding Abbé Journet. Should we invite him? For what date?

My dear friend, we wish you all very happy Christmas and Epiphany celebrations. Our friendship to you all.

---

57 Georges Dwelshauwers (1866–1937) was a clinical psychologist. He published numerous studies including *La synthèse mentale* (1908), *Les mécanismes subconcients* (1925), and *Traité de psychologie* (1928).

58 Abbé René Cadiou (1900–1973) was ordained in Quimper in 1928 before joining the faculty of theology at the Institut Catholique of Paris. He authored many books on Origen of Alexandria, notably *Introduction au système d'Origène* (1932) and *La jeunesse d'Origène* (1935).

Affectionately,
Jaq Maritain
[PS:] There is also a young French *agrégé* in philosophy whom I would also very much like to see attend these meetings – my friend Olivier Lacombe. Would you like me to invite him on your behalf?

No. 28, Letter from Jacques Maritain to Nikolai Berdyaev
(RGALI, dossier 1496, unit 605, folio no. 20)
+Pax
Meudon, 11 January [1929]
My dear friend,
Understood for the date: 29 January, 4 p.m. As for delivering a short introduction, I am afraid that would be quite impossible, please excuse me, but I am very tired and weighed down by migraines at the present moment. I think it would be much better for you to speak. Not a lecture, just an introduction laying out the goal of these meetings and opening things up for discussion. In any case, I think it would be preferable to have the first presentation be done by a Russian (Florovsky perhaps if it really bothers you to speak yourself. But I am sure the French would prefer to hear you). Du Bos has already told me he will come. I will call Massignon. As for Gilson, it is best that I not write to him, I do not know him well enough, or else I would do it, but a few days later after you have written to him. I think Massignon would be happy to get a letter from you, but I will alert him about it first. And I will take the liberty of inviting Olivier Lacombe whom I spoke to you about.

Attached are some addresses. Our friendship to you all.
Affectionately,
Jaq Maritain
[PS:] Abbé Journet has written me to say he is open to speaking some day at a Blvd Montparnasse meeting.

No. 29, Card from Jacques Maritain to Nikolai Berdyaev
(RGALI, dossier 1496, unit 605, folio no. 21)
+Pax
Meudon, 5 February 1929
My dear friend,
Excuse me for the slight delay in sending you the list I promised.[59] Here it is finally. About inviting the ecclesiastics, it would perhaps be best to wait for me to first see Monsignor Chaptal so that the incident with Father Bourgeois[60] does not repeat itself? I hope to see Monsignor Chaptal at the end of the week. I will write to you then.

I was delighted with the meeting at your home and especially by your presentation.[61] I spoke with Massignon by telephone and he would be happy to make some introductory remarks next time. We need only to choose a date.

Our kind regards to you and your family, my dear friend. Rest assured of my devotion and affection.
Jaq Maritain

No. 30, Card from Jacques Maritain to Nikolai Berdyaev
(RGALI, dossier 1496, unit 605, folio no. 22)
+Pax
Meudon, 9 February 1929
My dear friend,
I am sending this note in haste to say 1) Massignon is ready to do an introduction at your home on *Christine l'Admirable*, a little-known compassionate mystic of great interest. The date he proposes is Tuesday 26 February.

2) Abbé Journet wrote me to say his lecture could take place after Easter vacation, in other words sometime around April 15 (between the seventh and the fifteenth) would be his preference. Until then he is swamped with work and would find it very difficult to be available.

---

59 Maritain is referring to the list of people to be invited to the interfaith meeting that took place at the Russian students' centre in Boulevard Montparnasse. Maritain also refers to this list in his letter to Berdyaev of 9 February 1929.

60 In his letter of 2 November 1926, Maritain had suggested to Berdyaev that Father Vassili Bourgeois be invited to the interfaith meetings.

61 The first intimate gathering took place on Tuesday, 29 January 1929, in Clamart.

Our affectionate thoughts to all of you. With all my heart.
Jaq Maritain
[PS:] I think that you could invite Henry Gouhier[62] (the best disciple of Gilson) to the Clamart meetings.
11 February. I have received your letter. For us March 5th is perfect. As for Abbé Journet, I think it is materially impossible for him to be ready for the end of March. Try and invite him for April. I saw Monsignor Chaptal and he had no objections; he merely requested that I share with him the list I had made for you of the Catholics being invited. I just sent off the list to him. Could you please send me the address of Kartashev?
Affectionately,
J.M.

No. 31, Letter from Nikolai Berdyaev to Jacques Maritain
(BNU, Fonds Maritain)
Clamart, 10 February 1929
My dear friend!
I propose that our next meeting be at my home on Tuesday 5 March at 4 o'clock.[63] It is decided: Monsieur Massignon will give an introduction. But someone simply must act as moderator in order to prevent the anarchic tendency of our discussions. Should I go ahead and inform some of the French participants or will you do it yourself? It would be great to have Monsieur Du Bos at our meetings. The Catholic lecture about the Church for one of our Montparnasse meetings should take place near the end of March. I await your reply about the suitability of 5 March for the meeting at your home.

Our friendship to you all.
Cordially,
N. Berdyaev

---

62 Henri Gouhier (1898–1994) was a professor of philosophy who taught at the universities of Lille and Bordeaux, and later at Paris-Sorbonne.

63 Tuesday, 5 March 1929 was the day of the second "intimate" meeting at Clamart on the themes of "mysticisms and spiritualities."

No. 32, Letter from Jacques Maritain to Nikolai Berdyaev
(RGALI, dossier 1496, unit 605, folio no. 23)
+Pax
Meudon, 23 February 1929
Dear friend,
Pardon me for not being able to write to you sooner. Here is the list of French participants I will contact myself: Massignon, Du Bos, de Menasce, Abbé Altermann, Gouhier, Olivier Lacombe. I could also add Jean Daniélou[64] (a university *agrégé*), Dom Vincent Padovani of the Compagnie de Saint-Paul[65] (and maybe Abbé Cadiou).

You can be in charge of contacting: Fumet, Abbé Simeterre (if you think it proper to invite him), Dermenghen.

If you think there are not enough French participants (especially since one must always anticipate cases of flu!), let me know and I can see about proposing additional names. To be honest, I think the list is long enough as it is.

Our kind regards to you all.
Affectionately,
Jaq Maritain
[PS:] The meeting is definitely set for 5 March at your home.

No. 33, Letter from Jacques Maritain to Nikolai Berdyaev
(RGALI, dossier 1496, unit 605, folio no. 27)
+Pax
Meudon, 10 rue du Parc, 18 November 1929
My dear friend,
Yes, Tuesdays around 4 o'clock once a month at your place strikes me as entirely suitable for these intimate gatherings. Personally, 3 December as

64 Jean Daniélou (1905–1974) was a Jesuit theologian named cardinal in 1969.

65 Dom Vincent Padovani is mentioned several times by Maritain in his "Carnet 1929," *Cahiers Jacques Maritain* no. 69 (February 2015), in the entries for Monday, 25 March (page 40), Monday, 13 May (with Jean Daniélou), Thursday, 16 May (page 48), and Sunday, 26 May (page 50).

our first day works well for me. I am delighted at the prospect of hearing the presentation of M. Ilyin[66] on the question of Sophia.

On Monday 9 December I am unfortunately not available, as I have an appointment that cannot be moved. But on the 16th I am free. It would please me if it were possible for that day to schedule the lecture by Father Bulgakov[67] at the Montparnasse location. As for the continuation of the interfaith meetings, I confess that I no longer see much purpose in them. It seems to me we have already received what we could from that approach. We can speak again later about that.

I have notified Massignon, the Abbés and the younger participants about December 3.[68] Do you want to write to Du Bos, Gabriel Marcel, Fumet, and de Pange?[69] I will contact the others.

I have now reached out to Plon three times, and I have been promised that they are sending you the volumes of the "Roseau d'or" that you're missing. I am very annoyed by their negligence, and I am especially eager for you to receive my preface on Bergson.[70]

See you soon, my dear friend. Our warm regards to you all.

Affectionately,

Jaq Maritain

[PS:] Did you receive the book *Clairvoyance de Rome*[71] (about Action Française)?

---

66 Vladimir Nikolaevich Ilyin (1891–1974) was an Orthodox theologian.

67 Sergei Bulgakov (1871–1944) was an Orthodox priest and theologian. Expelled from Russia in 1922, he emigrated to France, where he taught at the Institut Saint-Serge in Paris.

68 The fifth intimate gathering would not take place on Tuesday, 3 December, but rather on Tuesday, 10 December 1929, as Maritain notes in his "Carnet 1929," *Cahiers Jacques Maritain* no. 69 (February 2015): 75: "At 4 o'clock at Berdyaev's, Orthodox-Catholic meeting, Ilyin speaks on sophiology."

69 Jean de Pange (1881–1957) was a writer and historian.

70 This preface was published in the eighth volume of the Roseau d'or, 4th series, no. 6 (July 1929): 5–131, present in Berdyaev's personal library in Clamart.

71 Jacques Maritain, *Clairvoyance de Rome* (Paris: Éditions Spes, 1929).

No. 34, Letter from Nikolai Berdyaev to Jacques Maritain
(BNU, Fonds Maritain)
Clamart, 29 November 1929
My dear friend!
Please send me a brief confirmation if Tuesday 10 December[72] suits you for the meeting at my place, and can we send out invitations? 3 December is impossible for the Russians because it's the eve of a major celebration of the Holy Virgin.

I also think it would be too soon after our meeting to schedule the lecture by Father Bulgakov for 16 December. Could we put it off until December 23 or 30 (both Mondays)? I await your reply.[73]

Our kind regards to you all.
Affectionately,
N. Berdyaev

No. 35, Letter from Jacques Maritain to Nikolai Berdyaev
(RGALI, dossier 1496, unit 605, folio no. 30)
+Pax
Meudon, 10 rue du Parc, 30 January 1930
My dear friend,
Gabriel Marcel sent me the enclosed letter from M. Puech[74] that I am sharing with you. Could you please respond directly to M. Puech since only you can say precisely what you wish.

It seems to me it would be best to tell him:

1) We are not asking for any specialized piece of work from him. It is not meant to be an exercise in erudition but more a discussion among friends.

72 Tuesday, 10 December 1929: the fifth intimate gathering in Clamart on the themes of "mysticisms and spiritualities"; Ilyin speaking on sophiology.

73 This lecture by Father Bulgakov seems not to have taken place.

74 Henri-Charles Puech (1902–1986) was *agrégé* in philosophy and a historian of religions. He held the chair in the history of religions at the Collège de France from 1952 to 1972.

2) We would like to have his opinion on the double question: What is the relationship between Pseudo-Dionysus[75] and properly Neo-Platonic mysticism, and what is his relation with Christian mysticism (not the kind that followed him but with that of Saint Paul, for example). In short, to what extent is Pseudo-Dionysus Neo-Platonic and to what extent is he Christian?

That is what I think would be best to say to him, but once again you're a better judge than I. The essential thing, I believe, is to set guidelines as much as possible for this academic, since otherwise erudition can have greater importance for him than "the thing itself."

Our kind regards to all of you.

Affectionately,
Jaq Maritain

No. 36, Letter from Nikolai Berdyaev to Jacques Maritain
(BNU, Fonds Maritain)
Clamart, 19 February 1930
My dear friend!

I finally had my meeting with Monsieur Puech. He has agreed to do a lecture for us on Pseudo-Dionysius and Neoplatonism, but not on 25 February, and in fact not before the second half of March. For 25 February, we do not have the time to improvise something. Let's plan on having the next meeting be with M. Puech at the end of March. And it is impossible to hold the meeting without your presence. When are you returning from Ireland?[76] Can we fix the date for the meeting as Tuesday 25 March? Please, my dear friend, send me an answer before your departure.

We could also hold the meeting on Tuesday 18 March, but will you be back by then?

Our friendly regards to you all.

Affectionately,
N. Berdyaev

---

75 Pseudo-Dionysius the Areopagite was a Syrian monk circa 500 CE whose writings were inspired by Neoplatonism.

76 Maritain was in Ireland and England from 10 to 21 March 1930.

No. 37, Letter from Jacques Maritain to Nikolai Berdyaev
(RGALI, dossier 1496, unit 605, folio no. 31)
+Pax
Meudon, 21 February 1930
My dear friend,
Yes, Tuesday 25 March[77] if you like would be good for me. I return from England on the 21st.[78]
Let's hope that M. Puech's presentation will not be too HISTORIC as that term is understood at the Sorbonne.

Our friendly regards to all of you.
Affectionately,
Jaq Maritain

No. 38, Letter from Jacques Maritain to Nikolai Berdyaev
(RGALI, dossier 1496, unit 605, folio no. 32)
+Pax
Meudon, 10 rue du Parc, [Thursday] 27 March 1930
My dear friend,
I do not know if you are thinking of pursuing further the painful incident on Monday[79] which, as you know, I deplored as much as you did. In any case, as I already said, if you wish to discuss the matter with the Cardinal of Paris, I am available to request such a meeting for you.

---

77 Tuesday, 25 March 1930, was the day of the seventh "intimate" gathering in Clamart on the themes of "mysticisms and spiritualities." Henri-Charles Puech gave a presentation on Pseudo-Dionysius.

78 On Maritain's stay in England, see "Carnet 1930," *Cahiers Jacques Maritain*, no. 70 (November 2015): 47–54. See also Olivier Rota, "La réception de Jacques Maritain par le catholicisme anglais," *Cahiers Jacques Maritain*, no. 50 (2005): 2–14.

79 See Maritain, "Carnet 1930," *Cahiers Jacques Maritain*, no. 70 (November 2015): 54: "Monday 24 March. Session at the Appeals Court about the union of Churches, presided over by the Cardinal. Report by Father de la Brière, M. Quénet, and M. Hemmer. M. Quénet scoffed. Body and soul of the church, one must also speak of the clothes. Berdyaev and Bulgakov left. They were right to do so. After Quénet, I left with Father Pressoir. Upset and indignant."

I plan on writing to Father Théry[80] for a new presentation on Pseudo-Dionysius.

Our kind regards to you all.

Affectionately,
Jaq Maritain

No. 39, Letter from Jacques Maritain to Nikolai Berdyaev
(RGALI, dossier 1496, unit 605, folio no. 51)
+Pax
Meudon, Friday [11 or 18 April 1930[81]]
My dear friend,
I enclose here the letter from Father Théry. We must find another "evaluator" ["*rapporteur*"]. For my part, unfortunately, I can think of no one.

We hope you are all well and wish you a pleasant Easter holiday.

Affectionately,
Jaq Maritain
[PS:] I went to see the Cardinal of Paris[82] and told him what I thought of M. Quénet's report.[83]

80 Father Gabriel (Hector) Théry (1891–1959) was a Dominican priest and professor of theology at Saulchoir and the Institut Catholique of Paris.

81 The precise date is missing, but the letter was written between 27 March and 20 April (Easter) 1930.

82 Jean Verdier (1864–1940) was named cardinal in December 1929. Maritain recorded in his "Carnet 1929" (page 59), for the date of Tuesday 8 April: "Visit … to Cardinal (M. Quénet)."

83 Abbé Charles-Alexandre Quénet (1883–1946) was the general vicar for foreigners and canon of Notre-Dame in Paris. Among his publications is the booklet *L'Unité de l'Église, les Églises séparées d'Orient et la réunion des Églises* (Paris: J. de Gigord, 1923). See André Mazon, "Nécrologie: abbé Charles Quénet," *Revue des Études Slaves* (1947): 279–83.

No. 40, Letter from Jacques Maritain to Nikolai Berdyaev
(RGALI, dossier 1496, unit 605, folio no. 52)
+Pax
Meudon, Easter Monday [21 April 1930]
My dear friend,
Certainly, an introduction by you on the problem of negative theology will be of great use to us. It is an absolutely central problem. This solution is excellent. Agreed for 6 May, if you like.

I am leaving tomorrow for Switzerland where I am to give three lectures.

Our best wishes to you all at this Easter time.

Affectionately,
Jaq Maritain

No. 41, Postcard from Jacques Maritain to Nikolai Berdyaev
(RGALI, dossier 1496, unit 605, folio no. 25)
Meudon, 28 April [1930[84]]
My dear friend,
I have found your card upon my return from Switzerland. Agreed for Tuesday 13 May.[85] That is also better for me.

Did you know that Gabriel Marcel has been sick? He's doing better but he still has two weeks of mandatory rest ahead of him.

I am glad that the book on Bergson interests you.[86]

Our friendly regards to you all.

Affectionately,
Jaq Maritain

---

84 The postcard is addressed to Monsieur Nikolai Berdyaev, 14 rue de St-Cloud, Clamart (Seine). The preceding envelope in the archive is dated 18-3-27 and addressed to 2 rue Martial Grandchamp, Clamart (Seine).

85 Tuesday, 13 May 1930 is the date of the eighth "intimate" gathering in Clamart on the themes of "mysticisms and spiritualities."

86 See Jacques Maritain, *La philosophie bergsonnienne: Études critiques* (Paris: Marcel Rivière & Cie, 1930).

No. 42, Letter from Jacques Maritain to Nikolai Berdyaev
(RGALI, dossier 1496, unit 605, folio no. 33)
+Pax
Meudon, 10 rue du Parc, 14 May 1930
My dear friend,
I still have a painful impression of yesterday's meeting. I was troubled to see that you were led to express thoughts that are deeply important to you within a less than peaceful setting that did not allow for a thorough discussion. That is why I prefer to say nothing about the serious question of evil that touches on God's reserved mysteries. I hope that my other remarks did not upset you. Even if I do not think the same way you do, know that I understand the problems you raise and have a great deal of respect for your thinking.

Do not forget to send me a copy of your *Dostoïevski*. It would also be good, I think, to send a copy to Abbé Journet at the Grand Séminaire de Fribourg in Switzerland. He can talk about it in *Nova et vetera*.

About the vexed questions of yesterday, I would like to make two points:

1) On theology's oversight over mysticism: it is to the extent that the mystic utters, in his way, theological propositions or, if you like, enters into the cataphatic domain, that theology checks him, as it were. And if it is to be done correctly, this oversight must take into account the distinctive characteristics of mystical language, in other words, by first of all translating into properly theological propositions the *speculative affirmations* with which the experimental language of the mystic is filled. (For example, I have the impression that while it is the vocabulary of Böhme,[87] Angelus Silesius[88] is using it for different purposes, notably for expressing above all his experience of love. Thus, the same words that have a value as gnosis in Böhme would be an experimental witnessing of love in Angelus Silesius, and for him filled with speculative affirmations entirely different from those in Böhme.) In fact, what theology is overseeing in this way is the mystic's *theology* and the recti-

---

87 Jakob Böhme (1575–1624) was raised Protestant, became interested in spiritual knowledge, and was the founder of German theosophy.

88 Angelus Silesius (1624–1677) was from Wrocław in Lower Silesia (present-day Poland), raised Protestant, studied the writings of Böhme, and wrote numerous religious hymns.

tude of his faith. It is clear that every branch of knowledge oversees itself. Mathematics judges the errors of mathematicians. And remember that the judge in the last instance is faith and the revealed truths that are superior to theology and from which theology derives all its force.

What matters is the interior *spirit* of the mystic, *Ecclesia de internis non judicat* [the church does not judge the interior disposition]. The mystic's *experience* itself, which takes place thanks to the gifts of the Holy Spirit, can only be judged by another mystic possessing the same Holy Spirit to a superior degree. *Spiritualis homo judicate omnia* [the spiritual man judges all things].

2) *Ungrund*: The fundamental criticism that I would make about this doctrine is the way it seeks in God something *deeper* than what *God himself revealed about himself and his intimate life*. What pride! About the intimate life of God we can know nothing more than revelation allows. And revelation tells us that God is one in three persons; it tells us nothing about an *Ungrund* that would be deeper. In truth, when Böhme gives a *human* idea – myth, symbol or concept, call it what you want – but in any case a *human* idea of *Ungrund* primacy over the dogmatically revealed truths and over the *divine* idea (the idea of the Holy Trinity); he is the one falling into cataphatic excess. *Gottheit*, *deitas*, that is the *Trinity*, there is nothing deeper in God. It is what reason cannot reach, what the Son must reveal to us (whereas unity is something reason can recognize).

The misunderstanding is so fundamental that in the remarkable text of Weigel[89] that you read to us, the Trinity – the most divine mystery of the Uncreated, the life of God himself in his deepest secret, that which Jesus Christ came to reveal to us – becomes a property of God *relative ad creaturas* [in relation to creatures]. I see this as an astonishing aberration. God *relative ad creaturas* is the God of philosophers, it is not the God of revelation. From Weigel there follows quite naturally Bruno[90] for whom the Trinity is only the three divine attributes (*relative ad creaturas*!) of Power, Wisdom, and Goodness. Through revelation we do not know God through

89 Valentin Weigel (1533–1588) was from the Electorate of Saxony and the author of a study of spirituality.

90 Giordano Bruno (1548–1600) was a Dominican friar from Naples. He was accused of heresy and burned at the stake in Rome.

his relation to creatures, we know God in himself and the creature in God and relation to God.

I hope we can see each other soon. Raïssa still has a bad sore throat, but she is doing a bit better, and I think that in another week she will be cured.

Our friendly regards to you all.

Affectionately,
Jaq Maritain

No. 43, Letter from Nikolai Berdyaev to Jacques Maritain
(BNU, Fonds Maritain)
Clamart, 23 May 1930
My dear friend!
Your letter raises such profound and important questions, and we really must discuss them tranquilly when we next meet. It is difficult for me to fully express my thoughts in a letter. I did not have the impression that the atmosphere at our last meeting was insufficiently calm. Russians always discuss matters passionately. I confess it is difficult for me to speak calmly when the topic is the problem of evil and suffering. I am deeply torn apart by this problem. Gnosis for me is not pride of knowledge, but the only possibility of not contending with God, and its source is in moral and spiritual experience. I hope to see you, my friend, in early June, and I hope that by that time Madame Maritain will already be feeling well. Will you be coming to our discussion with Massis[91] on the Orient and the Occident?[92] I will be sending you my *Dostoïevski.*

Our friendship to you all.

Affectionately,
N. Berdyaev

---

91 Henri Massis (1886–1970) was a literary critic and political essayist. He codirected the Roseau d'or series with Jacques Maritain. He was the editor-in-chief (1920–36) and then director (1936–44) of *La Revue universelle* and one of the lead authors of "Manifeste des intellectuels français pour la défense de l'Occident" (1935). He was elected to the Académie française in 1960.

92 A meeting at the Studio franco-russe that Maritain did not attend. He wrote to Robert Sébastien to apologize for his absence. See *Oeuvres complètes*, vol. 4, 1135.

No. 44, Letter from Jacques Maritain to Nikolai Berdyaev
(RGALI, dossier 1496, unit 605, folio no. 71)
+Pax
Meudon, Sunday [19 October 1930[93]]
My dear friend,
Agreed for Tuesday afternoon. I will be very happy to see you.[94]

Pardon me for not thanking you sooner for your *Esprit de Dostoïevski.* It had been on my mind to do so, but health problems got in the way. It is a strange thing that you and I have very different ideological structures behind our thinking, and yet everything you write is deeply interesting to me and inspires my deepest sympathy even when I oppose your arguments. This book on Dostoevsky strikes me as very important for understanding your conception of the world. It is full of admirable visions and is marvellously stimulating. It is the chapter on freedom that provokes in me the most reservations. This dialectic of Dostoevsky regarding freedom is certainly Christian, but a Christianity that operates thanks to a Hegelian ideology. I believe that if Dostoevsky had had a more explicit conception of a *supernatural* order, he would not have transposed into the weave of nature and, if I can put it this way, *metaphysicalized* the Pauline doctrine of law and freedom (since it is always to those points that we return). But we will speak more about all that.

See you soon. All our friendship to your dear family.
With all my heart.
Jaq Maritain
[PS:] Raïa and I thank you very much for the words of dedication on the first page of your book.[95]

---

93 The date is missing, but the publication of *L'Esprit de Dostoïevski* by Nikolai Berdyaev in 1929 (Paris: Éditions Saint-Michel), which is referred to in the letter, allows us to know the year and day, because Maritain met with Berdyaev on Tuesday, 21 October 1930.

94 For Tuesday, 21 October 1930, Maritain noted in his "Carnet 1930," *Cahiers Jacques Maritain*, no. 70 (November 2015): 102: "Berdiaev at 4:30 p.m."

95 This book with the dedication by Berdyaev was not found in the library of the Maritain archive at the BNU of Strasbourg.

No. 45, Letter from Jacques Maritain to Nikolai Berdyaev
(RGALI, dossier 1496, unit 605, folio no. 68)
+Pax
Meudon, Wednesday [22 October 1930[96]]
My dear friend,
I have thought about what you said to me yesterday concerning the publisher Saint-Michel. Here is what I advise – say you will give your manuscript to them on the following conditions:

1) The contract shall be signed within eight days.
2) In the contract the publisher shall agree to pay you an indemnity (2,000 francs, for example) if the work is not published within six months.

They have acted on this matter in a way that is sufficiently bizarre as to warrant you taking certain precautions.

Our affection to you all.
Yours,
J.M.

No. 46, Letter from Nikolai Berdyaev to Jacques Maritain
(BNU, Fonds Maritain)
Clamart, 20 November 1930
My dear friend!
We would so like to see you both at our place. Could you come to our home on Thursday November 27 or Monday December 1 around 4 p.m.? If those days do not suit you, we could say Thursday December 4 at the same time. We can talk then about the topics of our meetings. I await your reply. Kind regards to you all.
Cordially,
N. Berdyaev

96 The date is missing, but Maritain met Berdyaev on Tuesday, 21 October 1930. The contents of the letter mention Saint-Michel, the publisher of Nikolai Berdyaev's *L'Esprit de Dostoïevski* in 1929.

No. 47, Card from Jacques Maritain to Nikolai Berdyaev
(RGALI, Dossier 1496, unit 605, folio no. 36)
+ Pax
Meudon, Thursday evening [4 December 1930][97]
My dear friend,
I am sending this note to you in haste to say that the Tuesday that you have set for the meeting is not the 17th but December 16.[98] I hope you will have noticed that before sending out the invitations! Our kind regards to all of you.
Affectionately,
Jaq Maritain

No. 48, Letter from Jacques Maritain to Nikolai Berdyaev
(RGALI, dossier 1496, unit 605, folio no. 66)
+ Pax
Meudon, Thursday [18 December 1930[99]]
My dear friend,
Abbé Guérin, the chaplain of Catholic Youth Workers, will come to our home Sunday evening.[100] If you are free that evening, would you like to

---

97 The postage stamp of the card addressed to Nikolai Berdyaev, 14 rue de Saint-Cloud, Clamart (Seine), bears the date "6-12-30."

98 Tuesday, 16 December 1930: the ninth "intimate" meeting, with a presentation by Olivier Lacombe on the principle of identity and intelligence. See Maritain, "Carnet 1930," *Cahiers Jacques Maritain*, no. 70 (November 2015): 111; Jean de Pange, *Journal (1927–1930)* (Paris: Grasset, 1964), 354.

99 The complete date is missing but on Sunday, 21 December 1930, Abbé Guérin was present at Meudon with Berdyaev.

100 Abbé Georges Guérin (1891–1972) was general chaplain of the JOC (Jeunesse ouvrière chrétienne) from 1928 to 1950. He was present in Meudon on Sunday, 21 December 1930. See Maritain, "Carnet 1930," *Cahiers Jacques Maritain*, no. 70 (November 2015): 112: "Sunday 21. Mass (Father Bruno) … Abbé Guérin then Father Aupiais arrive during the presentation [of Abbé Lallement]. They stay for dinner, and also the young people, except for Izard. Marty, Deléage, Guyon, Jacqueline. Berdiaev after dinner." Abbé Guérin gave a lecture at Meudon on 8 December 1929. See Maritain, "Carnet 1929," *Cahiers Jacques Maritain*, no. 69 (February 2015): 74: "Sunday 8 December … At 3 p.m. a lecture by Abbé Guérin on the JOC movement (second Russian meeting of the year)." Father Francis Apiais (1877–1945).

come around 9 o'clock? I think you might find it interesting to speak with him. Our friendly regards to all of you.
Affectionately,
Jaq Maritain

No. 49, Letter from Jacques Maritain to Nikolai Berdyaev
(RGALI, dossier 1496, unit 605, folio no. 37)
+ Pax
Meudon, 17 February 1931
My dear friend,
Understood for [Tuesday] [February] 24.[101] I will send out the necessary invitations.

I am quite annoyed by the delay of *Léontieff*.[102] The delays are due both to the translation being unfinished and because of the overcrowding of the Roseau d'or program. The manuscripts already submitted to the publisher bring us through to next year. It should be noted that Plon is publishing much more slowly this year.

How to proceed?

It will be truly bothersome for me if I cannot publish this work in the Roseau. However, it is of some material importance that this volume appear quickly, so it is entirely clear that you are free to propose it to another publisher. We'll speak about that on Tuesday. Our friendly regards to all of you.
Affectionately,
Jaq Maritain

---

101 Tuesday, 24 February 1931: the eleventh "intimate" meeting in Clamart, with a presentation by Berdyaev. "He speaks about Jouhandeau's book, *Monsieur Goudeau intime* (NRF) in which he finds pages on the problem of evil." See Jean de Pange, *Journal (1927–1930)* (Paris: Grasset, 1964), 364.

102 This book was published later, and not by Plon but in a new series, Les îles, directed by Jacques Maritain: Nicolas Berdiaev, *Constantin Léontieff: Un penseur religieux russe du dix-neuvième siècle* (Paris: Desclée de Brouwer, 1937; first Russian edition, 1926).

No. 50, Letter from Nikolai Berdyaev to Jacques Maritain
(BNU, Fonds Maritain)
Clamart (Seine), 14 rue de Saint-Cloud, 6 October [1931]
My dear friend! We have only been back from Vichy a short time, and I would like to see you again to discuss certain matters. When could I come over? I am free next week on Tuesday (13 October) around 4:30 p.m., or Thursday (15 October) at the same time. But if those do not suit you, pick a day and time that is easiest for you. I hope you are all doing better now after the vacation.

Our friendly regards to all of you. Hope to see you soon.
Affectionately,
N. Berdyaev

No. 51, Letter from Jacques Maritain to Nikolai Berdyaev
(RGALI, dossier 1496, unit 605, folio no. 38)
+ Pax
Meudon, 27 October 1931
My dear friend,
I have been travelling these past days, forced to leave my home to attend meetings and devote all my time to an urgent piece of work. After having been in Chartres, then Chantilly, I am now in Bellevue! Excuse me for the delay in replying to you.

When I am back in Meudon, I will write you again to suggest a time to meet. (Perhaps next Sunday November 1? Could you come in the afternoon? Yes, that would certainly be the best day for me, if you're free then: Sunday afternoon.) I must speak to you about our meetings. I am so overwhelmed with overdue work and so completely exhausted that I doubt it will be possible for me to regularly attend our meetings this year, neither at your place nor the ones like we used to have at the home of Du Bos with Gabriel Marcel.[103] I am very upset about it all, but it seems materially impossible for me to maintain my former consistency. However, I certainly do not want

103 In 1930, Gabriel Marcel and Charles Du Bos hatched the ambitious project of a "Society for Christian Philosophy" with "lectures and discussion." Some meetings took place in Versailles et the home of Du Bos. Maritain accepted the idea on condition that they would be "above all friendly intellectual gatherings, entirely private," and fairly small. Maritain participated for a time

this to disrupt these meetings which are so beneficial. The trouble is that Massignon is in the same situation I am in. We have to find French philosophers who can attend regularly, and that is what I would like to speak with you about.

Since May, we've been plagued with health problems, and things have only started to get better over the last month, more or less. I hope you are all well. Our friendly regards to all of you.

Affectionately,

Jaq Maritain

No. 52, Letter from Nikolai Berdyaev to Jacques Maritain

(BNU, Fonds Maritain)

Clamart, 29 October [1931]

My dear friend!

I am sorry but next Sunday [1 November] I will not be able to come over. I will be hosting several people at my home then. But if you like, I can come see you the following Sunday (8 November) after 4 p.m. If that suits you, do not bother replying. If not, write me back and propose another day, but not Tuesday.

Affectionately,

N. Berdyaev

No. 53, Postcard from Jacques Maritain to Nikolai Berdyaev[104]

(RGALI, dossier 1496, unit 605, folio no. 39)

+ Pax

Meudon, 31 October 1931

My dear friend,

Unfortunately, the eighth is impossible because there is a meeting of students at my home. Next Saturday, November 7, I have to go to Paris and I

with Berdyaev. See Henri Bars, "Gabriel Marcel et Jacques Maritain," *Cahiers Jacques Maritain*, no. 19 (October 1989): 5–27, especially pages 10–11.

104 The postcard depicts the "Philosophers Alley" at the Château de Chantilly. Maritain had been in Chantilly, according to the letter sent to Nikolai Berdyaev on 27 October 1931.

think I will be free at 5:30 p.m. Would you like to meet, for example in the Boulevard Montparnasse at the Russian students' house?
Affectionately,
Jaq Maritain

No. 54, Letter from Jacques Maritain to Nikolai Berdyaev
(RGALI, dossier 1496, unit 105, folio no. 69)
+ Pax
Meudon, 10 rue du Parc, Friday [November–December 1931[105]]
Alas, my dear friend, here I am impeded by my work and end-of-year duties with not a single free afternoon. It would be wonderful if you could come to Meudon on Tuesday after dinner (excuse me for not inviting you to dine with us but my mother-in-law is very unwell at the moment). Friendly regards to all of you.
Affectionately,
Jaq Maritain

No. 55, Postcard from Jacques Maritain to Nikolai Berdyaev[106]
(RGALI, dossier 1496, unit 605, folio no. 40)
Chartreuse de Lucques, 30 November 1931
My dear friend,
I have been in Italy for a little over a week. I did some teaching in Milan and now I am getting a little rest at the Chartreuse de Lucques before returning to Paris. This explains why I have been late in replying to you. Will we finally manage to meet up? As soon as I am back, I will write to you again to propose a rendezvous. Friendly regards to all of you.
Affectionately,
Jaq Maritain

105 The year and month are not indicated, but Jacques Maritain's mother-in-law, Mamka, who lived with him in Meudon, was sick for several weeks between 12 November and 6 December 1931. See Maritain, "Carnet 1931," *Cahiers Jacques Maritain*, no. 73 (April 2017): 81: "Thursday 12 [November]. Mamka is suffering greatly these days with chest pains"; and page 87: "Sunday 6 [December]. Mamka is doing much better, we think it's through the grace of Saint Curé d'Ars." Raïssa's mother died in 1932.

106 The postcard depicts the Farneta Charterhouse near Lucca in Tuscany.

No. 56, Letter from Jacques Maritain to Nikolai Berdyaev
(RGALI, dossier 1496, unit 605, folio no. 41)
+ Pax
Meudon, 23 December 1931
My dear friend,
Enclosed are the two letters of introduction requested for Monsieur Klepinin.[107] I kept my wording rather general because I have forgotten the precise mission that leads him to want to meet Garric[108] and Abbé Guérin.

I was very pleased by what you said last Saturday in the rue Visconti.[109] It was so lively and direct as compared to the metaphysical, humanist sentimentality! My affectionate regards to you all.
Jaq Maritain

No. 57, Postcard from Jacques Maritain to Nikolai Berdyaev
(RGALI, dossier 1496, unit 605, folio no. 42)[110]
+ Pax
Meudon, 13 April 1932
My dear friend,
I was meaning to write to ask you to come over between 4 and 5. That day at our place there's a study meeting with the young people whom I spoke to you about at Clamart (most of whom work for the review *Esprit*). We will speak about properties, a discussion that has been going on for some time already, and I would be very happy to have you there and get

---

107 Dmitrii Klepinin (1904–1944) was of Russian origin and went into exile after the Revolution, first to Constantinople, then to a suburb of Belgrade, Serbia. In 1925 he enrolled at the Saint-Serge Institute of Orthodox Theology in Paris. In 1929 he received a scholarship for additional training at the New York Theological Seminary, where he studied the writings of Saint Paul. In 1937 he married and became an ordained Orthodox priest.

108 Robert Garric (1896–1967) was a Catholic writer and the founder in 1920 of the Équipes sociales, a group dedicated to social action and the formation of circles dedicated to education and technical training for the working classes.

109 Meetings of the Union for the Truth took place at 21, rue Visconti (Paris 6e).

110 The postcard depicts the façade of the Notre-Dame Cathedral in Paris.

your opinion on the matter.[111] We hope that Madame Berdyaev will be able to accompany you.
Affectionately,
Jaq Maritain

No. 58, Letter from Jacques Maritain to Nikolai Berdyaev
(RGALI, dossier 1496, unit 605, folio no. 43)
+ Pax
Meudon, 11 October 1932
My dear friend,
Have you found a translator for the third study that is to be collected in the Debate Questions?[112] Were you able to ask Madame Cain to do this work?[113] I would be grateful if you could write me about this matter because I am eager to see this volume appear. In eight days, Chuzeville,[114] who is now in Athens, will probably be back in Paris, and we can ask him to do this translation if on your end you've found nobody. But I would prefer it be Madame Cain, since it would probably go faster.

We very much enjoyed and admired your article in *Esprit*.[115]

---

111 See Maritain, "Carnet 1932," *Cahiers Jacques Maritain*, no. 74 (November 2017): 46: "Sunday 17 April. Meeting with fewer people (*Esprit* especially). Continuation on the Question of Property. Laloy comes with his wife, like last Sunday. Berdiaev at 5 p.m. I speak about *factibile* [what an artist creates] and *usus* [making use of something]. He says some quite remarkable things about the current state of Soviet philosophy."

112 See Nicolas Berdiaev, *Problème du communisme*, Questions disputées (Paris: Desclée de Brouwer, 1933), chapter III, "The 'General Line' of Soviet Philosophy." This study was published in Russian in the journal *Put'*, no. 34 (July 1932): 1–28.

113 Madame Lucienne Julien Cain had translated Berdyaev's *L'Esprit de Dostoïevski*.

114 Jean Chuzeville (1886–1962) was a literary critic and the translator of several works, notably a book by Theodor Haeker in the collection "Les Îles"; see OC XI, 858. On Haeker, see *Cahiers Jacques Maritain*, no. 31. Maritain noted that Chuzeville was present at a meeting about symbolism at the Studio franco-russe on Tuesday, 16 December 1930. See "Carnet 1930," *Cahiers Jacques Maritain*, no. 70 (November 2015): 111.

115 Nicolas Berdiaev, "Vérité et mensonge du communisme," *Esprit*, no. 31 (October 1932), 104–28.

See you soon I hope. Here we are still mired in health problems, it is truly overwhelming. Flu, colds, and fatigue!

Our kind regards to all of you.

Affectionately,
Jaq Maritain

No. 59, Postcard from Jacques Maritain to Nikolai Berdyaev
(RGALI, dossier 1496, unit 605, folio no. 44)[116]
+Pax
Toronto, 28 March 1933
My dear friend,
I want to tell you with what deep affection I think of you and yours. See you soon.
Affectionately,
Jacques Maritain

No. 60, Letter from Jacques Maritain to Nikolai Berdyaev
(RGALI, dossier 1496, unit 605, folio no. 45)[117]
+Pax
Meudon, 2 May 1933
My dear friend,
I would have liked to see you directly after my return from Canada.[118] But Raïssa and I feel so exhausted that we are leaving directly to get some rest, probably in the south, for three or four weeks. I will let you know as soon as I am back in Meudon.

Thank you for sending your two books (*Problème du communisme* and *Esprit et Liberté*) with the kind dedications. I will take *Esprit et Liberté* with me and be reading the book with great interest while in the south.

---

116 The postcard depicts the Canadian Bank of Commerce in Toronto, Canada.

117 The postcard depicts the façade of Notre-Dame Cathedral in Paris.

118 Jacques Maritain left France on 29 December 1932. He spent several months in Toronto giving courses and lectures at the Institute for Medieval Studies. He returned to Paris on 13 April 1933. See *Cahiers Jacques Maritain*, no. 76 (2018).

Like you, I suppose we will disagree, but I know that our amicable relations will not be affected.

Our warm thoughts go out to you and yours.

In sincere friendship.

Jacqs Maritain

No. 61, Letter from Nikolai Berdyaev to Jacques Maritain
(BNU, Fonds Maritain)
Clamart, 18 November 1933
My dear friend!

Thank you very much for sending your book.[119] Your dedication was deeply touching. I have already finished reading it. The study of the philosophy of freedom is very well written, as is everything else you've expressed, and with exemplary clarity. But you have once again proved to me that the Thomist philosophy is not a philosophy of freedom. If nature prevails over freedom, the latter cannot exist but is instead determined. And the resulting position is no better if you speak of metaphysical nature instead of physical nature. In Greek there is one word for both nature and the physical. For me, freewill is not the same thing as freedom. Our philosophies are of two different types: one, the primacy of freedom over being, the other the primacy of being over freedom. The second type is always intellectualist and freedom, for it, is not mysterious but grounded in reason. Nonetheless, I greatly sympathize with the second half of your book where you speak of temporal relations. In those pages I am often in total agreement with you. What separates us is a primordial feeling about life and the world. You are much more optimistic. Intellectualist and teleological philosophies are always optimistic. Me, I'm much more pessimistic and my philosophy is a tragic one (the result of the primacy of freedom over being and of the fundamental irrationality of the world). I do not find intellectualism in the Old Testament, nor the New, nor in the Apostolic Epistles. I only find it in Greek philosophy, in the writings of the pagan Aristotle. But we must talk about these questions when we see each other again, which I hope will be soon.

---

119 Jacques Maritain, *Du régime temporal et de la liberté*, Questions disputées (Paris: Desclée de Brouwer, 1933).

Friendly regards to you all.
Affectionately,
N. Berdyaev

No. 62, Letter from Jacques Maritain to Nikolai Berdyaev
(RGALI, dossier 1496, unit 605, folios no. 46 and 47)
+Pax
Meudon, 23 December 1933
My dear friend,
I received your letter at the very moment I was planning to write you. It has been too long since we saw each other last. Since my return from Canada I have been very tired, and the summer months were very difficult for Raïssa and myself.

I was hoping to read thoroughly your *Esprit et Liberté* so as to be able to talk about it with you. So far I have only been able to skim it – however enough to measure the importance of this work and to deplore the metaphysical dimension, which in my view is a destruction of metaphysics, generous and stimulating like everything from you, but a destruction all the same and a "catastrophe." I intend to take up your book again when I have more free time, study it in detail, and write an article about it in which I shall try to reduce certain misunderstandings. It will stand as both a marker of our philosophical differences and of the deep friendship that unites us. At the moment, however, I must prepare three talks that I am giving in Rome in March. After that, *Esprit et Liberté* will be my top priority.

I thank you for what you've written concerning my last book.[120] But I see there once again several misunderstandings, and an overly summary use of general ideas such as "primacy" of nature over freedom or freedom over being, "intellectualism," and so forth. I am fighting precisely against such simplifications.

If freedom necessarily presupposes spirit, and spirit presupposes being (and I too do not think that freedom is the same as free will, far from it! But if one denies free will one ruins freedom), a philosophy that affirms a primary, ontological absolute of freedom over being will not be a philosophy

120 Ibid.

of freedom, but a destruction of freedom. In my view, there is a primacy of freedom over being in the sense that freedom – what I call the freedom of exultation and freedom of autonomy – is at the highest level of spiritual being, which is the highest degree of being, and this freedom may be considered a fruit of being, of intelligence, and of love. But being is always the primordial root and *in this sense* there is a primacy of being; and there is also – and this is above all what I wished to underscore in the passages you are alluding to – a primacy of nature over freedom understood *in the sense of free will.* One cannot say things all at once in a book …

As for the optimism that you attribute to me (while ordinarily I am accused of pessimism), it amounts to affirming that God is Love and will triumph in the end, and that has nothing to do with Greek "intellectualism." It is the "optimism" of the Apocalypse, and I do not see how one can be a Christian if one does not have that conception of reality and of history. The Bible is far above philosophy and all philosophical systems, but there is definitely a certain *intellectualism* in the Bible, of course! The Bible places intelligence as the principal foundation of things, "in the beginning was the Word," it believes in the principle of contradiction, in the irreducible opposition of Yes and No, it believes in the reality of things, it tells us that if our eye is bad then our whole body will be in darkness. It is because it presupposes an intact reason that the madness of the Cross is the Divine Paradox in all its sublimity and divinely triumphs over reason.

Our friendly regards to you and yours and best wishes over the Christmas holidays. I hope we shall meet again soon. Let's try for early January.
Affectionately,
Jacques Maritain

No. 63, Letter from Jacques Maritain to Nikolai Berdyaev
(RGALI, dossier 1496, unit 605, folio no. 48)
+Pax
Meudon, 10 rue du Parc, 9 January 1934
My dear friend,
We would be so pleased if the three of you were able to come to dinner at our place on Tuesday January 23 at 7 p.m., are you free? I'm extending this invitation well in advance because our schedules are both so jam-packed,

and in this way I hope we will be able to set aside this evening with each other more easily.

We send the three of you our best wishes for the Christmas holidays in sincerest friendship.

Affectionately,
Jacqs Maritain

No. 64, Letter from Nikolai Berdyaev to Jacques Maritain
(BNU, Fonds Maritain)
Clamart, 12 January 1934
My dear friend!
We thank you for the invitation and we do want to come to your home, but Tuesday is not possible for me as it is the day of my course. Can you propose another day? The following days would be possible for me: Monday January 29, Thursday February 1, Friday February 2 or Saturday February 3. The preceding week is a very busy one for me. I hope to see you soon notwithstanding.

Friendly regards and best wishes to you all.

Affectionately,
N. Berdyaev
[p.s.] After completing my letter, on second thought, I realize that we are also free to come on *Thursday January* 25, and that would even be particularly convenient for me.

No. 65, Letter from Nikolai Berdyaev to Jacques Maritain
(BNU, Fonds Maritain)
Clamart, 12 February 1934
My dear friend!
We would so like to have you over before my departure. Could you all come to dinner at our place on February 27 around 7? I await your reply. Friendly regards to you all.
Affectionately,
N. Berdyaev

No. 66, Letter from Nikolai Berdyaev to Jacques Maritain
(BNU, Fonds Maritain)
Clamart, 19 April 1934
My dear friend!
I would so like to have attended your Saturday lecture in the "Union for the Truth" and taken part in the discussions.[121] Unfortunately, I was unable to do so. I feel thoroughly unwell. I am completely exhausted, and my arthritic pains are killing me. The doctor firmly recommends complete rest for the next while. As I was especially invited by Monsieur Guy-Grand[122] for that day, I ask that you convey to him the reason for my absence.

Father Florovsky asks that you give him a recommendation for Father Lebreton, he wants to have a scientific conversation with him, and also a recommendation for the Jesuit library in the rue Monsieur. He needs to use this library for his specialized studies. The two recommendations can be sent either to my address or directly to that of Father G. Florovsky (48, rue Babillot, Paris 13).

I would like to speak with you about your impression of Karl Barth.[123] In any case I hope to see you again soon.

Our friendly regards to all of you.
Affectionately,
N. Berdyaev

No. 67, Letter from Jacques Maritain to Nikolai Berdyaev
(RGALI, dossier 1496, unit 605, folio no. 49)
+Pax
Meudon, 25 April 1934
My dear friend,
I am very sorry to learn you are unwell and undergoing physical discomfort. Let me know if you can receive visitors without suffering further

121 Maritain noted in his "Carnet 1934," *Cahiers Jacques Maritain*, no. 77 (December 2018): 46: "Saturday 21 April. Presentation rue Visconti at Union for the Truth on *Régime temporal et liberté*."

122 Georges Guy-Grand (1879–1957) was the author of many works, notably *Pour connaître la pensée de Proudhon* (Paris: Bordas, 1947).

123 Karl Barth (1886–1968) was a Swiss Reformed pastor and professor of theology.

fatigue, in which case I will travel to Clamart as soon as I can. Unfortunately, I am being constantly called away, I have just returned from a trip that I did in haste directly after the meeting in the rue Visconti, and I must leave again in a few days for Nimègue where I am giving a lecture. I hope to meet with Pierre Van der Meer when I get back.

I apologized on your behalf to Monsieur Guy-Grand, who like everyone else regretted your absence on that day.

We shall make time to speak about Karl Barth. The tragedy seems to me to be this: he is a man who wishes that we listen to God alone, yet it is Barth and his personality that one is forced to listen to.

I hope to see you soon. Friendly regards to you all. Rest assured of my deep affection.

Jacqs Maritain

[p.s.] I am sending with this letter two cards for Father Florovsky. I know no one at rue Monsieur besides Father Doncoeur,[124] and I do not know who is in charge of the library.

No. 68, Letter from Jacques Maritain to Nikolai Berdyaev
(RGALI, dossier 1496, unit 605, folio no. 53)
Meudon, 28 September 1934
My dear friend,
Alas I was unable to go see you because of the retreat that occupied all our time, and tomorrow I set off for Canada.[125] I deeply regret not seeing you, it will have to be after me return, I plan on being back mid-November. You have my best wishes.

Friendly regards to all of you.

Affectionately,
Jacq Maritain

---

124 Paul Doncoeur (1880–1961) was a Jesuit writer.

125 Maritain noted in his "Carnet 1934," *Cahiers Jacques Maritain* no. 77 (December 2018): 69: "29 September, departure for Québec. Québec. Montréal. Ottawa. Toronto. Ann Arbor, Notre Dame. Chicago. New York. Washington. Return 16 November."

[p.s.] Have you received my *Leçons sur l'être*?[126] The publisher mishandled all the dedicated copies and the one to be sent to you disappeared. I wrote from out of town that you be sent another one, but I do not know if that request was carried out.

No. 69, Letter from Raïssa and Jacques Maritain to Nikolai and Lydia Berdyaev (RGALI, dossier 1496, unit 606, folio no. 1)
+
Meudon, 1 December 1934
Dear friends,
Jacques has returned and we would be pleased to see you at our place. Are you free on Sunday December 9 around 4 o'clock or earlier? That day we may have a study meeting on the question of Proudhon.[127] If you are not free on the 9th, would you be free to dine with us on Tuesday the 11th?

We send our warm regards to you, dear friends, as well as to your mother and sister.
Raïssa Maritain
[p.s.] Dear friend, please try to come to the meeting on Sunday, I would like that very much.[128] And come also on Tuesday December 11.
Affectionately, Jacques Maritain Pavlovitch[129]

126 Jacques Maritain, *Sept leçons sur l'être et les premiers principes de la raison spéculative* (Paris: Téqui, 1934).

127 Pierre-Joseph Proudhon (1809–1865) was an economist, philosopher, and political thinker at the dawn of French socialism.

128 Maritain noted in his "Carnet 1934," *Cahiers Jacques Maritain*, no. 77 (December 2018): 71: "Sunday 9 December. Study meeting. [Yves] Simon speaks on Proudhon. Berdyaev and Landsberg come."

129 Jacques Maritain Pavlovitch, literally "Jacques Maritain, son of Paul," which was the name of Jacques Maritain's father. This form of address appears for the first time in December 1934 and continues in their correspondence until April 1938. As for Nikolai Berdyaev, Jacques Maritain would address him as "Nicolas Alexandrovitch" on several occasions over a few years.

No. 70, Letter from Nikolai Berdyaev to Jacques Maritain
(BNU, Fonds Maritain)
Clamart, 28 December 1934
My dear friend!
Thank you very much for the invitation. We will come see you on Tuesday January 1 at around 7.[130] My sister-in-law[131] thanks you but will not be able to come. About food – well, do not trouble yourselves too much about me. I am able to eat veal, ham, vegetables, and oranges.

See you soon my friend.
Affectionately,
N. Berdyaev

No. 71, Letter from Nikolai Berdyaev to Jacques Maritain
(BNU, Fonds Maritain)
Clamart, 7 January [1935]
My dear friend Jakov Pavlovitch![132] I see that it will be very difficult to come to your place on Sunday January 13 even though I would very much like to hear you speak on the topic you have chosen.[133] However, I can organize things such that I could come on Sunday January 20 around 4 o'clock if the meeting is put off. You had told me that this might be possible.

In any case I hope to see you soon. Our kind regards to all of you.
Affectionately,
N. Berdyaev

---

130 Maritain noted in his "Carnet 1935," *Cahiers Jacques Maritain*, no. 78 (June 2019): 31: "Tuesday 1 January 1935. Many friends come to our house for a lunch prepared by Véra, Babet Jacob and Jeanne Linn: Berdiaev, the Linns."

131 Evgeniia Iudifovna.

132 Lydia Berdyaev, in her book *Profession: femme de philosophe* (Profession: Philosopher's wife) (Paris: Éditions Parole et Silence, 2020), 99, writes for the date Thursday, 28 February 1935: "Around 5 p.m. Jacques and Raïssa Maritain arrive, and Raïssa's sister Véra Oumantsova. Lieb also came and I said laughing, 'Here's the German Russian Fédor Ivanovitch and the Russian Frenchman Iakob Pavlovitch, because that's what we called Maritain."

133 Maritain noted in his "Carnet 1935," *Cahiers Jacques Maritain*, no. 78 (June 2019): 33: "Sunday 13 January. Study meeting (on the World and the Kingdom)."

No. 72, Letter from Nikolai Berdyaev to Jacques Maritain
(BNU, Fonds Maritain)
Clamart, 24 February 1935
My dear friend! Yesterday the Spanish philosopher Xirau was at my home.[134] He is a very nice man, but it was painful to see him stuck in such tragic circumstances. I so wanted to help him, and the idea came to me that perhaps Madame Ocampo could give him some advice.[135] One solution would be to become a professor in Argentina. You know Madame Ocampo better than I do. It would be great if you would write her a letter recommending Xirau and asking her to set up a time to meet with him. The meeting could be at our place, but that would be for Madame Ocampo to decide. I will write to Xirau once I have received your reply. If you think it is better that I write to Madame Ocampo myself, I will do so. Do I have the right address – 31, rue Raynouard? The Spanish tragedy is horrible.

Our friendship to you all.

Affectionately,
N. Berdyaev

No. 73, Letter from Jacques Maritain to Nikolai Berdyaev
(RGALI, dossier 1496, unit 605, folio no. 63)
+
Meudon, 25 March 1935
My dear Nicolas Alexandrovitch,[136]
Thumbing through my notebook, I have found the name of the woman you suggested to me. I am embarrassed to have such a bad memory. For some time now my distracted state has caused me dreadful problems.

I do not exactly recall what I was supposed to include in the letter. Here in any case is a letter of recommendation for Father Rouët de Journel,[137]

134 Joaquim Xirau i Palau (1895–1946) was a Spanish philosopher and pedagogue. He was a member of the "Barcelona School" and died in exile in Mexico.

135 Silvina Ocampo (1903–1993) was an Argentinian writer.

136 This form of address, "Nicolas Alexandrovitch," literally "Nicolas son of Alexander," appears for the first time in this letter from Jacques Maritain dated 25 March 1935.

137 Marie Joseph Rouët de Journal (1880–1974) was a Jesuit.

who I believe is in charge of aid at the Russian Refugees association. He is a very learned Jesuit whom I met once, but who unfortunately has a rather frosty personality.

If things do not work out with him, Madame B[erdyaev] can write on my recommendation to my friend Abbé Altermann, an administrator at the same church for foreigners in the rue de Sèvres. Alas, he has no funds whatsoever.

I hope you are doing well. Véra is in bed with pain in one leg. I'm just getting over the flu.

With our deepest affection.

Jacqs Pavlovitch

No. 74, Card from Jacques Maritain to Nikolai Berdyaev

(RGALI, dossier 1496, unit 605, folio no. 50)

+Pax

Meudon, Monday, 29 April 1935

My dear friend,

I am sending you this note to say it is indeed tomorrow, Tuesday April 30, that I will be giving my presentation to the *Esprit* group. In fact, I will be saying nothing new or all that interesting.

Some good news that we will be happy to discuss at greater length with you: Pierre and Christine Van der Meer are back. They finally realized that their place was not in a convent. For now, they are in Meudon and very near our place.

How are all of you doing? Here the past few weeks have been difficult. Véra was bedridden for more than a month with shin splints. She is only now getting up and about.

We would so like to see all of you soon. As soon as I can, I will write to you to propose a date.

Happy Easter to you all! Rest assured of my faithful friendship.

Yours,

Jacques Pavlovitch

No. 75, Letter from Nikolai Berdyaev to Jacques Maritain
(BNU, Fonds Maritain)
Clamart, 3 June 1935
My dear friend Jacques Pavlovitch!
We are inviting the Van der Meers to our place on June 10, 4:30 p.m. We would very much like to also have you come over that day. Soon I will be leaving for England and afterwards will be undertaking other travels. I hope to see you before my departure.

Kind regards to you all.
Affectionately,
N. Berdyaev

No. 76, Letter from Jacques Maritain to Nikolai Berdyaev
(RGALI, dossier 1496, unit 605, folio no. 70)
+
Meudon, Sunday, [9 June 1935][138]
My dear Nicolas Alexandrovitch,
I am so distracted lately that I wonder if I answered you? Pardon me if I forgot to do so. Alas, it is impossible for me to come see you tomorrow. I am travelling to Portugal and will be staying there for about ten days. I hope we can see each other after my return, if you yourself are not away at that time.

Our affection to you all.
Rest assured of my faithful friendship,
Jacques Pavlovitch

No. 77, Letter from Raïssa Maritain to Nikolai Berdyaev
(RGALI, dossier 1496, unit 606, folio no. 2)
Meudon, August 26, 1935
My dear friend,
I am reading your book, *La Destination de l'Homme*, passionately and enthusiastically! I have almost finished and have been speaking about it with

138 The date 9 June 1935, though missing from the letter, can be deduced from the contents of the preceding letter from Berdyaev, and from Maritain's letter which mentions his trip to Portugal from 10 to 17 June 1935.

Jacques (who will read it a bit later), and he shares my admiration for your work. We will probably not always be in complete agreement with all of your critical observations, but it is difficult to not feel at one with you regarding the positive and experimental aspects.

We would very much like to see you. Could you come to Meudon on Sunday with your wife? In the afternoon or in the evening for dinner? If not, name another day next week, Tuesday perhaps.

[Raïssa Maritain[139]]

No. 78, Letter from Nikolai Berdyaev to Raïssa Maritain
(BNU, Fonds Maritain)
Clamart, 28 August 1935

My dear friend!

I just received your letter and was very happy to read it. Your remarks about my book are all the more special because certainly there are some pages that could be displeasing to you and Jakov Pavlovitch.

We would have very much liked to come to your home, but tomorrow we are leaving for Vichy. I hope we will see each other at the end of September. I just got back from an interesting ten-day conference in Pontigny on asceticism. De Becker[140] will tell you about it.

Our kind regards to you.

Affectionately,
N. Berdyaev

139 The following page, which probably included a polite closing formula and signature, is missing.

140 Raymond De Becker (1912–1969) was a Belgian journalist.

No. 79, Letter from Nikolai and Lydia Berdyaev to Raïssa Maritain
(BNU, Fonds Maritain)
Clamart, 8 February 1936
Dear friend!
We are expecting you with your sister and the Van der Meers on Thursday February 20 around 5 p.m.[141] We have not seen you for a long time and are very happy at the prospect of seeing you again soon.
Affectionately,
Nikolai and Lydia Berdyaev

No. 80, Letter from Nikolai Berdyaev to Raïssa Maritain
(BNU, Fonds Maritain)
Clamart, 8 March 1936
My dear friend!
I will be coming to your home on Thursday March 12 around 4:30 p.m. It is better than coming to dinner. We will have a philosophical conversation. I do not know if Lydia can come because her sister is unwell.

Kind regards to you.
Affectionately,
N. Berdyaev

No. 81, Letter from Jacques Maritain to Nikolai Berdyaev
(RGALI, dossier 1496, unit 605, folio no. 67)
+Pax
Meudon, Wednesday evening [May-June, 1936[142]]
My dear friend,
Ah, how shall we get to your place on Saturday? Raïssa and Véra have great difficulty going on foot from our home to the station in Meudon and from the Clamart station to your home, and the modest taxi service that we

141 Raïssa and Véra were invited without Jacques Maritain, who was in North America from 3 January to 10 April 1936 for a series of courses and lectures. See "Carnet 1936," *Cahiers Jacques Maritain*, no. 79 (December 2019): 75–87.

142 The taxi strike at the time of the Front populaire allows us to date this letter to sometime in May or June of 1936, before the Berdyaevs left Paris for the summer.

ordinarily use is on strike. I think we will have to wait for the end of this taxi strike, which I doubt will last much longer, I hope. Could you tell me until what day we could still come to see you before your departure? Perhaps next Thursday, if the taxis are operating?

See you soon in any case. Our kind regards to all of you.

Rest assured of my faithful friendship.

Jacqs Maritain

[PS:] I will send you a telegram tomorrow, Friday, no matter what.

No. 82, Letter from Jacques Maritain to Nikolai Berdyaev
(RGALI, dossier 1496, unit 605, folio no. 54)
Off the coast of Bahia, 23 October 1936

Dear Nicolas Alexandrovitch,

I was not able to write you during my two-month stay in Argentina because of the huge amount of work I had to do.[143] However we were often thinking of you and of your dear home in Clamart with great affection. I hope this year we will be able to see each other more easily. During this dreadful agony that is wracking the world, and with the events in Spain that break my heart and throw me into an abyss of sadness, my thoughts are buoyed by a spirit of great fellowship. It will console us to see you and resume our conversations.

The welcome we received in Argentina was extraordinary – we will tell you all about it. And everywhere such enthusiasm for Léon Bloy. There is such a yearning for a Christian discourse! We have become quite attached to this country. But here too one must work hard to steer young people (sometimes the very best) away from the fascist temptation. I tried my best to do so.

Despite great fatigue, our health is not bad. (The sea has been rather rough from the start.) I hope all four of you are well. See you soon.

(We're expecting to arrive in Marseille on November 6.)

Our warmest thoughts go out to all of you.

Yours,

Jacques Pavlovitch

---

143 The stay in Argentina was from 19 August to 15 October 1936. Jacques, Raïssa, and Véra ieft France on 26 July and returned on 6 November 1936. See "Carnet 1936," *Cahiers Jacques Maritain*, no. 79 (December 2019): 89–94.

No. 83, Letter from Raïssa Maritain to Nikolai Berdyaev
(RGALI, dossier 1496, unit 605, folio no. 3)
Meudon, 29 November 1936
Dear friend,
Jacques has been in Rome for a week. He went there for the Thomist Congress. He will probably be back at the end of the week. We therefore cannot see you for another ten days or so. Jacques will write you. We are eager to see you again. Our return here was troubled by our radiator mess that took us two weeks to resolve. But all is well now.
Warm regards to you all.
Raïssa Maritain

No. 84, Letter from Jacques Maritain to Nikolai Berdyaev
(RGALI, dossier 1496, unit 605, folio no. 55)
Meudon, 7 December 1936
My dear Nicolas Alexandrovitch,
Here I am back from Rome. Finally! Will I now have a bit of stability?

We are so eager to see you. Would the three of you like to come to dinner in Meudon next Monday December 14? You have so much to tell us.

I hope you are all well. See you soon. To you all our deepest affection.
Яков Павлович[144]

No. 85, Letter from Jacques Maritain to Nikolai Berdyaev
(RGALI, dossier 1496, unit 605, folio no. 56)
Meudon, 10 rue du Parc, Tuesday, 5 January 1937
My dear Nicolas Alexandrovitch,
Next Sunday, January 10, some Spanish Catholic friends will come to our house. They are partisans of the republican government opposed to Franco. Bergamin[145]

---

144 "Jacques Pavlovitch" spelled in Cyrillic script.

145 José Bergamin (1895–1983) was a Spanish writer and dramaturge, a Catholic, and a supporter of the Spanish republic. He was named cultural attaché to the Spanish embassy in Paris. Maritain notes in his "Carnet 1936," *Cahiers Jacques Maritain*, no. 79 (December 2019): 96, that Bergamin was present in Meudon on Saturday, 26 December 1936. See also Yves Roullière, "José Bergamin et Jacques Maritain," *Cahiers Jacques Maritain*, no. 37 (1998): 16–41.

will be there and probably also the priest discussed by Semprun[146] in his letter in *Esprit* (published in the November issue).

I am inviting some friends over to hear them and discuss matters. It will be a small gathering and completely private, but one that I see as rather important. I urgently request that you join us. I consider your presence indispensable, my dear friend.[147] I would have liked to have given you more advance notice, but I only received Bergamin's answer this morning. I do so hope that you will be able to be free, and Madame Berdyaev as well.
Our affectionate thoughts to you all.
Jacques Maritain
[PS:] The meeting will begin at 3:30 p.m.

No. 86, Letter from Jacques Maritain to Nikolai Berdyaev
(RGALI, dossier 1496, unit 605, folio no. 35)
+
Meudon, Wednesday, [6 January 1937[148]]

My dear Nicolas Alexandrovitch,
Alas, I was unable to put off the meeting I spoke to you about. As your letter had still not arrived, I assumed it meant that you were able to come that day, and when the letter finally reached me, I had already sent out the invitations. I will be very sorry if you are unable to come, and I will try to find another time to speak about these troubling matters with you. Also, if by chance you are free then, would you like me to order you a taxi, and if so at what time? I have asked people to arrive for 3:30 p.m. If you prefer we could begin at 4 instead.

---

146 Jorge Sumprun (1923–2011) was a Spanish writer and politician. See Maritain's note recorded in his "Carnet 1936," *Cahiers Jacques Maritain*, no. 79 (December 2019): 95: "Wednesday 16 December: Sumprun and Mendizabal are present in Meudon a few days after my return."

147 Maritain records in his "Carnet 1937," *Cahiers Jacques Maritain*, no. 80 (June 2020): 25, for Sunday, 10 January 1937, the presence of Bergamin, Mendizabal, and about fifteen others, including Monsieur and Madame Berdyaev. He notes, "Bergamin's presentation is extraordinarily moving. This meeting has a powerfully humane character."

148 The date is missing, but the contents allow one to place the composition of this letter directly after the one of 5 January 1937.

We hope that Madame Berdyaev is completely well now. We send our best wishes to the three of you.

Rest assured of my deepest affection.

Jacques Pavlovitch

No. 87, Postcard from Jacques Maritain to Nikolai Berdyaev[149]
(RGALI, dossier 1496, unit 605, folio no. 57)
Meudon, 3 February 1937

Dear Nicolas Alexandrovitch,

Give us some news of you all. I hope you are now all well and that the flu has loosened its grip on your dear home.

The day after tomorrow I leave for Austria. I will be back sometime in mid-February. I count on seeing you then. Until that time, I send to all four of you our best wishes and affection.

Your friend,

Jacques Pavlovitch

No. 88, Letter from Nikolai Berdyaev to Jacques Maritain
(BNU, Fonds Maritain)
Clamart, 27 February 1937

My dear Jakov Pavlovitch!

We do so want to see you. We are no longer suffering from flu over here, though my mother-in-law is still in a terrible state. Could you come to our place on Thursday March 4 around 5 o'clock? If you're not free on March 4, then perhaps Thursday March 11. We can talk about our impressions of Vienna and many other topics. I await your reply.

Kind regards to you all.

N. Berdyaev

149 The postcard depicts a neighborhood (Calle Senador Nic. Habegger) of Reconquista, a city in the province of Santa Fe (Argentina). It was sent from Paris on 5 November 1937.

No. 89, Letter from Jacques Maritain to Nikolai Berdyaev
(RGALI, dossier 1496, unit 605, folio no. 72)
Meudon, Tuesday, [2 March 1937[150]]
Alas, my dear Nicolas Alexandrovitch, I brought a bronchial virus back from Austria that kept me bedridden for two weeks and from which I have still not fully recovered. Tomorrow I will take my first steps out to go see the doctor, but I do not think I will be able to go to Clamart the next day Thursday March 4. But we would be very glad if you and Madame Berdyaev could come to Meudon that day. It's the Mi-Carême[151] and classes are interrupted at the Institut Catholique. However, the following Thursday, if, as I expect, my bronchial tubes and throat are in working order, I plan to do my course at the Institut Catholique; therefore on March 11 it will also be impossible for us to go to your home.

I hope I will see you in two days on Thursday. We will then set a day for coming to Clamart.
Our deepest affection.
Jacques Pavlovitch

No. 90, Letter from Nikolai Berdyaev to Jacques Maritain
(BNU, Fonds Maritain)
Clamart, 16 March 1937
My dear Jakov Pavlovitch!
We must finally see each other. I propose that you come to our place on Monday, March 22 around 5 o'clock or Monday March 29 at the same time – or you can choose any day except Tuesday, Wednesday, or Saturday (Thursdays are always good for us). I hope to see you soon.

150 The date is missing, but the mention of Maritain's trip to Austria from Tuesday, 9 February, to Friday, 12 February 1937 (see "Carnet 1937," *Cahiers Jacques Maritain*, no. 80 [June 2020]: 30–2), allows one to identify the year and day.

151 Translator's note: A French festival that takes place on the twentieth day out of the forty that constitute the fast of Lent before Easter; thus "mid-Lent festival" would be a possible translation. The celebration, somewhat similar to Mardi Gras in New Orleans, dates from the Middle Ages and is still celebrated today in some communities and in parts of the West Indies.

Our kind regards to your household.
Affectionately,
N. Berdyaev

No. 91, Letter from Jacques Maritain to Nikolai Berdyaev
(RGALI, dossier 1496, unit 605, folio no. 58)
Meudon, Friday, [19 or 26 March 1937]
My dear Nicolas Alexandrovitch!
I have discovered your letter upon my return from Belgium.[152] We'll be very happy to come to your place on Monday March 29 at 5 o'clock.[153] It has been really too long since we were last able to see each other. I am curious to know your impressions of Austria – my own were bad, depressing, annihilating. We send you all our best wishes and deep affection.
Jacques Pavlovitch

No. 92, Letter from Nikolai Berdyaev to Raïssa Maritain
(BNU, Fonds Maritain)
Clamart, 25 May 1937
Dear friend!
I spoke with Jakov Pavlovitch about the lecture of Father Bulgakov, "Thomism and Sophiology." He told me that since you understand Russian that his lecture might interest you. It will take place Sunday, May 30 at 8:30 p.m. at 77, rue de Lourmel (15 arrondissement).

We need to meet some day. Our kind regards to you all.
Affectionately,
N. Berdyaev

---

152 Maritain made a trip to Belgium from 13–18 March 1937; see "Carnet 1937," *Cahiers Jacques Maritain*, no. 80 (June 2020): 36–7.

153 Maritain recorded in his "Carnet 1937," *Cahiers Jacques Maritain*, no. 80 (June 2020): 40, "Monday 20 March, 5 p.m. at Berdyaev's."

No. 93, Letter from Nikolai Berdyaev to Jacques Maritain
(BNU, Fonds Maritain)
Clamart, 7 December 1937
My dear friend!
We would like to see you. I am leaving for Holland on December 19 for two weeks. But perhaps we could see each other before my departure? Write and tell me the days that you would be available to come to our place, all three of you. Possible days for me would be, next week the Monday (December 13) and Wednesday (December 15) or Thursday (December 16) around 5 o'clock. I await your reply. If these days do not suit you, will have to put off a meeting until January after my return. It has been a long time since we saw you and we would so like to see you again.

Our kind regards to all of you.
Affectionately,
N. Berdyaev

No. 94, Letter from Jacques Maritain to Nikolai Berdyaev
(RGALI, dossier 1496, unit 605, folio no. 59)
Meudon, 9 December 1937
My dear friend,
I send this note in haste to tell you that we will be very happy to see you in Clamart next Wednesday December 15 at 5 o'clock.[154]
See you soon then. Our warm regards to you all.
Jacques Pavlovitch

No. 95, Letter from Jacques Maritain to Nikolai Berdyaev
(RGALI, dossier 1496, unit 605, folio no. 60)
Meudon, 10 rue du Parc, 5 March 1938
My dear friend,
Ah, so much time since we last saw each other! How did your trip to Holland go? How are all of you? We would so like to see you and hear your news.

154 Maritain recorded in his "Carnet 1937," *Cahiers Jacques Maritain*, no. 81 (January 2021): 40, "Wednesday 15 December. Mendizabal in Paris. Berdyaev."

Here we are swamped with work and troubles. Would it be possible for you to come for tea in Meudon next Saturday March 12 at 5 o'clock?
Our kind regards to you all.
Jacques Maritain
[PS:] We hope that Madame Berdyaev can accompany you.

No. 96, Letter from Nikolai Berdyaev to Jacques Maritain
(BNU, Fonds Maritain)
Clamart, 23 March 1938
My dear friend! The Russian philosopher Simeon Frank,[155] about whom we have already spoken to you, is asking me to write you. As his situation is exceedingly difficult, he is constantly hoping to receive a stipend for his scientific work from the Caisse nationale des recherches scientifiques. I have also written a letter to Brunschvicg[156] about Frank, and he said that it would be good to have a letter of recommendation from you. It is good to have lots of letters of recommendation, and it looks as though Frank will have letters from Le Senne,[157] Lavelle,[158] Jean Wahl,[159] Gabriel Marcel, and Gouhier. There were favourable reviews of Frank's book *La Connaissance et l'être* in the *Revue Thomiste* (no. 11) by Étienne Borne and in the *Études* issue of November 5, 1937. In the *Revue de philosophie* (no. 1, 1938) there is a long article about his book on Delesalle,[160] who very much admires

155 Simeon Frank (1877–1950) was a Russian philosopher who emigrated to France in 1922.

156 Léon Brunschvicg (1869–1944) was a specialist of the philosophy of science and the history of philosophy. He became a professor of the history of modern philosophy at the Sorbonne in 1927.

157 René Le Senne (1882–1954) was a French metaphysician and psychologist who was a part of the spiritualist movement.

158 Louis Lavelle (1883–1951) was a French metaphysician and leader of the philosophy of mind. He was elected to the Collège de France in 1941.

159 Jean Wahl (1888–1974) was a French philosopher and professor at the Sorbonne from 1936 to 1967, except during World War II, when he was fired on account of being Jewish and sent to the Drancy prison outside Paris. After his release in 1941, he fled to the United States until the end of the war.

160 Jacques Delessale (1912–1995) was a priest and professor in the Faculté des lettres of the University of Lille from 1945 to 1983.

Frank's book. In his application Frank says that he's writing a book entitled *Le Transrationnel, Introduction ontologique à la philosophie de la religion* (which is no good for the rationalists of the Sorbonne). It really would be great if you wrote a letter to support Frank, a Christian philosopher, and his application. The letter should be addressed to "Monsieur le president de la Caisse nationale des recherches scientifiques, Ministère de l'éducation nationale, 110 rue de Grenelle." The letter will be added to Frank's file. I would be very grateful if you were able to do this.

We hope to see you some day at our place. Our friendship to you all.
Affectionately,
N. Berdyaev

No. 97, Letter from Jacques Maritain to Nikolai Berdyaev
(RGALI, dossier 1496, unit 605, folio no. 61)
Meudon, 10 rue du Parc, 5 April 1937
Dear Nicolas Alexandrovitch,
I write this note to recommend to you a young poet among my friends, Jean Le Louët,[161] whom I admire very much and who wishes to have an interview with you. He is a philosopher as well as a poet, and I expect great things from him. He directs a youthful review, *Les Nouvelles Lettres*, and would be very happy to have you contribute to it. I am also contributing to this review.[162] I believe he wrote to you some time ago already. I would be very grateful if you'd be so kind as to send him a note to fix a meeting time. His address is: Jean Le Louët, 8 rue de la Petite-Arche, Paris [16th arrondissement].

I hope you are well. Here Raïssa was sick but she is doing better now. However, I am at the end of my tether. The doctor wants me to rest for three weeks. I am leaving to stay with friends near Strasbourg. The events we have been witnessing are heartbreaking.
We send you our deepest affection. Rest assured of my faithful friendship.
Jacques Pavlovitch

---

161 Jean Le Louët (1911–1982) was a poet and writer who directed the review *Les Nouvelles Lettres*.

162 In February 1939, Maritain published "Le crépuscule de la civilisation" (The twilight of civilization) in *Les Nouvelles Lettres* 1ère année, no. 5: 465–95.

No. 98, Letter from Nikolai Berdyaev to Jacques Maritain
(BNU, Fonds Maritain)
Clamart, 9 August 1938
My dear friend!
We so want to see you at our new house before our departure for Vichy (August 20). The best days for us would be Monday the 15th or Tuesday the 16th around 5 o'clock. I just got back from Pontigny. I am writing you though uncertain as to whether you are actually at home. I await your reply.

Our friendship to you all.
Affectionately,
N. Berdyaev
[PS:] New address: 83, rue Moulin de Pierre, Clamart (Seine).

No. 99, Letter from Jacques Maritain to Nikolai Berdyaev
(RGALI, dossier 1496, unit 605, folio no. 62)
Meudon, 9 March 1939
My dear friend,
Understood for Monday March 14. We look forward to your arrival around 5 o'clock. I hope that Madame Berdyaev will be able to accompany you.

Thank you for what you've told me about the study concerning the Jewish question.[163] I am glad that you found it accurate. I will send you soon a lecture that I gave about one month ago on the same subject.[164]

See you soon. Our faithful affection to you all.
Jacques Maritain

---

163 See Jacques Maritain, "Les Juifs parmi les nations" (The Jews among the nations), *La vie intellectuelle*, 10e année, n.s., vol. 56 (10 April 1938): 35–44. This text, published as an offprint by Éditions du Cerf, is present in the personal library of Berdyaev in Clamart with the dedication "à Nicolas Berdiaev, Bien amicalement, Jacques Maritain" (To Nikolai Berdyaev, with friendly regards, Jacques Maritain).

164 Some months after publishing the article-length version of "Les Juifs parmi les nations," Maritain published "Le mystère d'Israël" in *La Question d'Israël* 17e année, vol. 5, no. 69 (1 July 1939): 545–60.

No. 100, Letter from Nikolai Berdyaev to Jacques Maritain
(BNU, Fonds Maritain)
Clamart, 10 September 1939
My dear friend!
I am writing to you though I don't know if you are in Meudon. I would like to know where you are and what your plans are? We want to stay in our home in Clamart as long as possible. It certainly would be good to meet. Write me a short note if this letter reaches you.
Our friendship to you all.
Affectionately,
N. Berdyaev

No. 101, Letter from Nikolai Berdyaev to Jacques Maritain
(BNU, Fonds Maritain)
Clamart, 7 December 1939
My dear friend!
I was told that you would be returning to your home in Meudon. I am writing you to know if it is true. If so, I would like to see you at your place or mine to discuss things with you. Write back if you are in fact here. And how are you doing?
Our friendship to you all.
Affectionately,
N. Berdyaev

No. 102, Postcard from Jacques Maritain to Nikolai Berdyaev
(RGALI, dossier 1496, unit 605, folio no. 64)
Avoise (Sarthe), 10 December 1939
My dear friend,
We did not go back to Meudon so as to avoid unnecessarily moving all the papers that I had taken on vacation. For I am dispatched to America. The imminent departure has taken up all my time. Each time I go to Paris I hope to get to Clamart, but I am impeded by all the logistics and the countless errands that I must do. Raïssa and Véra want to accompany me – a hugely complicated situation for us. In two or three days we will have to make a decision. In any case, we are absolutely set on seeing you

before going. I will send word to let you know. See you soon. Our deepest friendship to you all.
Yours,
Jacqs Maritain

No. 103, A small card from Jacques Maritain to Nikolai Berdyaev
(RGALI, dossier 1496, unit 605, folio no. 65)
Meudon, 10 rue du Parc, [no date]
Dear friend,
This note to heartily recommend to you welcoming a young Belgian philosopher who would be pleased to make your acquaintance, Monsieur Sylvain De Coster.[165]
Affectionately,
Jacqs Maritain

No. 104, Letter from Jacques Maritain to Nikolai Berdyaev
(RGALI, dossier 1496, unit 605, folio no. 73)
French Embassy at the Holy See in Rome, 14 November 1945
My dear friend,
The young Ivanov, returning from Paris, has just informed us of the great misfortune that has befallen you. I wish to express the immense sadness for the three of us and with what painful affection we are all united with you and your sister-in-law. We loved Lydia deeply and admired her great spirit. I recall the last visit to Clamart where I saw her already very sick and that left me very worried for her. My dear Nikolai, words are useless, you know what we think, we cry and hope alongside you, and we are confident she accompanies you with her invisible presence. We embrace you fraternally, the two of you who remain, and are with you with all our hearts.
Jacques Maritain

165 Sylvain De Coster (1907–1983) was a sociologist of education.

No. 105, Letter from Nikolai Berdyaev to Jacques Maritain
(BNU, Fonds Maritain)
Clamart, 28 August 1946[166]
My dear friend!
We just got back. We were away for two months. We did a cure in Vichy and in Allevard. I found two packages you sent from America. I am greatly touched that you thought of me. Food supplies in Paris are still in a chaotic state which is why your packages were greeted with such pleasure.

After arriving at the house, my sister-in-law had an accident. She fell and broke her shoulder and must rest lying down for two months. As for me, I am crushed by the amount of work and meetings I have.

I would be happy to see you when you come to Paris and to discuss with you some worrisome matters.

My friendship to you all. And thanks again.
Affectionately,
N. Berdyaev

166 A letter addressed to Ambassador Jacques Maritain at the French Embassy near the Holy See in Rome.

Index